Fascism, populism
and the French Fifth Republic

Published in our
centenary year
↬ **2004** ↫
MANCHESTER
UNIVERSITY
PRESS

Fascism, populism and the French Fifth Republic

In the shadow of democracy

Catherine Fieschi

Manchester University Press
Manchester and New York

published exclusively in the USA by Palgrave

The right of Catherine Fieschi to be identified as the author
of this work has been asserted by her in accordance
with the Copyright, Designs and Patents Act 1988.

Published by
Manchester University Press
Oxford Road, Manchester M13 9NR, UK
and Room 400, 175 Fifth Avenue, New York, NY 10010, USA
www.manchesteruniversitypress.co.uk

Distributed exclusively in the USA by
Palgrave, 175 Fifth Avenue, New York,
NY 10010, USA

Distributed exclusively in Canada by
UBC Press, University of British Columbia, 2029 West Mall
Vancouver, BC, Canada V6T 1Z2

British Library Cataloguing-in-Publication Data
A catalogue record for this book is available from the British Library

Library of Congress Cataloging-in-Publication Data applied for

ISBN 0 7190 6208 X *hardback*
    0 7190 6209 8 *paperback*

First published 2004

13 12 11 10 09 08 07 06 05 04   10 9 8 7 6 5 4 3 2 1

Typeset by Helen Skelton, Brighton, UK
Printed in Great Britain
by CPI, Bath

This book is dedicated
to the memory of Georges Fieschi

Contents

Acknowledgements

The doctoral dissertation which served as the basis for this project would not have been possible without the kind and rigorous advice of my supervisor Hudson Meadwell at McGill University. I would like to thank the Department of Political Science at McGill University and the Social Sciences and Humanities Research Council of Canada for financial support. During those years I benefited from the generosity and commitment to higher education of my adopted country in a variety of ways, and in particular through the Province of Quebec's system of *Aide Financière aux Etudiants*.

I must also thank various members of the Front national who granted me interviews – first among them Jean-Marie Le Pen. But also, Bernard Antony, Bruno Gollnisch, Carl Lang, Jean-Yves Le Gallou and, finally, Sophie Brissaud, without whose help the higher echelons of the FN might never have been accessible.

At various stages of this project I was able to draw on the intellectual guidance and advice of two people in particular – for this I would like to thank John Gaffney and Colin Hay.

Over the years a number of peole contributed in many, varied and sometimes less tangible ways to this research project: Michèle Fieschi-Fouan, Jerôme Fouan, Isabelle Fieschi, John Gaffney and Luke Gaffney have been on the front lines for many years and unwavering in their support. And not far behind Elizabeth Baines, Alexander Costy, Gilles Denis, Linda Hoag and Emanuela Saccà.

Finally, in 2001 I had the good fortune of joining the School of Politics at the University of Nottingham: working in such a stimulating and friendly environment has been a real pleasure.

Introduction

The French *Front national* (hereafter FN) has been one of Europe's most successful and long-lasting parties of the far Right. Created in 1972 in an attempt to federate the diverse currents, groups, leagues and movements of the far Right in France, the party went – until 1999 – from strength to strength, achieving high scores in almost all major French elections as well as in European elections. Most spectacularly, in 2002 the French public found itself – through a combination of factors – faced with an unexpected choice in the second round of the country's presidential elections: the run-off was between the incumbent President Chirac and, to the nation's shock, the FN's Jean-Marie Le Pen. Much has been written since on Le Pen's extraordinary showing in 2002. Was France to be forever 'tempted' by options on the far, or robust, Right? Was this an unwelcome repeat of France's flirtation with fascism in the 1930s? How had Le Pen, at the head of a party which had been all but written off by French and foreign commentators alike since a serious internal crisis in 1999, made such a comeback, and scored over 17 per cent of the national vote?

This project is an attempt to answer some of these questions by taking a long view of the development of the far Right in France. It culminates with an analysis of the FN and an explanation for its success (as well as its obvious limits), but sets both in the context of ideological and institutional developments that pre-date the party's creation by decades and, perhaps, centuries.

As such, this is less a book about the FN than a book about the conditions which allow a phenomenon such as the FN to emerge. Keeping this in mind, therefore, the project brings together disparate strands of analysis and a broad literature that covers electoral phenomena, party politics, institutional analysis, historical inquiry and ideological developments in an attempt to offer a more complete but also a more rigorous account of the reasons behind the success of the FN as the most contemporary manifestation of the far Right in France and of the political and historical context that sired it.

A rich but limited literature

The party's willingness to endorse and propagate ideas associated with the far Right (an anti-immigration stance, toughness on law and order issues, ultra-conservative views on the family and a propensity for hierarchical and authoritarian social models), its seemingly unstoppable rise, the boisterous personality of its leader Jean-Marie Le Pen and the failure of France's other parties to marginalise it successfully, all of these factors have contributed to turning the study of the FN and its antecedents into a vibrant research area. Electoral specialists, discourse analysts, historians, party politics analysts and scholars of comparative politics have taken part in describing, analysing and attempting to understand the party. However, as is argued in Chapter 1, only a few of the studies carried out yield a picture comprehensive enough to explain the emergence, rise and success of the FN at a time when the far Right seemed discredited in most Western democracies and in a place such as France, namely a Republic with entrenched liberal democratic credentials. But, as shall also emerge from Chapter 1, existing studies on the FN do contribute to a multifaceted picture of the party and therefore to an understanding of it. The shortcomings of the literature are often the result of an overly focused – or else under-theorised – study: electoral studies for example, take voter preferences as their overwhelming concern; the analyses of FN discourse tend to remain oblivious to the general political and institutional context. The historical case studies privilege explanations which – understandably – do much to contextualise the FN's emergence and rise but cannot give a proper indication of the originality of the phenomenon or of the political mechanisms which account for its occurrence. Finally, political party analysts grant too much importance to party strategy and not enough to circumstance, habit or leadership or 'external' factors. This fragmented view is not conducive to a 'thick' understanding of the FN, an understanding which captures the nature of the party within French and European contexts and thus the complex set of circumstances that accounts for its success.

Two conclusions can be drawn from the literature on the FN and its shortcomings. The first of these is that the party's emergence and success is best understood through an approach which draws a variety of analyses into a more comprehensive model. This means the development of an approach sensitive to historical and ideological factors as well as to their expression in political discourse on the one hand, and to issues of mobilisation and party political strategy on the other. A further focus on institutions serves as a prism through which to take into account the context's opportunities and constraints and the impact of these on the mobilisation strategies of parties.

The aims of the project and the approach adopted

This book has three main aims. The first is to demonstrate that a valid understanding of the emergence and success of the FN must be based on a view of the party which takes into account its ideological profile as a vehicle for far-Right[1] ideas, its position in the historical development and evolution of far-Right ideologies in France, and its tactics as a political party in the institutional context of an industrial liberal democracy, the French Fifth Republic.

The second aim of the book is to demonstrate that the study of French politics should distance itself from the exceptionalist bias of much of the literature. French politics and the French polity should be taken as unexceptional exceptions. French specificity is best taken into account with the tools appropriate to comparative political inquiry, since French politics, while specifically French, is subject to the drives, pressures, constraints and tensions generated by the many factors it shares with other industrial democracies.

Finally, in terms of its methodological claims, the book seeks to illustrate the potential of the historical institutionalist approach in combination with a theory of ideology and change. It therefore expands the epistemological potential of historical institutionalism by recognising the importance of the role of ideas (and systems of ideas) in mediating relationships between institutions and political actors.

The literature on the FN, as Chapter 1 will illustrate, makes little of the institutional context in which this variant of the far Right in France has met with such success. The argument here is that the FN has been able to take advantage of a set of political opportunities provided within the Fifth Republic. In contrast to other movements or parties of the far Right in France, the FN has been both more

successful and more durable. In contrast to other parties of the far
Right in Europe, this success has seldom translated into participation
in government. The first, it is argued, is the result of the capacity of
the FN to adapt to the exigencies of Fifth Republican politics on
the one hand and the institutionalisation of a form of rally politics
which privilege populist agendas in the Fifth Republic on the
other. While the economic climate, tensions associated with post-
industrialism, the personality of Jean-Marie Le Pen and a host of
other factors have undoubtedly contributed to the rise and success of
the FN, it is argued here that the relationship between the institutional
framework of the Fifth Republic (and the concomitant presidentialisation of French politics) and a set of political concepts constitutive
of various far-Right ideologies are more important explanatory variables, and, perhaps, the condition which enables these other variables
to have effects. The second, limited participation in government,
stems from the constraints placed upon the FN by these very same
factors.

After this first chapter devoted to a survey of the literature on the
study of the far Right in Europe and more specifically on the FN,
Chapter 2 elaborates a model of ideational institutionalism. This
chapter takes as its departure the literature on structures of political
opportunity and argues that, just as mobilisation on the Left has
been studied as an exploitation of existing opportunities in a given
system, so too can be mobilisation on the far Right. The literature on
structures of political opportunity however, relies on a restrictive view
of institutions. While institutions are conceived of as opportunities as
well as constraints, the literature on opportunity structures normally
fails to take into account the effects of institutions in a suitably dynamic
manner. In order to rectify this view, neo-institutionalist approaches to
institutions are introduced. Subsequent chapters define the nature of
French institutions on the one hand and the nature of the French far
Right on the other: Chapter 3 provides an overview of the concept of
presidentialism and argues that a proper definition of institutions, such
as the one set out in Chapter 2, should allow for a reconceptualisation
of the institution of the presidency and therefore a better understanding of the presidency's effects (presidentialism). The chapter
concludes with an examination of French presidentialism and presidential practices and a discussion of France's difficult acceptance of
strong executive rule in the Republic. Here the weaknesses of the
Third and Fourth Republics are analysed. It is suggested that a better
understanding of France under both of these regimes (and of the

evolution of French parties and the French party system) is gained if modern liberal democratic politics are understood as driven by a tension between two contradictory drives (a representative party drive and a plebiscitary rally drive). In the case of France, it is argued that the Fifth Republic institutionally incorporates, if not reconciles, these two drives for the first time, thus creating new structures of political opportunities for political parties and political actors.

Chapters 4, 5 and 6 turn to fascism, French fascism and the far Right in France, with Chapters 5 and 6 addressing the particular case of the FN. In these chapters the argument is made that, until the Fifth Republic and the institutionalisation of the effects of a strong Presidency, rally politics occurred alongside 'normal' politics and were, therefore, generally ephemeral. Thus, I argue, much as Fascism needed a certain set of historical and institutional circumstances to emerge, so too did the ideological stance of the FN. Chapter 5 therefore argues that having started as a proto-fascist movement and party, the FN evolved over time to take advantage of the political opportunity struc-tures of the Fifth Republic. These opportunities were linked to the institutionalisation of the rally drive. Hence, it is argued, the FN adopted a strategy and a discourse which drew upon and developed the party's existing rally element. The nature of fascism in France is seen to be profoundly transformed by the privileging of the concept of populism. The morphology of the ideology developed and adopted by the FN makes populism a core concept – if not *the* core concept – while other concepts (central to fascism) such as palyngenetic renewal are relegated to a secondary role. The FN became more successful as it transformed fascism and privileged a national populism more in tune with the presidentialism of the institutions of the Fifth Republic and its associated rally politics. The last chapter, Chapter 6, illustrates the party's evolving stance between 1972 and 2002 and its move away from fascism and toward populism.

The conclusion revisits the research findings in light of the FN's more recent electoral fortunes. It shows that, whilst the party was weakened by the internal split it suffered in 1998/1999, by 2002 Le Pen was nevertheless able to take second place (with 15 per cent of the vote) in the first round of France's presidential election. The conclu-sion thus draws attention to the fact that both the split in the FN and its resilience to crisis should be understood as stemming from the same ideological and institutional dynamics.

Notes

1 The term 'far Right' has been chosen deliberately as the most neutral. It refers, simply, to parties ideologically situated far on the Right of the political spectrum.

Chapter 1

Understanding the far Right in France and Europe: institutional blind-spots

Since the early 1980s extremist formations on the far Right of the ideological spectrum have either become more vocal or have succeeded in attracting a level of support unprecedented since the end of the Second World War. Most scholars have noted this rise with a mixture of concern and scholarly interest. Why the increase in levels of support for Right-wing extremism? What did the re-emergence of far-Right parties say about the party-systems within which they were emerging? Would they last? Were they comparable across national boundaries and, finally, did they differ substantially from the movements of the turn of the century, the inter-war period or those indeed of the war itself, or were they merely as some authors claimed 'old wine in new bottles'? Whatever the answer might be in the long term, their appearance on the political scene has prompted political scientists and historians to pay closer attention to the fringes of the political Right. This chapter provides a brief account of the main strands of the literature devoted to the study of the rise of Right-wing extremism in Europe and more specifically of the FN in France. Finally, it sets out an alternative explanation for the success of the FN in France.

Right-wing extremism in Western Europe: tentative explanations

Explanations concerning the rise of far-Right movements and parties in Western Europe fall into two distinct categories. The first set of explanations examines the rise of the far Right in Europe as part of what has become known as 'new politics'. These authors address the issues raised most prominently by Inglehart's thesis of the silent revolution[1] and attribute the rise of movements and parties of the far Right to changes in values and their translation in party-system preferences and configurations. More particularly, the movements and parties of the far Right are depicted as reactions or backlashes against the culture of post-materialism identified by Inglehart. Here, these parties are seen as a new phenomenon reflecting specific and distinct attitudinal and value changes in the electorate.

The second category of explanations relies more explicitly on socio-economic factors, highlighting the transformation of modes of production and modes of consumption and emphasising their effects on levels of employment and standards of living. These explanations depict the far Right as resulting from a general disenchantment with traditional parties, unease in the face of an increasingly unpredictable political and economic future, and fears relating to the growing immigrant population in various Western European countries. They generally depict far-Right movements and parties as single-issue, protest parties and their supporters as disillusioned voters venting their frustrations.

Thus, while the first set of explanations posits deep and lasting transformations, the second essentially views support for the far Right as episodes of protest. It is fairly easy to see, however, that these explanations are related to one another: fears concerning loss of status and control – and the xenophobic attitudes often created by such fears – can be linked to the dislocations and transformations provoked and engendered by a post-industrial society and post-Fordist modes of production, for example. Also, the concurrent loss of faith in mainstream parties, and the crisis of representation invoked by many authors, might explain the changes in values which have been isolated by some authors as responsible for the rise of far-Right extremism.

A further feature of these explanations needs to be highlighted: most of these authors are well aware of the complex nature of their object of study, and all of them acknowledge the relevance of other factors besides those that they think are central or determinant. None of them isolates one single factor as responsible for the rise or resurgence of various forms of Right-wing extremism in Western Europe. This suggests that few, if any, authors rely on single-factor theories.

Aside from the categories of explanations delineated above, an important additional parameter must be taken into account, namely the role granted by authors in either of the two categories to a historical and/or analytical connection between Fascism and the current movements and parties of the far Right. For some authors, far-Right parties are historically (if not necessarily ideologically) connected to fascism. For others, the parties and movements are a new political form completely disconnected from fascism and for whom fascism does not even constitute an analytical vantage point from which they can be examined, analysed or labelled.

New politics and old Right

Piero Ignazi's work has become archetypal of one approach to the study of the far Right. In a 1992 article he interpreted the far Right in Europe as a consequence of changes in values and mass beliefs.[2] Ignazi was attempting to apply Inglehart's[3] idea of a 'silent revolution' in ideological beliefs to the other (far Right) end of the political spectrum. Further, he depicted the far Right as a back-lash against those new politics and those post-materialist ideas which for Inglehart were taking hold of the European electorate and public more generally.

Ignazi's thesis focused essentially on developments in the party system. He concluded that, given the higher volatility of European electorates and the (simultaneously) predicted rise in new parties, far-Right parties were a logical consequence of party-system change. Yet, Ignazi argued, the resurgence of the far-Right parties was unforeseen and took the academic community by surprise. His main concern was to account for Inglehart's failure to notice and to explain the rise of far-Right parties. Ignazi's argument is straightforward: if there really was a transformation in political values and an emergence of new politics as Inglehart argued, these transformations could not have affected only half of the political spectrum (i.e. the Left with which Inglehart is concerned), but should also have affected the political spectrum's other extreme, the Right. 'In a sense,' writes Ignazi,

> it could be said that the Greens and the ERPs [Extreme Right Parties] are, respectively, the legitimate and the unwanted children of the New Politics; as the Greens come out of the silent revolution, the ERPs derive from a reaction to it, a sort of 'silent counter-revolution.'[4]

Ignazi goes further. The ERPs, he insists, are not just unaccounted for, they are at odds with the idea of a society increasingly concerned with post-materialist values. In terms of values, post-materialism (and increasing wealth) should have eradicated the need (or, at least, the expression of the need) to express values of the far Right. Furthermore, in party-political terms, why, asks Ignazi, has the space taken up by the new politics not 'shrunk' the political space available for the ERPs?

Ignazi examines spatial criteria, the ideological content of the ERPs and, finally, their attitude to the political system. His conclusions can be summarised in the following way: by looking at how the parties are organised on the Left/Right continuum, Ignazi provides a broad overview of the Right pole of the political spectrum.[5] The list yields new parties and more established parties, thus Ignazi concludes it is necessary to use a more substantive criterion to determine the nature of these parties. Here, Ignazi makes what he calls a 'bold statement':[6]

> The only ideological corpus for the extreme right has been provided by fascism … First, fascism is the only ideology more or less unanimously recognised as an extreme right ideology. Second, fascist ideology … is different and, in some ways alien from conservative thought. Third, up until the 1970s, all extreme right groups and parties referred to and were inspired by the most influential party of this tendency in Europe, the Italian MSI which was patently, by any standard, a neofascist party.[7]

Ignazi draws up a list of ERPs which he deems connected to fascism. This list, while extensive, does not contain the French FN (it does contain the German *Nationaldemokratische Partei Deutschland* (NPD) and *Deutsche Volksunion* (DVU), the Italian *Movimento Sociale Italiano* (MSI), the Spanish *Frente Nacional* (FN) and others). Finally, Ignazi examines the parties' attitude to the political system and concludes that all of the parties initially isolated as potential ERPs exhibit an anti-system attitude and a desire to undermine the legitimacy of the system.

Ignazi classifies his parties in the following manner: for a party to be classified as extreme Right it should exhibit either an anti-system attitude or a connection to fascism. If it exhibits only the second or both it is classified an old ERP (such as the Italian MSI); if it exhibits only the first – an anti-system attitude – it is classified as a new ERP. In another article, taking the MSI and the FN respectively as archetypal old and new ERPs,[8] Ignazi underscores the differences between the two types. Two things are noteworthy: the first is his classification of all the parties he examines under the label of extreme Right; the second is the fact that even when he concludes, with respect to some cases such as the FN, that the party no longer has any real connection to fascism, it is interesting to note that fascism (for the reasons he outlines) still serves as a matrix from which these parties have emancipated themselves. In other words, while the verdict may be that some of the parties are no longer fascist, they nevertheless have to pass – or fail in this case – the fascist litmus test. This, in contrast to the approaches described in the next section, means that no matter what the parties are seen ultimately to represent ideologically, they are nevertheless analysed – in terms of their ideological commitments – through an analytical grid structured by fascism. For an author such as Ignazi, no understanding of these parties is seen to be possible before their relationship to fascism – even if this relationship is now weak or non-existent – has been carefully ascertained. Yet, another category of explanations depends on discarding the litmus test and arrives at conclusions on the nature of these parties with only cursory attention paid to fascism.

Traditional politics and the new Right

Perhaps the most influential interpretation of the resurgence of Right-wing extremism in Europe are those explanations put forth by Hans Georg Betz, not least because it constitutes a refutation of Ignazi's analytical standpoint. The author argues that the type of Right-wing extremism present in Europe today has nothing to do with fascism and, therefore, should be analysed quite separately. For Betz,

> What distinguishes the recent wave of Right-wing mobilisation from earlier ones is, first, the extent to which various Right-wing movements and parties have successfully established themselves within roughly the same time span in a substantial number of Western democracies; second, the extent to which they have managed to influence the political discourse on a range of significant socio-cultural and socio-political issues; and, third, the extent to which they have succeeded in gaining significant political offices and positions.[9]

More importantly, Betz argues that we are 'witnessing the emergence of a new politics of the Right, promoted by a new type of Right-wing political party'.[10] The argument here is that these parties no longer cling to the ideological relics of fascism; they have, according to the author, traded in a fascist outlook (and look) for 'the tools of contemporary political marketing'.[11] Betz's argument relies on his contention that, in order to be neo-fascist, Right-wing extremist or far-Right parties must fulfil at least two criteria: firstly they must exhibit a programmatic rejection of the democratic rules of the game of individual liberty, and of the principle of individual equality and equal rights for all members of the political community, and support and strive for the replacement of the existing community by an authoritarian system in which rights are based on ascribed characteristics (such as ethnicity, religion or race). Secondly, the parties must endorse violence and the propagation of violence to achieve these ends.[12]

Betz argues that none of the contemporary parties can therefore be labelled neo-fascist, Right-wing extremist or far Right. Rather, Betz contends, these parties have in common their programmatic radicalism and their populist appeal. From this perspective then, these parties are to be understood as part of a new wave of radical,[13] Right-wing populism.

> Radical Right-wing populist parties are radical in their rejection of the established socio-cultural and socio-political system and their advocacy of individual achievement, a free marketplace, and a drastic reduction of the role of the state. They are right-wing in their rejection of individual and social equality, in their opposition to the social integration of marginalised groups, and in their appeal to xenophobia, if not overt racism. They are populist in their instrumentalisation of sentiments of anxiety and disenchantment and in their appeal to the common man and his allegedly superior common sense.[14]

Betz's argument concerning populism and his analysis of the populist appeal of the parties is convincing, and most authors would agree with the populist label for a range of European parties of the far Right (indeed the present argument is rooted in the importance of populism for the FN – but treats populism as an integral part of fascism).[15] What is less convincing is the rest of Betz's argument concerning the labelling of the parties and the definition of fascism.

The first objection to Betz's argument concerns the manner in which he discards the possibility of labelling the parties and movements under scrutiny 'far Right', 'neo-fascist' or 'Right-wing extremist'. His argument that the movements have to satisfy the two criteria he outlines is, at best, applicable to the notion of neo-fascism, but certainly not to the other two terms whose flexibility renders the question of a strict two-part set of criteria superfluous and unhelpful. Cas Mudde's influential analysis of Right-wing extremism[16] as a political ideology, for example, allows for a more flexible definition of Right-wing extremism and one which does not include violence. In his typology, most parties excluded by Betz would fit within the rigorous, yet more realistic, boundaries of his definition of Right-wing extremism.

Further, a working definition of fascism would no doubt include the two sets of criteria he outlines but, even then, it is arguable that neo-fascist parties would go to great lengths to adopt a democratic exterior only to discard it when it suited them. The notion that a rhetorical allegiance to democracy and a wafer-thin commitment to democratic institutions should be enough to remove the neo-fascist label from these parties seems, at best, naive and betrays a misunderstanding of the ideological thrust of fascism. Secondly, let us not forget that it is neo-fascism which is evoked by Betz and not fascism *per se*. A neo-fascism, i.e. a *new* version of fascism, might well incorporate or even rely upon, a different rhetorical appeal. Following on from this, the claim that these parties express a fundamental ideological realignment also seems to be wishful thinking. Third, and most importantly, it can be argued that Betz's populism – while probably a correct label – arrives much like the genie in the machine, with little in the way of explanation. Betz seems to be arguing that these parties turned to populism simply because the time of fascism has passed and the use of the media allowed – in fact, demanded – a more palatable populist approach. Yet, populism has ideological roots which date from well before the rise of neo-populist parties in Europe; it has connections to other Right-wing ideological forms including fascism. None of these problems are explored.

The crux of these criticisms can be summarised in the following manner: while Betz convinces the reader of the usefulness of the populist label, this label remains disconnected from the history of the Right in Europe. The ahistorical quality of the analysis therefore prevents the author from considering a version of populism which may – or may not – have links to fascism; which may – or may not – be radical; which may – or may not – be a response to particular conditions.

Betz's discarding of fascism and neo-fascism is not so much wrong as unhelpful since he is led to discard the ideological baggage with which many parties (such as the MSI in Italy, the French FN and the German *Republikaner*) have had to contend. Hiving populism off from the issue of the historical legacy of the Right does not help.

In the same volume Stephen Immerfall analyses the neo-populist agenda.[17] The chapter, an analysis of the sources of neo-populism, relies on fear and the 'profound and largely psychological, crisis of the 'popular classes'[18] as major explanatory variables. Social alienation, cultural estrangement and feelings of isolation are also referred to as contributing to the success of neo-populism. Again, the interpretation by Immerfall – which complements that of Betz – is that these new politics are largely the result of ahistorical factors such as feelings of relative deprivation and other psychological factors. Aside from the slight condescension which emanates from such explanations, the main point of criticism against them is that they do not explain a turn to *Right-wing* populism. Why is this populism Right-wing? While they may account for a radicalisation of the popular classes and for a populist 'turn', they do not properly account for the Right-wing nature of the radicalism or of the populism. The refusal to entertain the possibility of fascism's influence on many of the groups or parties does much to account, it seems, for this lacuna.

A futher influential analysis of the far Right is that elaborated by Kitschelt in 1995.[19] In his work *The Radical Right in Western Europe*, Kitschelt puts forward a thesis that draws on his *The Transformation of European Social Democracy* (1994) in which he argues that the economy of advanced capitalism (a post-industrial capitalism) has given rise to a new set of cleavages – a left-libertarian and a right-authoritarian pole – both of which cut across traditional class cleavages. Interestingly, Kitschelt's argument, like Ignazi's, draws on the conception of a post-industrial politics and the emergence of new cleavages drawn by these politics. But this is where the similarity ends.

The emergence of these new cleavages, argues Kitschelt, compels parties to draw votes from a new set of alliances. In the case of the radical Right, Kitschelt's argument is twofold. First and foremost, he argues that it is only under these conditions of post-industrial capitalism (with developed welfare states, convergence of the traditional Left and the traditional Right) that the radical Right can be successful and, secondly, that in order to be electorally successful, radical Right-wing parties need to find what he calls 'the winning formula'. In their case, the winning formula is an appeal that combines pro-market liberalism and authoritarian ethno-centrism. This ideological 'package' attracts a viable coalition of voters (independent businessmen, farmers and the working class) numerous and motivated enough to carry the radical Right to power. For Kitschelt, the prototype of what he terms the 'New Radical Right' party is the French FN and the author makes a distinction between the New Radical Right and anti-statist populism (the archetype of which he argues, is the Austrian *Freihheitliche Partei Österreichs* (FPÖ)).

Kitschelt's is a rich and systematic study of the radical Right in Europe: he identifies powerfully effective variables and the study is large scale. The argument is also extremely compelling because it brings together notions (which will be used a little further on in this study) of opportunity structures, ideological appeals and electoral coalitions in post-industrial democracies. Unfortunately, a number of issues make the argument less convincing than it might have been. One of the main problems with Kitschelt's work is that it relies on a distinction between New Radical Right and anti-statist populist parties. To some extent, even when the work was written the distinction between these types was tenuous; further, time has shown that the parties that Kitschelt had most strongly associated with either type have moved to embrace features of the other: one of the main arguments of this book is that the FN has moved toward an increasing populism. Another problem with the study is, quite simply, the fit between the stipulated elements of the coalition and the reality. Most parties of the far Right in Europe have increased their working-class vote – and this across the board – and most parties have moved to embrace a racist, or at least ethnocentric appeal. So, if the distinction hinges in part on different types of coalitions characterising different types of parties, those distinctions have been eroded. And, in the case of the FN, both Perrineau and Mayer make quite clear, for example, with regard to the 1988 election presidential election, that support for the party did not come from the pro-market voters – in fact quite the opposite: the FN drew its support from those who were least liberal in economic terms.[20]

In conclusion, both sets of explanations which we have examined seem unsatisfactory (and a detailed examination of the FN will support this assessment): the first because, while it posits a difference between new and old Right, does little to explain the springs of new and old Right support. The second because of its failure to contextualise – historically and institutionally – the ideological concepts upon which it relies.

The *Front national* in comparative perspective

In an analysis of the FN (uncharacteristically inclined to set the FN within, if not a comparative framework, certainly a comparative outlook), Nonna Mayer highlights the fact that the rise of the FN coincides with the rise of other similar movements in Europe and that the FN is simply more successful than they are. Three years later, Mayer's words have an added weight: while I aim to explain why the FN has been more successful at every political level and for a longer period of time than most other far-Right parties in France and perhaps than most far-Right parties in Europe, the last few years have held unprecedented success – and certainly enormous flux – for the party family of the far Right in Europe.

Some countries have seen little change in the strength of their far Right parties. In Germany, for example, while the high score in favour of the DVU in the Saxe-Anhalt Landtag elections in April 1998 (12.9 per cent) led commentators to fear the possibility of the far Right's entry into the Bundestag elections of September 1998, this did not happen. Moreover, the DVU's membership has been in free-fall since 1992. While the relative youthfulness of the vote (30 per cent of the far-Right vote is cast by voters who are under thirty) and the party's increasing recruitment in the more popular and working-class sectors of society (19 per cent of the working-class vote; 17 per cent of the unemployed vote) is alarming, the party is not seen to pose a real threat in electoral terms for the time being. Further, despite Franz Shönhuber's relatively charismatic personality, the *Republikaner*'s most recent electoral results (1.8 per cent in the autumn 1998 parliamentary elections) suggest that they, too, are on the wane.[21]

The relative weakness of the far Right in Germany and in countries such as Spain is comforting, but it is an exception. Throughout Europe, the 1990s and early years of the new millennium saw an increased support for parties on the far Right. Italy saw its Fascist party mutate almost overnight in 1995 (along with the rest of its party system). During that year, the MSI transformed itself into the *Alleanza Nazionale* (AN) at the Congress of Fiuggi from which the new party's manifesto '*Le tesi di Fiuggi*' is taken. Despite this transformation, and the repudiation of Fascism and its racial laws, the party was divided (with the older generation refusing to adopt leader Gianfranco Fini's post-Fascism and remaining faithful to the Fascism of the Salò Republic). However, as a coalition partner of the short-lived first Berlusconi government, but more importantly of the second Berlusconi government (2001–), Fini's AN has retained a crucial position of power with twenty-four seats in the chamber of deputies (12 per cent of the vote).[22]

Scandinavian countries have contributed their share of far Right successes in recent years: most of them can be interpreted as a backlash against the developed welfare states and the relatively liberal immigration policies adopted by most of these countries. The consequences have been that in Norway the Progress Party collected 15.7 per cent of the vote in the 1997 legislative elections. Most strikingly, in Denmark, the Danish People's Party collected 12 per cent of the vote and twenty-two seats in the autumn 2001 election.[23]

However, the countries in which the far Right is most successful today (FN aside) are Austria, Belgian Flanders and the Netherlands. The Belgian far Right's current incarnation, the *Vlaams Blok*, founded in 1978 by Karel Dillen, has in the past few years hovered around the 12 per cent mark in Flanders and is Anvers' most powerful political force. In the elections of 13 June 1999 the *Vlaams Blok* gained 9.8 per cent of the vote and fifteen seats in the national assembly; this success swelled to 11.6 per cent of the vote and eighteen seats in the elections held in May 2003.[24]

Austria's FPÖ, led by Jorg Haider, is a populist party which thrives on the Austrian fear of the flood of refugees from Central and Eastern Europe. The story of the FPÖ is a well-documented one: a flirtation with Austrian centrist politics in the immediate aftermath of the Second World War, a subsequent return to a harder political line under the leadership of Jorg Haider, and the international condemnation following its staggering success in the October 1999 elections in which the party gained 27 per cent of the vote and thanks to which it entered into a coalition government with the Conservative party. The recent past has been less kind: internal strife and tensions between the party's leading politicians led to the resignation of the FPÖ government and to early elections. These elections confirmed the FPÖ's fall from grace as it collected a mere 10 per cent of the vote, and while still a junior coalition partner (their reduced power serving the now very dominant Conservative party well), the FPÖ is struggling to maintain itself as the third party of Austrian politics.[25]

Finally, while its star is already dimming in the constellation of the far-Right party family, the meteoric rise and equally abrupt decline of the *Listj Pim Fortuyn* (LPF) in the Netherlands cannot remain unmentioned. Created in 2001 in anticipation of the Spring 2002 election by the maverick and flamboyant Dutch politician Pim Fortuyn, the LPF rose to prominence on the back of a mix of policies that succeeded in fusing far-Right issues of immigration, asylum rights and criminality with the more traditionally tolerant Dutch themes of ecology and libertarian attitudes to sexuality and drugs. Fortuyn, an outspoken and openly homosexual economics lecturer, took the party from its creation to 17 per cent of the vote in the space of less than a year. His assassination in mid-campaign, however, left the party without its main source of appeal and, with their leader gone, the LPF struggled to maintain its status within the governmental coalition. Again, internal strife and leadership changes led to the calling of early elections in 2003 in which the LPF fell to 5.7 per cent of the vote.[26]

A number of things are striking about the recent successes of these parties: the first, and perhaps least surprising, is that success seems to arise in systems with proportional representation. Secondly, it is not only proportional representation that seems to be an explanatory factor, but also the nature of political power and its exercise in these particular contexts. By this, I mean that the Netherlands, Austria, Belgium and Denmark all harbour systems that are variously described as consociational, or proportional. Politics is carried out in a spirit of compromise and designed to reach consensus. The case of Italy is slightly more complicated in that consensus was reached through the domination of the system by one (hegemonic) party of government and at the exclusion of another. However, all of these systems can be said to have been somewhat immobile and/or marked by long periods of consensus politics. The far-Right parties burst on to the scene in a way that can be partially interpreted as a surge of support for non-consensual politics.

Thirdly and finally, what is also striking about these parties is their relatively short-lived success if and when in power: the fortunes of the FPÖ and the LPF are the best illustrations of the fact that while the electoral systems at work in the Netherlands and Austria might make them more easily permeable to the far Right in electoral terms, the tradition which allows the parties to break into the system conversely imposes limits on these parties' formulation and implementation of policy once in government – to the point where they, in fact, are unable to maintain public support and their own internal coherence beyond a few years, or sometimes, as in the case of the LPF, a few months. The case of Italy is, again, slightly different but worth including in this broad comparison. Though the first Berlusconi coalition government fell rapidly (due to the tension between the AN and the third partner Umberto Bossi's *Lega Nord* (Northern League)), the second Berlusconi government seems to have fared slightly better. A number of things can explain this: the fact that the coalition might have learnt from previous mistakes; The AN's and Fini's more flexible approach to governing in coalition and their increasingly watered-down post-Fascism and, finally, the parties' more seasoned approach to isolating and catering to their allies outside government.

What is of interest here, however, is how the French FN compares with these other parties: it shares some of the features evoked above while also differing substantially from many of them. For example, the FN has existed for much longer than most of the parties, but it emerged as a successful party only a decade after its creation. As such

it cannot be understood simply as a flash-in-the-pan protest movement, or the short-lived effects of voter frustration and an electorally
volatile climate. On the other hand, the more recent successes of
the FN seem to place it alongside these far-Right parties who seem
to have been able to capitalise on the public's growing sense of
disillusionment with a form of politics that left voters feeling as though
they were permanently shut out of a process dependent strictly on elite
bargaining and elite consensus.

Most commentators take the Dreux elections in 1983 as the FN's
first significant electoral success. In Dreux the FN gained 16.7 per cent
of the vote and a few weeks later it garnered 9.3 per cent of the vote
in the Parisian suburb of Aulnay-sous-Bois. It is clear that the Dreux
score opened up a political space for the FN. The far Right seemed
then, as it often does, to rise from its ashes.[27] From that point onwards,
aided and abetted by the use of Le Pen's party that François Mitterrand
made against the conventional Right, the FN scored 11 per cent in the
1984 European elections; 9.7 per cent in the 1986 legislative elections;
14.4 per cent in the 1988 presidential election; 9.8 per cent in the
1988 legislative elections (although this time it did not gain any seats
given that the election was not held under PR); 11.9 per cent in the
1989 European elections; 13.28 per cent in the 1992 regional elections; 12.7 per cent in the 1993 legislative elections; 10.5 per cent in
the 1994 European elections; 15.3 per cent in the 1995 presidential
election; 15 per cent in the 1997 legislative elections; and finally 15 per
cent in the 1998 regional elections. The trend apparent here is that of
a stridently extremist party maintaining itself consistently above the
10 per cent mark for nearly a decade and a half. This is a party which,
at the time of writing, has held seats in the European parliament for
nearly fifteen years, which has governed four major towns (including
Toulon France's fourteenth largest city and major port) since the
municipal elections of 1995 and whose leader was the third most
popular candidate in France's most important national election in
1995.[28]

What is apparent therefore, is that the FN did well consistently and
in various types of elections. Legislative elections, despite the national
scores, are notoriously stacked against it but, in all elections at the
national, regional or municipal level the FN had become a political
force to be reckoned with. The most recent European election in
June of 1999 witnessed the FN's worse result in fifteen years following
the movement's split into two rival parties, while 2002 saw Le Pen's
most significant success in the presidential election (16.9 per cent of

the vote), as well as the FN's more modest score in the June 2002 legislative elections (11.1 per cent of the vote). What is noteworthy however, and what this book shall seek to highlight and explain, is the fact that the FN was systemically successful over nearly two decades. Poured over in quick succession, even the FN's more mediocre results in legislative elections (9.7 per cent in 1986; 9.8 per cent in 1988; 12.7 per cent in 1993; 15 per cent in 1997 and 11.1 per cent in 2002), while they may pale in comparison to Le Pen's more personal scores in the presidential elections (14.4 per cent in 1988; 15 per cent in 1995; 16.9 per cent in 2002), indicate a party able to maintain itself in both types of electoral contests, despite the impossibility of translating electoral significance into governmental participation.

This, in fact, is where the FN differs significantly from the other 'successful' far-Right parties in that it has never had a powerful position in any government and, in fact, has never governed at the national level. Aside from a brief spell between 1986 and 1988 during which it held a handful of seats in the National Assembly, the very same party that has consistently delivered a significant proportion of the vote over the past two-and-a-half decades in France has never been in a situation in which it is confronted with the tensions inherent in governing.

The interest of this puzzle goes beyond the obvious electoral systems answer. There is no doubt that the absence of proportional representation clearly impacts on the nature of the FN's success. That much is established. However, what is not explained is that which accounts for its continued and growing strength over decades, its ability to overcome – what looked like terminal – internal party strife in 1999/2000 and, overall, its importance on the French party-political and ideological scene, to the extent that it is not erroneous to claim that the FN was setting the political agenda in France for the better part of the late 1980s and 1990s. Finally, the FN is widely held to have granted Chirac an overwhelming – though less-than-legitimate – 80 per cent victory in the second round of the 2002 presidential election and prompted the implosion of the left coalition.

What the literature on the FN does not take into account is precisely this systemic, institutional aspect of the FN's success (and conversely the systemic, institutionally determined aspect of the FN's setbacks). In other words, the ebb and flow of the FN's political fortunes – in the broadest sense of the expression – need to be analysed. Yet much of the analytical work on the party does not succeed in these terms. As such, the next section looks at the literature available on the FN, explains its shortcomings, and indicates the manner in which this book seeks to remedy them.

France: depictions and analyses of the *Front national*

The FN as a response to crisis

The FN as a response to economic crisis

Alain Bihr's influential book *Pour en finir avec le Front national*, while slightly dated (it was published in 1992),[29] is the best and quintessential expression of a neo-Marxist analysis of the FN combined with a traditional French view of the relevance of French exceptionalism (a trait present in many of the French works on the FN and one which reflects both French academics' notorious mistrust of comparative methods as well as their unabashedly French understanding of France as a nation unlike any other). As a neo-Marxist, Bihr analyses the FN as the expression of the culmination of a number of crises in French society and politics.

Bihr pinpoints four main crises which he sees as the sources of the FN's success: the crisis of the hegemonic bloc, the crisis of the working-class movement, the crisis of the nation-state and a cultural crisis. Using a Gramscian analysis of power blocs,[30] Bihr begins with what he labels the 'crisis of the hegemonic bloc', i.e. the crisis of the alliance of, on the one hand, farmers, small capitalists and shopkeepers, and the political class on the other. The tacit political agreement was that the Republic would not undermine these first three sectors and that they, in return, would support the regime. According to Bihr this bargain – a bargain which flourished under the Third Republic – was undermined to begin with in the 1930s (a fact which he sees as partly explaining the middle-class triumvirate's support for Vichy), further damaged after the war as the country modernised and, finally, broken when de Gaulle chose to support the Common Market in the mid-1960s. Post-war changes which brought about a concentration of capital and then a centralisation of capital in the hands of a capitalist bourgeoisie, transformed the life of the middle classes upon whom the existence of the Republican regime depended. Between 1954 and 1975 for example, the number of small shopkeepers declined from 1,250,000 to 950,000;[31] the proportion of the population which constituted these middle classes supportive of the Republic went from 31 per cent to 14 per cent of the total population.[32]

Bihr's argument therefore is that this middle class felt cheated and duped, its very existence threatened by a regime it had helped to support and entrench. To these frustrated middle-class voters, Bihr adds the actions and attitudes of their progeny who, having benefited from a more open education system and increased access to professions – which had been out of their parents' or grandparents' reach – find themselves in a difficult political and social situation belonging neither to their parents' circles nor to those circles to which they are professionally entitled to belong but from which they nevertheless remain socially excluded. For Bihr it is this uneasy, educated but ostracised generation which fuelled the radical movements of 1968.

In order to square the circle and bring the analysis up to date, Bihr then argues that the old middle-class bloc thus finds itself stuck between the radical 1968 generation on the one hand and the representatives of transnational finance capital on the other. This, he goes on to say, creates a reactionary bloc whose faith in the system is shaken even further when, as a result of the Left's election to power in 1981, the Left strikes an alliance with capital in 1983. Caught between a new hegemonic Left-wing bloc and a Right unwilling to defend its interests, the traditional middle classes become radicalised, thus lending their support to the FN.[33]

Bihr's other three crises stem from this political-economic moment: the transnationalisation of capital provokes a crisis of the nation-state by calling into question the legitimacy of the state; this in turn provokes a crisis in representation which affects political parties and their role within this contested state. The transnationalisation of capital and the crisis of the nation-state also transform class relations and politics. Working-class organisations could no longer play their roles as mediators and representatives, thus leading to a fragmentation of the workers as a group, which in turn led to a transformation of working-class consciousness[34] (resentment, alienation and, as of 1983, disappointment with the Socialist government). This for Bihr explains the transformation of the working class and its vulnerability to the anti-political themes taken up by the FN and thus its surprising support for the party in recent years.

Bihr's analysis is relevant, but not merely for France. Therein lies the problem: the explanation is partly convincing because the crisis of the nation-state, the rupture of the social-democratic compromise, and the crisis of the working-class movement all apply to most Western nations in the second half of the twentieth century. Yet, Bihr's conclusion points out that the far Right is more powerful in France than anywhere else in Western Europe. There is here a real problem of cause and effect.

The author, however, is not oblivious to this problem but his response depends on a thesis of French exceptionalism. The list of accentuating circumstances designed to bolster the explanatory framework and make it fit the French case is long: the role of the Left in power since 1981, the management of the economic crisis of the early 1980s (the high interest rates, the subsequent dismantling of entire sectors of the French economy), the unemployment rate, France's colonial past, Vichy, Jacobinism, the role of the *Parti Communiste Français* (PCF) … and the list goes on.[35]

The point here is that Bihr is right: all of these factors must have played a part in the construction of a political situation favourable to the rise of the FN. But in many ways his argument goes no further than that.

The FN as a response to political crisis

Other authors also tend to privilege explanations for the rise of the FN as responses to crises although most of them are not Marxists or neo-Marxists. Often therefore, the crisis is not an economic one but a more strictly political one, a crisis in representation or a more generally diagnosed social malaise.

Both Birenbaum and Ignazi for example[36] can be seen to point to a 'crisis of representation' in French politics. Such texts draw upon electoral analyses such as those of Pascal Perrineau who uses electoral figures in order to illustrate the extent and scope of the crisis and thus strengthen the argument concerning its severity and the plausibility of attributing the far-Right vote to it.

Perrineau's 1997 book *Le symptôme Le Pen* also draws on the concept of a crisis of representation. The first part covers familiar ground and the emergence of the FN, the second offers a 'profile' of FN voters and concludes that young males, with a low level of education make up the (then growing) bulk of the FN electorate. While the usual suspects (fear of immigration, threat of unemployment and general insecurity)[37] seem responsible – as they were in the early 1980s – for the decision to cast a vote for the FN, Perrineau underscores what he calls the 'diabolical causality'[38] which has transformed the circumstances of crisis and social dislocation into a causal reasoning in which the character of the immigrant figures as the devil himself.

> Just as late 19th century France had lent a compliant ear to the great
> themes of the 'judeo-maçonic conspiracy', late 20th century France ...
> surrenders to the myth of the 'fifth column' of immigrants. The electoral
> terrain of this modern demonology is that of an urban, socially anomic
> France in which – much as in the early 19th century – there develops the
> theme of 'the dangerous classes'. In the late 20th century, however, these
> are defined by ethnic origins rather than by social background.[39]

This, according to Perrineau, produces what he calls the 'vote of
resentment'.[40] The resentment is generated by a transformation of
society from industrial to post-industrial capitalism. The increased
differentiation of the salaried classes between intellectual and unskilled
manual labour, those who fear for their jobs and those who do not, and
the growing sense of powerlessness in the face of this widening gap has
led to the quest for scapegoats. The immigrant embodies mobile,
cosmopolitan and international society which is seen as responsible for
the precariousness of everyday life. The book's main conclusion is that
French society is in the throes of major transformations, hence the
French public's tendency to turn to 'negative politicisation':[41]

> Whereas the 1960s and 1970s had generated a whole series of social
> movements which had called into question social hierarchies, demanded
> equality, attempted to weaken borders, defended the rights of minorities
> and demanded a redistribution of power, the 1980s and 1990s are years
> of anti-egalitarian visions of society, withdrawal into national myths, the
> exclusion of minorities and the upholding of strong national power.[42]

The conclusion is thus reminiscent of those of Ignazi and of Michael
Minkenberg[43] who also claim that the resurgence of the far Right in
Europe is an authoritarian and materialistic response to the post-materialist revolution. Perrineau reads the events of the 2002 elections as
confirmation of his thesis and argues that what he refers to as the 'deaf-
ening protest' of the 2002 presidential elections is one more manifestation of the FN's will to express a sort of civic break (*fracture civique*)
through the rejection by the electorate of the governing elite.[44]

    While all of these authors present thorough analyses of the FN
they all converge on a range of explanations which places political crisis
at the centre of things. This political crisis, however, is extremely ill
defined. One slides from the idea of a crisis of representation (in which
individuals abandon political parties who fail to represent them
adequately), to an all-encompassing crisis of civilisation which leads
individuals to question not only the nature of the party system and its
validity or the efficiency or trust-worthiness of political parties, but

more fundamental things such as the nature of their social ties to the community, or their entire value system. Notions of crisis such as the latter are less than helpful: such vague civilisational crisis can explain any number of things. Strikingly, none of these authors who take crisis as their central explanatory variable focus, in particular, on a crisis of institutions.

What the authors share on the other hand is a strong sense of French exceptionalism in these matters. There is no attempt at comparison in any of these works with other European countries (let alone countries outside the European Union), and aside from Ignazi's willingness (and need) to venture beyond the realm of French political studies, none of the authors makes any attempt to use social science tools or arguments elaborated by non-French academic communities.[45] Further, French exceptionalism could be part of a valid argument if it were integrated into an explanation as to why the FN takes the shape that it does and works as it does, given the institutional context and particular historical trajectories of far-Right parties in France. In a context where the FN is particularly successful but not alone in Europe as a far-Right party, the case for French exceptionalism should be made – and taken – with a pinch of salt. It is the particular opportunities afforded the FN in the French context which might be exceptional – or at least, possibly, unique – but using ideas of post-materialism, Europeanisation and post-industrialism to make a case for the French exception in matters of far Right votes seems little short of strange and unimaginative.

The FN as an electoral machine

Much of the literature on the FN focuses rather more specifically on the voters attracted to it rather than on the party *per se*. Perrineau's 1997 book would also fit into this category if it were not for the fact that the book's aim is to elucidate the nature of a national crisis rather than to explain the motivations behind a vote for Le Pen. Perrineau's earlier contributions on the FN, on the other hand, are more straightforwardly electoral studies. In *Vote de crise*[46] (a tome devoted to the study of the 1995 presidential elections results) as well as in his contributions to the 1989 *Le Front national à découvert*, Perrineau focuses on electoral results in order to explain the increase in the FN's votes in formerly Left-wing bastions. In his 1989 work, he pioneered what was to become the received interpretation of the FN's electoral success:

from 1971 to 1982 the FN's electoral gains were non-existent, Dreux's municipal election of 1983 (henceforth referred to as the 'Dreux effect')[47] was to change all that and mark a reversal of fortune for the party.

Perrineau's corollary argument is that the FN progressed in striking fashion in former Left-wing bastions because a popular electorate – long faithful to the Left – unmoved by the personalised Lepenism of the 1980s, worn out by the deepening social and economic crisis and by fifteen years of a regular alternating of Left and Right in power, seemed willing to turn to the FN as an unexplored 'third way'.[48]

The increasing reliance on the Left's disaffected voters is one of the striking things about the FN's electoral evolution, and Perrineau's analysis is the most thorough on this point. During the 1980s FN voters were drawn overwhelmingly from the traditional Right (the *Rassemblement pour la France* (RPR) and the *Union pour la Démocratie Française* (UDF)), by 1995 however (and this remained true until 1999) the cohort of voters exhibited significantly higher levels of votes from the parties of the Left (socialist and communist). Most of the vote transfers came from former socialist bastions in Northern France, few transfers came from former communist strongholds (this is important as it argues against the traditionally held view that the French communist party's decline was partly created by the rise of the FN and a haemorrhaging of communist votes to the FN).[49]

Using post-election polls as a source of data, Perrineau further concludes that in 1988 out of a hundred voters two were from the far Left, ten from the Left, twenty-one from the Centre, twenty from the Right and forty-five from the far Right; in 1995 these figures were five from the far Left, thirteen from the Left, twenty-nine from the Centre, twenty-three from the Right and thirty from the far Right.[50] Ultimately, the FN still draws most of its voters from an electorate which is happy to label itself 'Right' or 'far Right', nevertheless the evolution detected by Perrineau is significant given that it underscores the party's appeal to a dual electorate and thus the complexity of the FN's political positioning.[51]

Nonna Mayer is another author whose work has mostly focused on electoral aspects of the FN. In an article published in 1997 and then subsequently expanded into a 1999 monograph, Mayer examines the evolution of the FN vote.[52] The 1997 article confirms the implantation of the FN at every level of French political life. Mayer stresses the stability of the FN vote and underscores, in particular, the stability of the mobilising themes: immigration, insecurity and unemployment.

The only slight shift between 1995 and 1997 is that unemployment seems to come first in the range of concerns expressed by FN voters (as opposed to immigration coming first in the past), but this is also the case for voters of every other party. Clearly in 1997 the high rate of unemployment, and thus the threat of unemployment, was uppermost in every French voter's mind.[53] The electoral geography of the FN, and the profile of the average FN voter (young, male and with a low level of education) are also confirmed. The aim of the article is thus essentially to emphasise the stability of every aspect of the party in terms of electoral gains, all the while underscoring the changing nature of the links between the FN and its voters.

In particular Mayer emphasises the fact that what initially could have been conceived as a protest vote seemed to be increasingly characterised by identification with the leader of the FN. For example, in 1995 47 per cent of the voters indicated that they voted for Le Pen in the first round of the election in order to express their resentment against other political parties (only 38 per cent said they had voted for Le Pen in the hopes that he would go on to the second round). By 1997, 46 per cent of the voters declared that they had voted for the FN because he was their first choice candidate (and only 38 per cent in order to protest against other parties).

Along the same lines, Mayer argues that whereas until 1996 FN voters were those exhibiting the lowest level of attachment to their candidate's party, by 1997 half of those who had voted for Le Pen in the legislative elections said they had done so because they had faith in the party.[54] While this last figure should be interpreted in the context of a legislative election where, given the nature of the contest, party attachment is bound to outweigh leadership attachments, this shift in the nature of support for the party was also detected by other analysts[55] and seems to reveal an evolution in the type of link between the FN and its supporters.

This leads Mayer to conclude that 'National Frontism' has replaced 'Lepenism'. Mayer's 1999 book is a more detailed analysis of the same themes. More interestingly, the work represents an attempt at countering the domination within French academic circles of the analyses of Perrineau. As such, where Perrineau talks of '*gaucho-Lepenisme*', for example, Mayer counter-argues with a more subtle diagnosis of a '*vote niniste*' (*ni droite/ni gauche* – neither Left nor Right). Where Perrineau sees the effects of French exceptionalism, Mayer sees a phenomenon eerily similar to those found in the rest of Europe.

More specifically, Mayer's work is a study – in light of the recent split within the FN – of the decisional process which leads an individual to vote for the FN. In this, her analysis is somewhat different from those of other electoral specialists given that her argument is that one needs to look not so much at the electorate of the FN but, rather, at the process which leads to a vote for the FN.[56] The typical FN voter remains, as established since the late 1980s, male, young and with a low level of education. Using the American studies on the appeal of authoritarian personalities as well as analyses of the psychological springs of fascism,[57] Mayer concludes that an ethnocentric and authoritarian view of the world and social relationships is characteristic of a majority of FN voters.[58] Furthermore, the majority of FN voters seem overwhelmingly swayed by the force of 'simple ideas' which appeals to a cohort with a low level of education and relatively depressing prospects.[59] In an attempt to determine whether education or personality is the determining factor in a vote for the FN, Mayer concludes that a high score on the intolerance scale will generally overrule a high level of education but that generally speaking, education seems to play a determinant role in the development of a tolerant personality, thus leading Mayer to conclude that the link between level of education and the FN vote is very strong.[60]

The most important point in Mayer's study is her conclusion that the FN vote is made up of three distinct types of voters. On the one hand there are supporters who belong firmly to the Right or the far Right of the political spectrum and which represent half the FN vote. On the other hand , there are voters two-thirds of whom see themselves as '*ni-nistes*', and one third of whom would label themselves Left wing – or formerly so. Mayer illustrates through a set of figures going back to 1988 how the vote for Le Pen may be a working-class vote without necessarily qualifying as a Left-wing vote.[61] This is an important qualification to the conventional wisdom of the past ten years. Mayer's conclusion also enables her to give a plausible explanation for the split into two of the FN in 1999. According to the author, the split reflects the dual nature of the vote and therefore the double composition of the party's electoral constituency.[62]

Mayer's volume is undeniably the most thorough and accessible of FN voter analyses. By drawing on and referring to the work of North American and European political scientists she also introduces a theoretical dimension which is absent from the works of French electoral analysts. Her attempt to introduce an element of comparison into her work and the conclusion that the motivations of FN voters are nothing extraordinary in late-twentieth-century Europe is nothing short of revolutionary in French academic circles. Ultimately however, this is a sensitive electoral analysis, but little more.

The ideational world of the FN: in the beginning was the idea

A final and particularly interesting area of the literature on the FN is that which focuses on the ideas or ideology of the FN. French authors such as Milza, Taguieff and Winock converge on the idea that the FN is a vehicle for a form of populism. Milza's contribution is one of the clearest and most informative accounts of the FN's ideas. In a chapter entitled '*Le Front national: droite extrême ... ou national-populisme*',[63] Milza draws upon his previous work on French fascism in order to answer what he regards as the main questions concerning the ideological identity of the FN.[64] Is the FN fascist? Is it a form of counter-revolutionary Right reactivated by anti-communism on the one hand and the anxieties linked to a post-industrial society on the other? Is it a form of national-populism? For Milza the answer to whether the FN is fascist is a resounding 'no'. The author however, painstakingly affirms that while the FN is not fascist, this fact should not lead analysts to under-estimate either the importance of fascism in France or the odious nature of the FN even if it is not fascist. For Milza, fascism as a totalitarian phenomenon remained marginal in France: it remained – to use his terminology – a 'virtuality'.[65] However, fascism, if it did not give rise to a totalitarian regime, did, according to Milza, spawn an ideological tradition and while it may not have been born in France (as Sternhell claims[66]) it can be seen to have deep French roots.

According to the author, the FN has broken with the explicitly fascist aims and tactics of its founding members in order to fulfil strategic imperatives which could not be fulfilled in a world in which liberal democracy dictates political behaviour. The fact that the FN has not been a mass party (such as the *Parti national fasciste* of 1921, or even Jacques Doriot's *Parti populaire français*, influential in the 1930s) coupled with its firmly far-Right credentials[67] prohibits the use of the fascist label.

As to whether the FN should be considered a part of the counter-revolutionary Right, Milza's answer is that the FN should be understood as a combination of counter-revolutionary ultra-conservatism and Vichy's national-populist doctrine. Thus, it combines a nostalgia for Vichy's national revolution and the ideas of the counter-revolutionary Right such as a strong state and a natural, established (God-given) social order.

P. A. Taguieff is one of the rare authors whose main concern has been to delineate the contours of the ideology of the FN. For Taguieff, who was one of the first to draw on the idea of national populism in assessing the FN,[68] the tradition within which the FN should be interpreted has dual commitments: an organicist model of society on the one hand and social Darwinism on the other. The first suggests a drive to 'preserve', 'maintain' and 'conserve'; the second has overtones of struggle and victory over adversaries. To some extent these drives are in opposition to one another but according to Taguieff they are linked by the concept of reaction.[69] In literary spheres, argues Taguieff, the synthesis of these two drives is expressed under the label of the 'conservative revolution'. In the national-populist political tradition it is the concept of reaction which provides the linkage and subsequently the synthesis between the two contradictory poles: '[Reaction] operates the synthesis of the equally valued attitudes of conservation and domination, of defense and attack, of taking root and expansion, of respect for the past and a future-oriented offensive.'[70]

In Taguieff's analysis then, Le Pen is portrayed as someone whose function is that of the 'great unifier'. The heterogeneity of the FN's doctrine requires the presence of a leader capable of synthesising the contradictions of this fundamentally unstable set of doctrinal tenets.

The literature examined in this last section is undoubtedly the most enlightening on the FN's ideology and it shall figure more prominently in the rest of this book. There are, however, two identifiable lacunae. The first is that, in most of these texts, ideas seem to float, gas-like, from one era to the next, briefly incarnated by one movement or another but the manner in which they are transmitted, transformed and exploited remains relatively unexplored. While the populism of Betz's analysis was reduced to party-political expressions with little in the way of an account of the formation of ideas or even, more modestly, of the ideological content of the labels, the converse is true here: the ideas are only tangentially related to their political expressions and when discourse analysis is used, the words themselves are not expressly linked to tangible political phenomena.

Secondly, these authors inevitably characterise the ideas of neo-fascism, populism or national-populism as attacks on the Republic and Republican institutions, which they might well be. But here, the first criticism perhaps explains the second: the reluctance of these authors to tie the ideas of the FN to a set of political realities may explain their failure to recognise that the Fifth Republic which they see as permanently under attack from these ideas and the parties and movements associated with them, is partly responsible for the success of their political expression in the FN.

Overall, what is characteristic of all of the literature surveyed so far is the conspicuous absence of institutions and the institutional contexts as explanatory variables. Whether it be the analyses of the FN that privilege crisis as an explanation or those which examine the electorate of the FN more particularly or, finally, those examined in this last section which take as their main focus the ideological stance and the ideas of the FN, none of these analyses incorporate institutions as part of the explanatory matrix.

Even in the case of electoral or voter studies, the institutions within which these electoral choices are made remain absent and their impact on the nature of the choices available remain unexplored. The aim of the next chapter is precisely to elaborate a framework for the understanding of the FN which takes institutions and ideas into account as explanatory variables.

Notes

1 R. Inglehart, *The Silent Revolution* (Princeton, NJ: Princeton University Press, 1977); see also R. Inglehart, 'Value change in industrial society', *American Political Science Review*, 81 (1987), 1289–303.

2 P. Ignazi, 'The silent counter-revolution: hhypotheses on the emergence of extreme Right-wing parties in Europe', *European Journal of Political Research*, 22 (1992), 3–34.

3 Inglehart, *The Silent Revolution*.

4 Ignazi, 'The silent counter-revolution', p. 6.

5 Ignazi, 'The silent counter-revolution', p. 6.

6 Ignazi, 'The silent counter-revolution', p. 9.

7 Ignazi, 'The silent counter-revolution', p. 9.

8 P. Ignazi, 'New and old extreme right parties: the French *Front national* and the Italian *Movimento Sociale*', *European Journal of Political Research*, 22 (1992), 101–21.

9 H. G. Betz, 'Introduction' in H. G. Betz and S. Immerfall, eds, *The New Politics of the Right* (London: Macmillan, 1998), p. 1.

10 Betz, 'Introduction', p. 1.

11 Betz, 'Introduction', p. 2.

12 Betz, 'Introduction', p. 3.

13 Betz's distinction between 'extremist' and 'radical' is not satisfactorily drawn. Nevertheless, basing ourselves on Betz's argument, it would seem

that for this author 'extremism' is associated with violent rejection whereas 'radicalism' entails espousing fundamental change. The distinction is perhaps most apt when applied to two different areas: radicalism applies to programmes whereas extremism applies to tactics. In conclusion however, if it is the case that the two words refer to different areas then the distinction is not particularly useful. (see Betz, 'Introduction', pp. 3–4).

14 H. G. Betz, 'The new politics of resentment: radical right-wing populist parties in Western Europe', *Comparative Politics*, 25:4 (1993), 413.

15 For a detailed account see H. G. Betz, *Radical Right-Wing Populism in Western Europe* (New York: St. Martin's Press, 1994). In particular see Chapter 1 for his definition of populism.

16 C. Mudde, 'Right-wing extremism analyzed: a comparative analysis of three alleged right-wing extremist parties (NPD, NDP, CP'86)', *European Journal of Political Research*, 27 (1995), 204–24.

17 S. Immerfall, 'The neo-populist agenda', in Betz and Immerfall, eds, *The New Politics*, pp. 249–61.

18 Immerfall, 'The neo-populist agenda', p. 251.

19 H. Kitschelt (with R. McGann), *The Radical Right in Western Europe* (Ann Arbor, MI: University of Michigan Press, 1995).

20 P. Perrineau, *Le symptôme Le Pen: radiographie des électeurs du Front national* (Paris: Fayard, 1997); N. Mayer, *Ces français qui votent FN* (Paris: Flammarion, 1999).

21 On the *Republikaner* see M. Minkenberg, 'The new right in Germany: the transformation of conservatism and the extreme right', *European Journal of Political Research*, 22 (July 1992), 55–81; E. Zimmerman and T. Saalfeld, 'The three waves of West German right-wing extremism', in P. H. Merkl and L. Weinberg, eds, *Encounters with the Contemporary Radical Right* (Boulder, CO: Westview Press, 1993), pp. 50–7; see also C. Mudde, *The Ideology of the Extreme Right* (Manchester: Manchester University Press, 2000).

22 For material on the MSI and the AN see R. Griffin, 'The 'post-Fascism' of the *Alleanza Nazionale*: a case study in ideological morphology', *Journal of Political Ideologies*, 1: 2 (1996), 123–45; P. Ignazi, *Il polo escluso. Profilo del Movimento Sociale Italiano* (Bologna: Il Mulino, 1989); also by Ignazi, *Postfascisti?* (Bologna: Il Mulino, 1995); R. Chiarani, 'The Italian far right', in L. Cheles, R. Ferguson and M. Vaughan, eds, *The Far Right in Western Europe* (London: Longman, 1995).

23 For a general treatment of the far Right in Scandinavia see L. Svåsand, 'Scandinavian right-wing radicalism', in Betz and Immerfall, eds, *The New Politics*, pp. 77–93.

24 See M. Swyngedoun, 'The extreme right in Belgium: of a non-existent *Front National* and an omnipresent *Vlaams Blok*', in Betz and Immerfall, eds, *The New Politics*, pp. 59–75.

25 On the FPÖ see Max Riedlsperger ' The Freedom Party of Austria: from protest to radical right populism', in Betz and Immerfall, eds, *The New Politics*, pp. 27–43; see also K. R. Luther, 'Austria: a democracy under threat from the Freedom Party?', *Parliamentary Affairs*, 53: 3 (July 2000), 426–42.

26 On the LPF see E. Jones, 'Politics beyond accommodation? The May 2002 Dutch parliamentary elections', *Dutch Crossings*, 26: 1 (Summer 2002), 61–78.

27 In a January 1984 SOFRES poll (which each month measures public support for politicians) 9 per cent of people interviewed declared that they had 'a high opinion' (*'une bonne opinion'*) of the FN and 9 per cent were of the opinion that they 'would like to see Jean-Marie Le Pen play an important role in the months and years to come' (*'jouer un rôle important dans les mois et les années à venir'*). Baromètre Figaro-SOFRES (January 1984).

28 The best sources – used here – for an analysis of the FN's electoral results are P. Perrineau and N. Mayer, eds, *Le Front national à découvert*, second edition (Paris: Presses de Sciences Po, 1996) and Perrineau, *Le symptôme*.

29 A. Bihr, *Pour en finir avec le Front national* (Paris: Syros, 1992).

30 Bihr, *Pour en finir*, pp. 47–50.

31 Bihr, *Pour en finir*, p. 57.

32 Bihr, *Pour en finir*, p. 57.

33 Bihr, *Pour en finir*, pp. 47–77.

34 Bihr, *Pour en finir*, pp. 91–98.

35 Bihr, *Pour en finir*, pp. 275–85.

36 G. Birenbaum, *Le Front national en politique* (Paris: Balland, 1992); P. Ignazi, 'Un nouvel acteur politique,' in P. Perrineau and N. Mayer, eds, *Le Front national à découvert*, pp. 63–80.

37 In the 1997 regional elections 65 per cent of FN voters cited insecurity as a primary motivation for their vote; 67 per cent cited immigration and 67 per cent fear of unemployment (compared with the average of 22 per cent, 22 per cent and 75 per cent of the general population respectively). Perrineau, *Le symptôme*, pp. 177–8.

38 Perrineau, *Le symptôme*, pp. 180–3.

39 Perrineau, *Le symptôme*, p. 181.

40 Here Perrineau cites the German philosopher Max Scheler (p. 182), but his diagnosis has also much in common with a more recent one namely Hans Georg Betz's mentioned in the previous section.

41 Perrineau, *Le symptôme*, p. 243.

42 Perrineau, *Le symptôme*, p. 244.

43 M. Minkenberg, 'The new right in France and Germany. *Nouvelle Droite, Neue Rechte* and the new right radical parties', in P. Merkl, ed., *The Revival of Right-wing Extremism in the Nineties* (London: Frank Cass, 1997), pp. 65–90.

44 P. Perrineau, 'La surprise Lepéniste et ses suites legislatives', in P. Perrineau and C. Ysmal, *Le vote de tout les refus* (Paris: Presses de Science Po, 2003), pp. 199–222.

45 This should be qualified: Perrineau cites, in passing and without specific references, Inglehart, Merkl, and Minkenberg once in the last four pages of his conclusion. Perrineau, *Le symptôme*, pp. 244–7.

46 P. Perrineau, 'La dynamique du vote Le Pen: le poids du gaucho-lepénisme', in P. Perrineau and C. Ysmal, eds, *Le vote de crise: l'élection présidentielle de 1995* (Paris: Presses de Science Po, 1995), pp. 243–61.

47 The best – and apparently only – analysis of the Dreux municipal elections is to be found in an article by P. Bréchon and S. Kumar Mitra, 'The National Front in France: the emergence of an extreme right protest movement', *Comparative Politics*, 25 (October 1992), 63–82 (on Dreux see more specifically pp. 71–8). The authors show that the themes of immigration and insecurity were key mobilising themes for the FN as early as 1984. They also conclude that the FN is essentially a protest movement rather than a party.

48 Perrineau, 'La dynamique', p. 252.

49 According to Perrineau, the correlation established between measures of the evolution of the socialist electorate and that of the FN electorate is of –0.78. The correlation established between measures of the evolution of the communist electorate and the evolution of the FN electorate is of 0.15. Perrineau, 'La dynamique', p. 254.

50 Perrineau, *Le symptôme*, p. 256. All figures used by Perrineau are from a SOFRES post-election poll held between 20–23 May 1995.

51 Authors such as Pierre Martin have taken issue with Perrineau's analysis: using the same figures as Perrineau (and in particular the SOFRES poll which gave evidence as to the fact that Le Pen voters were less motivated than the average voter by traditionally Left-wing themes (such as the maintenance of certain standards of social provisions, or the fight against exclusion for example), Martin assures the reader that Perrineau's hypothesis of a 'gaucho-lepénisme' is nowhere confirmed. His argument is that what is in evidence is not so much a move to the Left of the Le Pen electorate so much as a move to the Right of the working-class electorate: '[T]here are both transfers from the Left to the mainstream Right, as well as transfers from the mainstream Right and the Left to the FN' (p. 7). This evolution according to him is symptomatic of the impact of the immigration question on the French political scene after 1981. The ultimate aim of Martin's demonstration, and in keeping with the political views of the Fondation Saint Simon, is to lift the burden of the rise of the FN from the shoulders of the French Left, and transfer this burden on to the behaviour of the parties of the Right. P. Martin, 'Le vote Le Pen', *Notes de la Fondation Saint-Simon* (Paris: October–November, 1996), pp. 1–2.

52 N. Mayer, 'Du vote lepéniste au vote frontiste', *Revue française de science politique*, 47, 3-4 (June–August, 1997), pp. 438–53; N. Mayer, *Ces français qui votent FN* (Paris: Flammarion, 1999).

53 Mayer, 'Du vote lepéniste', p. 443.

54 Mayer, *Ces français*, pp. 85–203.

55 H. Le Bras, 'Trois composantes des moeurs en France', in N. Mayer, ed., *Les modèles explicatifs du vote* (Paris: l'Harmattan, 1997); P. Perrineau, 'Les étapes d'une implantation électorale', in P. Perrineau and N. Mayer, eds, *Le Front national à découvert*, pp. 37–62.

56 Mayer, *Ces français*, p. 12.

57 For these purposes Mayer refers to the main – dated – texts such as Adorno's work on *The Authoritarian Personality* (New York, NY: Harper and Row, 1950) or E. L. Hartley, *Problems in Prejudice* (New York, NY: King's Crown Press, 1946) but also to more recent work such as

B. Altemeyer, *The Authoritarian Specter* (Cambridge, MA: Harvard University Press, 1996) or her own 'La perception de l'autre', in P. Perrineau and C. Ysmal, *Le vote surprise: les élections législatives des 25 mai et 1er juin 1997* (Paris: Presses de Science Po, 1998), pp. 267–84.

58 Mayer, *Ces français*, pp. 57–60.

59 The figures cited by Mayer are interesting: individuals without the French baccalaureate (high-school diploma equivalent) are three times more likely to vote for the FN than those who have the diploma; furthermore, this proportion has steadily grown over the past decade. Finally Mayer highlights the generational difference on this count: the low level of education is less of a determining factor for older cohorts but seems to make a dramatic difference in the younger one. Mayer, *Ces français*, pp. 69–70, Table 1.

60 Although there is a caveat to this statement: Mayer also notes that in cases of extreme intolerance (i.e. very high scores on the intolerance scale), a higher level of education seems to encourage the individual to vote for the FN. Mayer, *Ces français*, p. 72.

61 Mayer, *Ces français*, pp. 214–19.

62 Mayer isolates, firstly, a social cleavage: the '*ni-nistes*' are generally of modest origin: in 1997 two-thirds of them had a link to the working class, 41 per cent of them quit school at 14 while 90 per cent do not have a baccalaureate. The '*droitistes*' on the other hand are from relatively affluent social backgrounds, nearly one-third of this cohort has a baccalaureate, 39 per cent of them (as against 22 per cent in the *ni-nistes* group) are in well-paid professional work. Ideologically this last group is overwhelmingly more Catholic, they are generally far more disapproving of homosexuality and abortion and on the whole the *ni-nistes* seem more tolerant as a cohort (toward different ways of life, opinions, practices, criminality and justice). The *ni-nistes* hold Left-wing social beliefs, are more willing to defend welfare provision standards and are globally more supportive of state intervention and of public-sector action. They are also more likely than the '*droitistes*' to mobilise in order to safeguard what they regard as their rights. Finally, politically, the two groups are diametrically opposed: the ni-nistes exhibit little faith in politics, they are overwhelmingly drawn from backgrounds where at least one (and usually both) parents considered themselves 'apolitical' and their defining characteristic is their suspicion regarding the political class and political elites. The figures are striking: 85 per cent of the *ni-nistes* declare that they feel don't feel close to any political party (as compared with 60 per cent of the *droitistes* and 44 per cent of the non-FN voters); 89 per cent of them say have faith in neither the Left- nor the Right-wing parties to govern the country (as compared with 57 per cent of the *droitistes* and 31 per cent of the non-FN voters); 70 per cent of them feel that politicians are unconcerned with ordinary people like them (as opposed to 49 per cent of the *droitistes* and 26 per cent of the non-FN voters). Mayer, *Ces français*, pp. 223–45.

63 P. Milza, 'Le Front national: droite extrême … ou national-populisme?' in J. F. Sirinelli, ed., *Histoires des droites en France, Vol. 1* (Paris: NRF/Gallimard, 1992), pp. 691–729.

64 See P. Milza, *Les fascismes* (Paris: Imprimerie nationale, 1985); P. Milza, *Fascisme français. Passé et présent* (Paris: Flammarion, 1987).

65 Milza, 'Droite extrême', p. 708.

66 Z. Sternhell, *Les origines françaises du fascisme* (Paris: Seuil, Coll. Points, 1983).

67 It is interesting to note that for Milza the FN is unequivocally part of the extreme Right: it strives for long term transformations of the social order, for the establishment of a strong state and it is stridently against liberal democracy. Radical direct action and recourse to violence are, for Milza, a potential but not a requisite part of the extreme Right.

68 P. A. Taguieff, 'La doctrine du national-populism en France', *Études*, 364: 1 (1986), 27–46; P. A.Taguieff, 'Mobilisation national-populiste en France: vote xénophobe et nouvel anti-sémitisme politique', *Lignes* (March 1990), 91–136; P. A. Taguieff, 'La métaphysique de Jean-Marie Le Pen', and 'Un programme révolutionnaire?' in P. Perrineau and N. Mayer, eds, *Le Front national à découvert*, pp. 173–94 and pp. 195–227.

69 Taguieff, 'La métaphysique', pp. 174–5.

70 Taguieff, 'La métaphysique', p. 175.

Chapter 2

Institutions, opportunites and ideologies

As underscored in the previous chapter, the literature on the French *Front national* fails to take into account the institutional context in which this party has emerged and evolved. The aim of this chapter is to outline a theoretical framework in which institutions and institutional change figure prominently. To do this, two bodies of literature will be evaluated and used: the first centres around theories of mobilisation and, in particular, the study of political opportunity structures; the second is the new-institutionalist literature. Finally, Michael Freeden's work on 'ideological morphology' will also be examined and integrated into a model of ideational institutionalism. This framework will then be applied to the FN in order to explain its success from the early 1980s onward. The FN is an organisation seeking entry into a wider institutional context. It is also a political actor seeking legitimacy through further institutionalisation. Thus, this study does not look at how policies are constrained by institutions, or how institutions constrain the impact of political ideas,[1] or even how ideas constrain policy making, but, rather, we pick things up at another point in the cycle of ideas, institutions and policy making and ask how institutional innovations bring about changes in ideas – or renew the legitimacy of older ones – all of which in turn affect other institutions (and organisations) and their chances of survival or success. Picking up the cycle at this particular point, and from this particular angle, allows for the emphasis to be placed on the role of opportunities as well as constraints.

One useful way of conceiving of the two variables in this book would be to say that the institutions of the Fifth Republic constitute the dominant paradigm (infused with a set of what Campbell refers to as 'paradigmatic ideas') which the FN attempts to permeate by adopting a set of programmatic ideas not extraneous to the dominant paradigm.[2] The literature on political opportunity structures permits an initial formalisation of this reasoning and the manner in which mobilisation is linked to institutions is thereby illustrated. Further, one could argue that the literature on new social movements (hereafter NSMs) deals with challenges posed to political systems,[3] and as such it is useful to look at the FN in those same terms, as a challenge coming from the Right rather than from the Left. Along these lines it is also worth pointing out that the Fifth Republic, particularly in its foundational moments, turns every political actor, party or movement – aside from the Gaullists – into an 'outsider' and therefore into an actor which, much as NSMs often need to do, must learn to gain entry into a political system.[4]

Introducing the structure of political opportunity

Notions of political opportunity structures are far from new. Those scholars who elaborated the political opportunity structure framework of analysis for the study of NSMs, however, were particularly concerned with examining and measuring the manner in which opportunities in a given political system structure mobilisation, social movement activity and social movement 'success'.

The systematic examination of structures of political opportunity is relatively recent. In 1973 Peter Eisinger defined them as a set of institutional variables which he used to analyse and explain riots in American cities.[5] Notions of 'open' and 'closed' local government were also applied by Tilly to the nation.[6] Both authors emphasised the fact that movements elaborate strategies which are a reflection of the environment in which they live. Snyder and Tilly for example had already looked at the waves of mobilisation in France in the 1830s and concluded that mobilisation was more closely linked to electoral opportunities and regime changes than to grievances or levels of deprivation.[7] In other words, movements were as much reactive as they were active: they were dependent on shifting alliances at the elite level, dependent on the actions of other social movements, dependent, finally, on the institutional balance of power in a given place at a given time. Social movements according to these authors were, therefore, not only affected by their internal mechanisms, crises and resources, but also by factors which were exogenous to their own organisational structures and parameters.

Kitschelt's 1986 article[8] is the first in which the institutions constitutive of political opportunity structures are stable governmental structures which vary from country to country and explain variations in the impact and success of the movements across countries. Other authors build on this notion in order to explain variations within a single country: how did shifting coalitions, electoral agendas, changes in personnel, alterations in foreign policy and other more fundamental changes (regime changes, institutional reforms) create more or less favourable conditions for social movements?

It is worthwhile pointing out here that theories of political opportunity structures owe much to theories of resource mobilisation. Like resource mobilisation theories, political-opportunity-structures approaches conceive of social movements as rational, collective enterprises whose aim is to further their cause using all available resources in the most efficient manner possible. Unlike the resource mobilisation approach, however, political-opportunity-structures theories emphasise the movements' external resources rather than their internal resources. As Kitschelt writes,

> the emphasis [of the present comparison of anti-nuclear movements] is on relating the strategic choices and societal impacts of movements to specific properties of the external political opportunity structures that movements face.[9]

In a 1992 article Kriesi, Koopmans, Duyvendak and Giugni present their findings regarding the level of general mobilisation in France, Germany, the Netherlands and Switzerland;[10] These findings confirm the relevance of the political process in measuring the level of mobilisation in these various countries.

Aside from contributing to the renewed emphasis in the study of political processes, these authors also offer a concise definition and presentation of theories of structures of political opportunity.[11] Following Kriesi's distinctions[12] the authors put forth three sets of properties pertaining to political systems:

> Its formal institutional structure, its informal procedures and prevailing strategies with regard to challengers, and the configuration of power relevant for the confrontation of challengers. The first two sets of properties provide the general setting for the mobilisation of collective action; they also contain the relevant configurations of power. Together with the general setting, the relevant configuration of power specifies the strategies of the 'authorities' or the 'members of the system' with regard to the mobilisation of the 'challengers'. Theses strategies, in turn, define (a) the

extent to which challenging collective action will be facilitated or repressed by 'members of the system' (b) the chances of success such actions may have, and (c) the chances of success if no such actions take place, which may be either positive, if the government is reform-oriented, or negative if the government in power is hostile to the movement.[13]

Of general significance is the emphasis placed on political processes and their impact on movements. Two aspects of this definition are of particular relevance:

1. the emphasis placed upon those elements which shape the config-uration of power as well as how the latter creates opportunities;
2. the acknowledgement of the web of political opportunities which are created by the political context. This aspect will be examined below, criticised and modified – thanks to the contributions made by new institutionalist theories.

Structures of political opportunity and the general political setting

Formal institutional structures

With respect to what they refer to as the 'overall institutional setting', Kriesi *et al.* follow state-centred theories.[14] They therefore use the distinction often made between weak states and strong states. According to these authors:

> weak states are defined by their openness on the input side and by their lack of capacity to impose themselves on the output side. Conversely, strong states are defined as closed and having a high capacity to impose themselves. The internal structure of state institutions – the degree of their internal coherence or fragmentation – is thought to determine the overall strength or weakness of the state.[15]

Put differently by Sid Tarrow:

> The argument runs that centralized states with effective policy instru-ments at their command attract collective actors to the summit of the political system, while decentralized states provide a multitude of targets at the system's base.[16]

In many ways the argument put forth by Kriesi and Tarrow (as well as separately by Duyvendak),[17] draws on the existing literature on state capacity, without entering into the details of the argument.[18] This means, to some extent, that the analysis of state strength is minimal. Nevertheless it concurs with the various studies which have been carried out in this field, and in particular with most examinations of the French state (both on the part of state theorists as well as others), which argue that the French state, by being both centralised and the home of a strong executive, can be seen as having a high capacity for policy implementation while at the same time being difficult to penetrate.

These issues require some comment as the state of the literature reveals one of the many paradoxes which pervade the study of France and illustrates the necessity for what follows in this chapter. The French state has been portrayed as a monolithic, impregnable fortress. Nevertheless, Vincent Wright, Jack Hayward and Ezra Suleiman as well as Pierre Birnbaum have all repeatedly pointed to the caricatural nature of this depiction. Wright for example devoted an entire chapter of his *The Government and Politics of France* to the debunking of various myths about the French state and the system of public administration in France:

> The power and influence of the administration are less great than the critics contend … There are, in practice, real limits to administrative power. In the first place it should be remembered that the state is ubiquitous but it is not omnipresent: France is not a totalitarian society and civil society is extensive and flourishing. Secondly, it should be noted that in some areas there has been an attempt since the 1960s to disengage the state …[19]

These remarks lead to the conclusion that the French state is not as impregnable as once was thought because there is access by means of various forms of nepotism and the characteristically named '*filières*' (loosely translated as 'pathways') which grant informal, privileged and unofficial access to 'outsiders'.[20]

Hayward expresses this view in the following manner:

> National uniformity conceived of as a comprehensive code of standardized rules imposed on all and sundry by Parisian officials as the guardians of republican virtue, is the principle that is supposed to be the keynote of the relationship between the French government and the citizen. Practice is different … To maintain the appearance of impartiality, the agents of the state take refuge in bureaucratic impersonality. They deal with 'categories' and not 'cases'. The objects of these regulations have no choice except to 'pull strings', to bribe or to revolt.[21]

These authors therefore, recognise that the fortress is assailable in unofficial practice if not in official theory. Although it is important to note Wright's conclusion on this: 'The practice,' he writes, 'is not necessarily corrupt: France is not a "banana republic". The appropriate organs of the state may adopt other attitudes.'[22] He then goes on to cite collusion with certain groups, genuine collaboration to form a symbiotic relationship (on this Wright draws on Suleiman's argument),[23] toleration or discrimination for political reasons.

What becomes apparent is that the generalised view of the monolithic French state has undergone a process of qualification for some years now. For most experienced analysts of the French state it appears to be more accessible to outsiders than it once was. To some extent, the reality of research suggests that the traditionally held view was in many respects a caricature and never existed in full form. However, the qualifications of the caricature seem, themselves, to lead to a caricatural view of France: despite caveats that 'France is not a banana republic' the impression one is left with is that the access granted by the French state is being granted almost exclusively via informal networks and back-room deals, thus strengthening the view that the state is indeed as impermeable to outsiders as ever, except where slightly corrupt.

This is where theories of political opportunity structures can make a worthwhile contribution. While these theories lead to the wrong conclusion about France, they nevertheless point in the right direction by allowing for the treatment of the French case as an institutional setting capable of granting opportunities and not just as a political setting accessible only through nepotism and slightly corrupt informal practices.

Informal procedures and dominant strategies

The theoretical distinction here is between 'exclusive' strategies (which repress, confront or polarise) and 'inclusive' strategies (which facilitate, enhance cooperation and often bring the assimilation of the challengers or their ideas into the system).[24] According to the authors, political systems fall into one or the other category. France and Germany tend toward exclusion and repression, while Switzerland and the Netherlands tend toward more integrative strategies.

By combining the strong-state/weak-state distinction with the exclusive/integrative one, the authors arrive at a matrix into which they slot the four countries whose mobilisational events they intend to analyse. Full exclusion is characterised by the combination of a strong state with an exclusionary dominant strategy. This situation amounts to no formal (institutional) or informal (prevailing modes and strategies) access to the polity. This situation of complete exclusion is contrasted with that of complete inclusion which the authors refer to as 'full procedural integration' – a situation whereby the combination of a weak state and facilitated access to the system conspire to give challengers access but with little chances of procedural or policy impact as the state is too weak to implement much of what the challengers seek.

Two combinations allow for intermediate cases: a situation termed 'informal cooptation' refers to a strong state offering no formal entry into the polity but informal facilitation of access, while another intermediate case, referred to as 'formalistic inclusion', offers the possibility of a weak state presenting multiple access points (thus a facilitative prevailing strategy) but with no real possibility of significant concessions or implementation of policy.[25]

France is seen here as a case of full exclusion, combining a strong state and an exclusive, sometimes repressive, attitude to challengers. Other authors have made similar points. According to Crozier, for example, the centralisation of the French state has a significance that goes beyond the desire to concentrate power at the top:

> It is an extremely centralised system, almost by nature. But the profound significance of this extreme centralisation which is recognised by all, is ... the placing of sufficient distance, or a protective screen, between those people who have the right to make a decision and those people who will be affected by this decision.[26]

The notion of inclusive and exclusive strategies is economical and useful but is in need of some modification. Phil Cerny rejects outright the notion that France can be understood as having either a closed formal institutional system or exclusive informal strategies. According to him, France is remarkably open to political contestation and (writing on terrorism) he makes the following remarks:

> Recourse to terrorism seems disproportionate in a society which offers so many other means of expressing political, sometimes revolutionary, opposition ... where radical activists can have recourse to a variety of more or less efficient forms of alternative political behaviour.[27]

Cerny's view however does not seem to fit the reality either: most NSMs do in fact emerge only with difficulty in France, and research findings confirm this.[28] The view of full exclusion, however, is not

supported and this project illustrates the importance of selective inclusion[29] of challengers – in the French system. The system is open to
those whose programmatic ideas can be accommodated in dominant
institutions. The conclusions put forth by Kriesi regarding institutions
and the French polity are somewhat flawed, but these problems can be
remedied: first, some of the literature on new institutionalism and
historical institutionalism can be used to strengthen the analysis of the
nature of institutions, and the consequences of institutional change.
Second, their arguments about the opportunities for challengers made
available by formal and informal structures need to be modified.

Refining theories of political opportunity: the contribution of the new institutionalists

The characterisation of institutions by political-opportunity-structures
theorists is in need of some amendment for the POS to be usefully
applied to the French case. This, in turn, leads to a very different view
of France from that which emerges from Kriesi's conclusions, one
which helps to understand the success of movements/parties such as
the FN.

The first problem arises from the dichotomy between 'formal'
institutional arrangements and more 'informal' procedures. This
distinction reveals too narrow an understanding of institutions and
how they function. The second problem is the resulting conception of
France as a closed and exclusive polity. While France can be seen as a
closed polity for some movements, it offers institutional access – in
various forms and through various means – to others.

The new institutionalist literature enables one to address both
objections in turn. Adding an institutional level of analysis to the
initial theory of structures of political opportunity constitutes one of
this book's main aims as it is concerned with the way in which a proper
conceptualisation of institutions – combined with an understanding of
how ideologies develop and evolve – can explain political action.

The new institutionalism and an initial redefinition of institutions

As remarked by Kenneth Shepsle, in a 1986 article in which he criti-
cises the gains of the behavioural revolution,

> Our ability to describe (and less frequently, to explain) behavior ... has diminished the attention once given to institutional context and actual outcomes. On net the behavioral revolution has probably been of positive value. But along with the many scientific benefits, we have been burdened by the cost of the restricted scope in our analyses.[31]

This remark by Shepsle reflects the purpose of the new institutionalism: to re-insert the study of institutions within the science of politics. The new institutionalism yields a view of institutions which is more conducive to a dynamic understanding of politics and of the political process.

Peter Hall's definition is a good starting point, as for him institutions comprise the following:

> formal rules and compliance procedures and standard operating practices that structure the relationship between individuals in various units of the polity and the economy.[32]

Several aspects of this definition warrant discussion. First, what is striking about this definition is the emphasis on 'procedure' and 'practice'. Institutions here are conceived of as much more than a set of formal rules. The shift away from a rule-bound (static, rigid and immobile) to a more fluid, and perhaps more complex, conception of institutions is obvious. It is important to keep in mind, however, that this evolution did not begin with the new institutionalists' renewal of interests in institutions: conceptions of institutions have evolved regularly, and the 1960s and 1970s saw the first move away from a narrowly legalistic understanding of institutions toward a redefining of them which came to encompass more informally organised political actors such interest and pressure groups.[33]

However, it is the literature on the new institutionalism which succeeded in turning institutions as frameworks into institutions as frameworks of relationships – and relationships entail both practice and mediation. As classical institutionalists held, institutions *do* structure political relations amongst various actors in the political and social and economic sphere, but – and this is one of the new institutionalists' main contributions – they do so partly through the relationships they have with one another – from institution to institution – and through the relationships they construct between political actors – which are or are not yet fully institutionalised. Krasner pinpoints this interconnectedness of institutions in a 1988 article in which he argues that horizontal linkage, or 'breadth', is one of the two key aspects of institutionalism (the other being vertical depth). His reasoning high-lights this important dimension of institutions:

> Breadth refers to the number of links that a particular activity has with other activities, to the number of changes that would have to be made if a particular form of activity were altered.[34]

This means that institutions can be conceived of as three-dimensional: they are at once a framework, the relationships enacted within this framework and the pattern of these relationships over time.

Thus, another important element connected to historical institu-tionalism's emphasis on practice is that of temporality. In Peter Hall's definition of institutions the idea that practices are 'standard', in other words that they are routinised, often ritualised, dictated and expected by either formal rules or implicit convention, is central. Institutions are thereby located in the realm of action and practice as well as in the realm of structure. This is remarkable because the instances of repeti-tion – and therefore patterns of actions over time – are what endows institutions with their paradoxical nature. Action and the reification (or ossification) of that action are contained in the very nature of institu-tions and therefore gives them inherent qualities tending toward both action and inertia.[35] So institutions survive, evolve and break down through a dialectical process. The dialectic is exhausted when the repe-tition of action over time in expected patterns finally turns into an ossi-fication of action. Notions of 'repetition' and 'standardisation' might seem to impart a kind of timelessness to institutions, a sense that they are outside history. Such a conclusion would be erroneous in this case and it is important to note that here the repetition, standardisation and ritualisation of institutions are intrinsically connected to the historical context from which they spring. Historical institutionalism, in fact, is focused on historically specific patterns and contextually bound routin-isation. While institutions emerge as patterns of practice, the practices themselves are shaped by specific historical circumstances.[36]

To conclude this section and for the purposes of this analysis, insti-tutions will be taken to mean complex frameworks of ritualised rules, procedures and norms as well as the practice of their elaboration and implementation by actors (corporate or individual) who are in some way employed, mandated or appointed to carry out the aims of the institutions according to their ascribed roles within it. Such a definition thus recognises that institutions do things and that, as such, to some extent they should be understood as containing an organisational component.

The distinct contribution of historical institutionalism

As argued by Hall and Taylor,[37] the new institutionalism can be viewed as containing three distinct branches. Our argument here hinges in great part on the idea that one of the three varieties (historical institutionalism) is of particular relevance to the study of the far Right and is the most original of the three.

March and Olsen's seminal 1984 article[38] contains the most concise statement of the historical institutionalists' purpose. They summarise their main ideas in the following manner:

> The ideas deemphasize the dependence of the polity on society in favor of an interdependence between relatively autonomous social and political institutions; they deemphasize the simple primacy of micro processes and efficient histories in favor of relatively complex processes and historical inefficiency; they deemphasize metaphors of choice and allocative outcomes in favor of other logics of action and the centrality of meaning and symbolic action.[39]

Taking the paragraph as a reliable summary of their general intent, several issues need to be addressed. Firstly, March and Olsen's 'deemphasis' on choice is interesting given the rational-choice logic which animates whole areas of this literature. Their approach underscores the wish of many historical institutionalists to view institutions as not just contexts in which choices get made.[40]

March and Olsen – as well as Skocpol,[41] Hall and Katzenstein as historical institutionalists – emphasise the primacy of institutions, not only as shaping the choice of strategy but also as shaping the goals, preferences, points of reference and capacities of the political actor. So, while all new institutionalists try to move away from an exclusively society-centred understanding of politics in an attempt to illustrate and explain how institutions affect society (and not only the other way around), rational-choice institutionalists grant institutions the power to shape the context in which choices are made, while historical institutionalists go even further by allowing institutions to have a role in preference formation and goal orientation.[42]

Historical institutionalists' most important claim is that political preferences are not shaped by exogenous political forces. Political preferences are endogenous and shaped within a system of political institutions. On this Ellen Immergut is particularly enlightening as she reaches for a Rousseaun understanding of institutions and argues when discussing historical institutionalism:

> Citizen's preferences are not, as the pluralists thought, efficiently trans-mitted to political leaders via interest groups and political parties; instead the representation of interests is shaped by collective actors and institu-tions that bear traces of their own history ... [p]olitical economies – like political systems are structured by dense interactions among economic, social, and political actors that work according to different logics in differ-ent contexts.[43]

In sum 'Definitions of interests are viewed as political results that must be analysed and not as starting points for political action to be taken at face value'.[44]

Thelen and Steinmo define historical institutionalism as an approach which takes institutions to be 'both formal organisations and informal rules and procedures that structure conduct'.[45] It is worth noting that historical institutionalism's blurring of the line between organisations and institutions is perceptible here once again. Also note-worthy is the fact that the formal and informal are explicitly connected.

Historical institutionalism, as underscored by Hay, is 'historical' because of its 'incorporation as a fundamental premise, of the insight that institutions so defined are a sedimentation of both intended and unintended consequences of prior agency'.[46] Thus, historical institu-tionalism is well placed to recognise the relevance of both praxis and temporality to the definition of institutions and is poised to contribute to the reformulation of the relationship between structure and agency, ideas and institutions.

Each of the three schools of new institutionalism (rational-choice, sociological, and historical institutionalism) can best be understood as premised on a fundamentally different conception of the relationship between institutions and individuals. But the question formulated by Hall and Taylor (can historical institutionalism 'develop a distinctive response to the question: how do institutions relate to individual action?'),[47] is somewhat misleading and, perhaps, not altogether effi-cient in exploiting the originality of historical institutionalism. In order to be useful with respect to their own definition of institutions (one to which this project in part subscribes) the question should emphasise the mediated nature of relationships, political and other.

Our preliminary conclusion that it is not 'how' institutions relate to individuals, but rather, 'what' mediates the relationship between the two which is the relevant question.

Rational-choice institutionalism: exogenous mediation

Rational-choice institutionalism has contributed to our understanding of strategic individual action,[48] but if one asks the question what mediates the relationship between rational, interest-maximising individuals and institutions the answer is 'information'. The relationship here is based on an individual's preferences which are fixed and exogenous (i.e. not shaped by institutions) and a mediating mechanism which is also exogenous, information. Epistemologically, this means that the relationship between individuals and institutions is one characterised by remoteness. In a sense this brings to the fore the main problem with rational-choice interpretations of behaviour, in that the mediating factor in the relationship is unreliable.[49] Behaviour appears irrational simply because it is based on rational calculations effected on the basis of partial or erroneous information. In theoretical terms therefore the mediating factor appears to add to the complexity of the relationship without granting the relationship the 'tightness' or relative closeness necessary for the mediation to be effective. More importantly, as alluded to earlier on, institutions derive some of their power and legitimacy from our expectations repeatedly met over time; in the rational-choice model the unreliable nature of information – as well as its crucial role – leads to two possible consequences. The first is the potentially static nature of political arrangements. This would go some way toward giving an additional explanation to rational-choice strategic dilemmas and the quasi-impossibility of moving beyond Nash equilibrium situations. The second consequence is that rational-choice institutionalists would therefore necessarily construe institutions as repeatedly unmet expectations, which fundamentally alters the nature of the concept. As such the links between individuals and institutions are not clarified as a 'relationship', but rather as decoding on the part of individuals and structuring outcomes on the part of institutions.

Sociological institutionalism: internalised mediation

Sociological institutionalism yields a broader definition of institutions. While this broadness has contributed to political science's rethinking of institutions and as such has served as the impetus for many of the lines of inquiry associated with new institutionalism, the approach presents some problems. For the purposes of this chapter the most important one is that the definition of institutions given by sociological institutionalists makes institutions somewhat indistinguishable from many other factors. Richard Scott for example refers to institutions as 'frames of meaning' which serve as templates for human action.[50] By abolish-ing – with little justification – the difference between institutions and context, or institutions and culture, sociological institutionalists abolish the useful distinction which allows one to distinguish institu-tions from the rest (from myths, from ideas, from norms and roles, ideologies and, as stated earlier, from organisations). To the question what mediates the relationship between individuals and institutions, therefore, the sociological institutionalists' answer would be, very little: the characteristic of the relationship is that, over time, it becomes immediate as roles and norms are internalised.

While we would not dispute that individuals' personalities are in part shaped by the framework in which they live and evolve, the line between the psychological make-up of the individual and institutional imperatives becomes so blurred as to almost disappear. Where the problem with rational-choice institutionalism was the exogenous nature of the mediating factor, the problem with sociological institu-tionalism is its quasi-endogenous nature – i.e. the disappearance of the mediating factor.

Historical institutionalism: toward ideational mediation

Historical institutionalism allows for a relationship between individuals and institutions which has more analytical and epistemological purchase, in part because, to the question, what mediates the relation-ship between institutions and individuals?, the answer is history and practice. Institutions as characterised by historical institutionalism are historically specific patterns of practice. However, the emphasis on context, historical and cultural, while helpful, remains to some extent unspecified. Historical institutionalism's emphasis on the 'intended and unintended consequences of prior agency'[51] suggests that added specification is required regarding what kind of mediating factor is at work between the individuals (agency) and institutions as practices enacted by individuals. What is suggested here is that, without doing violence to historical institutionalism's central commitments (history and practice), it is worth incorporating systems of ideas – ideologies – as the mediating factor in this model.

Historical institutionalism makes much of intended and uninten-ded consequences, alternative rationalities and the fact that causality is a contextual phenomenon. According to these theorists, shifts of ideas can dramatically affect the manner in which institutions impact on behaviour, while at the same time, shifts in institutional configurations will affect the relevance of certain ideas. The relationship between ideas and institutions is thus a dynamic one, and in historical institutionalist terms, the two are intrinsically dependent on one another. Institutions are thus granted their complexity, their unpredictability, their inefficiency and quirkiness, while they in turn impart upon ideas the ebb of flow of currency and legitimacy. Institutions do indeed facilitate or inhibit the organisation of interests by granting them currency or legitimacy or status – or not doing so – but this goes further as institutions create the parameters within which a set of ideas will or will not be relevant, and thus the parameters within which interests are constructed and articulated. I would go further than that and suggest such shaping does not just 'shape beliefs regarding the efficacy of different types of political action',[52] but, simply put, it shapes belief. If belief in efficacy shift and interests adapt, chances are that beliefs are changing. This is an important as it focuses in on the point at which ideas and institutions are most intimately connected, perhaps in their most symbiotic state.

Earlier in this discussion two main problems were identified with the model of political opportunity structures. Theorists working on structures of political opportunity were said to draw too sharp a distinction between formal institutions and informal procedures and prevailing strategies; secondly, they were seen as misgauging the nature of the opportunities afforded social and political movements in, and by, the French polity.

An incorporation of historical institutionalist insights into the model along the lines delineated throughout this chapter's two previous sections addresses both of these problems. Firstly, historical institutionalism can allow researchers to posit an intrinsic link (absent from the framework of political opportunity structures) between formal institutions and dominant strategies. Historical institutionalism creates a more appropriate distinction, more congruent with neo-institutionalist premises and historical institutionalist aims, not bet-ween formal institutions and informal procedures, but, rather between formal and informal institutions. As underscored by Jack Knight,[53] informal institutions constitute the foundations of society and formal institutions are 'designed and created on this foundation' of informal institutions.

The distinction is an important one because it both enlarges the definition of institutions while potentially underscoring the difference between intended and unintended consequences, thus pointing to institutions' often haphazard emergence, consolidation, change and breakdown. With respect to theories of political opportunity structures, this means that institutions as reconceived through new institutionalist approaches can encompass a broader range of things, including the unintended consequences of formal institutions (for example, the effects of the Presidency – presidentialism – on the French structure of political opportunity).

The second query formulated regarding the structure of political opportunities, concerned these theorists' conception of the French polity as closed and exclusive.

Again, historical institutionalism can be seen to make a significant contribution here: institutions as conceived of in historical institutionalist terms grant polities a much less static quality. The first point therefore is that the formal and informal institutions of any given polity are in a constant state of flux which precludes long-term, categorical conclusions. Secondly, historical institutionalism's emphasis on history and practice places a premium on temporality and action. It turns institutions into possible instances of opportunity which – contrary to what political-opportunity-structures theories stipulate, – appear and disappear depending on the actors' (institutional and non-institutional) interpretation of the context. These opportunities and constraints are not fixed; they are also in a constant state of flux, as constraints can be turned by actors into opportunities and vice versa.

It is here, however, that taking into account ideologies as mediating factors has the most theoretical purchase. Once ideas and more specifically systems of ideas such as ideologies are incorporated into political opportunity structures, opportunities can be perceived as in part defined by the 'fit' between the dominant institutional paradigm and the programmatic ideas of the actors seeking to penetrate it.[54]

Michael Freeden's work allows for a definition and conceptualisation of ideologies which puts them in a particular relationship to context and, more specifically, to institutions. His theory of ideology relies on the concept of ideological morphology.[55] The model and theory have been elaborated in order to bridge the perennial gap between theory and action from which theories of ideology suffer (as Freeden writes, 'Ideologies need, after all to straddle the world of political thought and political action, for one of their central functions is to link the two').[56] In this respect, Freeden's model also allows one to link agency and structure.[57]

Having established the differences and similarities between political philosophies and ideologies in an earlier section of his work, Freeden concludes that:

Ideologies serve as the bridging mechanism between contestability and determinacy, converting the inevitable variety of options into the monolithic certainty which is the unavoidable feature of political decision. *Because ideologies involve concerted action, they relate to the sphere of organization; because they involve decisions, they relate to control; and because they involve language they relate to the attempted injection of certainty into indeterminacy.*[58] [my emphasis]

The aim of institutions and the institutionalisation of practice is to make language coterminous with the reality of a repeated practice over time, hence the identification of a tendency toward both action (practice) and inertia (reification of that action over time). The aim of ideologies is to make language coterminous with the repeated action or decision over time. Either of these aims – decision making or action in the political sphere – can only be fulfilled at the expense of indeterminacy.[59]

Central to Freeden's analysis[60] is the notion that ideologies consist of clusters of concepts which give specific meaning to essentially debated, contested political meanings. Ideologies are made up of core, adjacent and peripheral concepts and these three types of concepts are characteristic of the morphology of ideologies. Each ideology consists of one or more core concepts, these core concepts are in a close relationship to a series of adjacent ones, finally they are also associated – but more loosely – with a series of, more ephemeral, peripheral concepts. Freeden illustrates these relationships through the case of liberalism: 'For instance, an examination of observed liberalisms might establish that liberty is situated within their core, that human rights, democracy and equality are adjacent to liberty, and that nationalism is to be found on their periphery.'[61]

The core concepts are deemed ineliminable: if they are missing, or disappear, then we are dealing with another ideology or ideological construct. Despite Freeden's label, the 'peripheral' concepts are the ones that 'breathe life' into the core ones. The adjacent concepts 'adapt' or 'tailor' the core to context, to historical instance, and institutional situation as well as to social and cultural context. More particularly they play a crucial role in helping to define the core concepts – for example, they flesh out the particular understanding of 'liberty' as a core concept present in liberalism – by their very proximity to the core. The linkages between the core and adjacent concepts are central to the exact understanding and meaning of the core. The fact that these relationships among concepts are mutually influential means that the patterns of these relationships will give each ideology its unique shape and potential for transformation. It is thus important to note that the relationship between these concepts is as important as the nature of these concepts.[62]

The core concepts are thus defined and contextualised through the adjacent concepts. The adjacent concepts are mutable. Core concepts on the other hand are not allowed to travel or become peripheral, lest the ideology in question be fundamentally transformed. Freeden makes much of a very useful analogy between the types of furniture in a room and the elements present in an ideology. He also stresses that the relationship of the objects in a room to one another and how they are arranged is what gives the room its distinctiveness and argues that the same can be said for the relationships between the core, adjacent and peripheral concepts constitutive of an ideology.[63]

Through this model ideologies lose any static characteristic and the boundaries between them become much more permeable. On the other hand, the morphological approach renders ideologies more recognisable and identifiable over time as they evolve and shed components or develop others thus generating 'hybrid' or new ideologies.

As Griffin points out:

> On one level they [ideologies] have something in common with myths in the way they blend rational propositions, emotional inclinations, cultural values, and utopian goals. They also share certain properties with organic phenomena in that they are essentially protean in their capacity constantly to adapt to different cultural environments and changing political circumstances, readily producing mutations which deviate from earlier species.[64]

The idea of possible mutations is central to Freeden's model and is crucial to the present argument which revolves around the notion that institutions and ideologies are in a symbiotic relationship because both are dependent on a dialectical relationship structured by time and language. As institutions create a web of opportunities for parties and movements they also profoundly influence the ideologies of the parties and movements. Conversely, the actions of parties and movements must be put in the foreground and set against their institutional backdrops. An adequate operationalisation of institutions as concepts needs to encapsulate their complex role and more crucially reflect their dual nature, i.e., reflect the fact that they are both processes and rules that govern processes. They are both practice over time and the framework for these practices.[65]

The political-opportunity-structures theorists' failure to recognise the *extent* of the dynamism proper to institutions (the fact that institutions not only structure opportunities but create them) and to the political setting as whole in effect turns into a 'qualitative' failure to assign to institutions their proper role in creating opportunities.

Margaret Weir's concept of 'bounded innovation'[66] seems particularly apt for the present purposes. Weir argues that the interaction of ideas and politics over time creates 'a pattern of bounded innovation'.[67] When writing about employment policy in the US from the late 1920s to the 1980s she stipulates that: 'Central to this narrowing process' – the selection of one policy over another – 'was the creation of institutions, whose existence channelled the flow of ideas, created incentives for political actors, and helped to determine the political meaning of policy choices.'[68]

Weir's approach views institutions as suitably dynamic entities, capable both of channelling and of creating incentives. But it also presents another interesting feature: it acknowledges that institutions, by their actions, create political meaning; by channelling decisions; structuring choices and preferences and creating opportunities for various actors, they determine and ascribe sense to actions, meaning to decisions, in short they turn events and actions into politics by infusing them with a political meaning bound to the political context. In this sense, institutions are actors in the political process and historical institutionalism with its potential emphasis on temporality appears to offer the researcher the most efficient tools for investigation.

Preliminary methodological conclusions

Two preliminary conclusions are of significance for the remainder of this book and for the case study in particular. The first conclusion is related to the historical institutionalist methodology: as stated throughout this chapter, the aim is to delineate the contours of the relationship between ideas and political institutions. Historical institutionalism allows one to incorporate into this study a theory of ideology whose basic dynamism can take into account institutional shifts and historical context.

Secondly, this discussion shows that the concept of a structure of political opportunities is a valuable tool and fruitful starting point for this analysis: it emphasises the relevance of institutions and of the political context to the study of mobilisation. The aim now is to apply this framework to the case of the far Right in France and, ultimately to the *Front national.*

What the next few chapters illustrate is the impact of the evolution of the institution of the Presidency in France on the French far Right as well as the manner in which ideas that are intrinsic to the far Right in France impact on the institution's evolution. The argument suggests that a set of institutional transformations created a new opportunity structure for the far Right in France, which adapted and transformed itself from a set of proto-fascist movements into the much more Fifth Republic-friendly *Front national*.

Notes

1 The best reference here is Peter Hall, 'Conclusion: the politics of Keynesian ideas,' in P. Hall, ed., *The Political Power of Economic Ideas* (Princeton, NJ: Princeton University Press, 1989), pp. 361–91.

2 This terminology is borrowed from John Campbell, 'Institutional analysis and the role of ideas in political economy', *Theory and Society*, 27 (1998), 377–409. In his article Campbell elaborates a four-part typology of ideas based on the distinction between normative and cognitive ideas on the one hand and background and foreground ideas on the other. The result is four types of ideas: programmatic, paradigmatic, ideas as frames and ideas as public sentiments.

3 For this it is useful to turn to Tarrow's definition of a 'new social movement': 'A social movement is a set of collective challenges by people with common purposes and solidarity in sustained interaction with elites, opponents and authorities.' S. Tarrow, *Power in Movement: Social Movements, Collective Action, and Politics* (Cambridge: Cambridge University Press, 1994), pp. 3–4. The FN fulfils all the criteria.

4 One could argue that the literature surrounding the analysis of political opportunity structures is designed to explain a movement's entry into the system rather than the manner in which it fares once it is inside the system. Such a point, while legitimate, does not take into account the view of institutions which will be elaborated in this chapter and throughout this book. If institutions are given their wider meaning (and this requires looking at other theoretical frameworks) then the notion that they are political opportunities for political actors can be extended to the full life-span of the actor in question.

5 Peter Eisinger, 'The conditions of protest behavior in American cities', *American Political Science Review*, 67 (1973), 11–28.

6 C. Tilly, *From Mobilisation to Revolution* (Reading, MA: Addison-Wesley, 1978); see also C. Tilly, 'Social movements and national politics', in C. Bright and S. Harding, eds, *Statemaking and Social Movements* (Ann Arbor, MI: University of Michigan Press, 1984), pp. 297–317.

7 D. Snyder and C. Tilly, 'Hardship and collective violence in France, 1883–1960', *American Sociological Review*, 37 (1972), 520–32.

8 H. Kitschelt, 'Political opportunity structures and political protest: anti-nuclear movements in four democracies', *British Journal of Political Science*, 16 (1986), 57–85.

9 Kitschelt, Political Opportunity Structures, 59–60.

10 H. Kriesi, R. Koopmans, J. W. Duyvendak and M. Giugni, 'New social movements and political opportunities in Western Europe', *European Journal of Political Research*, 22 (1992), 219–44.

11 Although Tarrow can be seen as having put forth the structure of political opportunities approach as early as 1989 (see S. Tarrow, *Struggle, Politics and Reform: Collective Action, Social Movements and Cycles of Protest*, second edition (Ithaca, NY: Cornell University, Western Societies Program Occasional Paper 21, 1989).

12 H. Kriesi, 'The political opportunity structure of new social movements: its impact on their mobilization', in J. C. Jenkins and B. Klandermans, eds, *The Politics of Social Protest: Comparative Perspectives on States and Social Movements* (London: UCL Press, 1995), pp. 167–98. Initially published in 1991 by Wissenschaftszentrum Berlin für Sozialforschung, FSIII 91–103.

13 Kriesi *et al.*, 'New social movements', p. 220.

14 Kriesi *et al.*, 'New social movements', p. 222.

15 Kriesi *et al.*, 'New social movements', p. 222.

16 Tarrow, *Power in Movement*, p. 89.

17 J. W. Duyvendak, *Le poids du politique: nouveaux mouvements sociaux en France* (Paris: L'Harmattan, 1994), especially the second section.

18 Most authors writing on the state and particularly on state strength/weakness or 'state capacity' take Tocqueville's analysis as a starting point, but there is no broad agreement as to what the state consists of nor what it is able or entitled to do. The literature on the state points to a move away from pluralist theories of the state emphasising civil society, groups of individuals and competing interests, and toward an approach through which the state can be treated as a political actor in its own right. In this approach the problems posed are those of rule and control rather than of distribution or redistribution and the emphasis is placed on institutions and institutional variables and constraints. (For a good discussion of this shift see S. Krasner, 'Approaches to the state: alternative conceptions and historical dynamics', *Comparative Politics*, 16: 2 (January 1984), 223–46). It is important to keep in mind that the notions of state strength put forth by the political opportunity structures literature is a simplified version of what is in fact a richer literature. In essence authors who work on political opportunity structures often draw only on P. Katzenstein's *Between Power and Plenty* (Madison, WI: University of Wisconsin Press, 1978) discussion. The structure of political-opportunities arguments on the state can all be traced to the author's typology of weak and strong states.

19 V. Wright, *The Government and Politics of France*, third edition (London: Unwin Hyman, 1989), pp. 129–30.

20 Although to some extent this confirms the argument being criticised: centralised states need to provide 'informal' routes outside the norm.

21 J. Hayward, *Governing France: The One and Indivisible Republic*, second edition (London, Weidenfeld and Nicholson, 1983), pp. 23–4.

22 Wright, *Government*, p. 290.

23 On this see E. Suleiman, *Power and Bureaucracy in France: The Administrative Elite* (Princeton, NJ: Princeton University Press, 1974) and *Les notaires: les pouvoirs d'une corporation* (Paris: Seuil, 1987).

24 Kriesi *at al.*, 'New social movements', p. 222.

25 Kriesi *et al.*, 'New social movements', pp. 222–31.

26 M. Crozier, *La société bloquée* (Paris, Seuil, 1970), p. 95.

27 P. Cerny, 'Non-terrorism and the politics of repressive tolerance', in P. Cerny, ed., *Social Movements and Protest in France* (London, Frances Pinter, 1982), p. 121.

28 See for example, R. Ladrech, 'Social movements and party systems: the French Socialist Party and the new social movements', *West European Politics*, 12: 3 (1989), 262–79; J. W. Duyvendak, *Le poids*; J. W. Duyvendak, 'Une "communauté homosexuelle" en France et aux Pays-Bas: de blocs, tribus et liens', *Sociétés*, 39 (1993), 75–81; See also the works of Touraine who, despite leaving the state out of his analysis, puts forth the idea that French society is difficult to penetrate. On this see also Tarrow's argument in *Power in Movement*, pp. 177–86. Here Tarrow highlights the differences between the disruptive French student movement of May 1968 and the less strident American women's movement. Tarrow's conclusion is that the French student movement's failure and the success of the American women's movement can be attributed to different structures of political opportunity which the French students, in this case, failed to use. Whereas the women's movement used a discourse and tactics which enabled it to be integrated into the political mainstream and into public debate and, thus, make political headway, the French student movement used tactics and a discourse which isolated it from a public it was never able to capture. What the students did not do was to exploit the structure of opportunities as it was offered to them. However, Tarrow underscores the fact that the French structure of political opportunities is narrower and perhaps less accessible than the American one. Lastly, though conclusions diverge, most recent works on France highlight the significance of the role of the Left in power in France (on and off from 1981 to the present) and the changing impact of the French Communist party on Left-wing mobilisation.

29 Duyvendak tentatively makes this point in his 1994 work, *Le poids*, although his arguments differ from mine.

30 The literature on the new institutionalism has already made some significant contributions in bringing institutions back into the study of mobilisation. For a discussion see E. Amenta and Y. Zylan, 'It happened here: political opportunity, the new institutionalism and the Townsend movement' in Stanford M. Lyman, ed., *Social Movements, Critiques, Concepts, Case-Studies* (London, Macmillan, 1995), pp. 199–233.

31 K. Shepsle, 'Institutional equilibrium and equilibrium institutions', in Herbert Weisberg, ed., *Political Science: The Science of Politics* (New York, NY: Agathon Press, 1986), p. 52.

32 P. Hall, *Governing the Economy: the Politics of State Intervention in Britain and France* (New York and Oxford: Oxford University Press, 1986), p. 19.

33 Robert Dahl, *Who Governs? Democracy and Power in an American City* (New Haven, CT: Yale University Press, 1961).

34 S. Krasner, 'Sovereignty: an institutional perspective', *Comparative Political Studies*, 21: 1 (April 1988), 74.

35 On this notion of a dialectical approach to institutions see C. Hay, '"Punctuated evolution" and the uneven temporality of institutional change: the "crisis" of Keynesianism and the rise of neo-liberalism in Britain', paper presented to the Eleventh Conference of Europeanists (Baltimore, 26–28 February, 1998). In this paper Hay proposes a dialectical approach to institutional analysis which is an attempted synthesis of what he refers to as 'more discursive' strands of neo-institutionalism. In many ways this is concurrent with the present approach which maintains a separation between institutions and ideas.

36 Despite this emphasis on practice, this research wishes to distance itself from functionalist approaches which characterise most rational-choice and indeed much new institutionalist research in general. Practices are separate from the function(s) an institution performs. In other words, the practices referred to here are to be conceived of as those actions (both ordinary and extraordinary) which allows the institution to perform tasks (be it a function or something else) and which sustains them over time. Change in what constitutes the institution or what it does on a daily basis may or may not affect its function. The two might be, but are not necessarily, connected.

37 P. Hall and R. Taylor, 'Political science and the three new institutionalisms', *Political Studies*, 44: 5 (December 1996), 936–57.

38 J. G. March and J. P. Olsen, 'The new institutionalism: organizational factors in political life', *American Political Science Review*, 78 (1984), 734–49.

39 March and Olsen, 'The new institutionalism', p. 738.

40 Rational-choice theorists for example give institutions weight as context and structure. In other words institutions, in the rational-choice model, are of crucial importance essentially because they structure the rules of the game in which humans are thought to be endlessly calculating benefits, arranging fixed preferences and maximising outcomes. When the rules of the game change so do the calculations for the maximisation of outcomes, hence the need to take institutions into account.

41 See in particular T. Skocpol, *Protecting Soldiers and Mothers: The Political Origins of Social Policy in the United States* (Cambridge, MA: Belknap Harvard, 1992). See also, T. Skocpol, 'Bringing the state back in: strategies of analysis in current research', in P. Evans, D. Rueschmeyer and T. Skocpol, eds, *Bringing the State Back In* (Cambridge: Cambridge University Press, 1985).

42 For a discussion of the role of institutions in preference formation see Peter Hall 'The movement from Keynesianism to monetarism: institutional analysis and British economic policy in the 1970s', in S. Steinmo, K. Thelen and F. Longstreth, eds, *Structuring Politics: Historical*

   Institutionalism in Comparative Analysis (Cambridge: Cambridge
   University Press, 1992), pp. 90–113.
43 E. Immergut, 'The theoretical core of the new institutionalism', *Politics
   and Society*, 26 (March 1998) 17.
44 Immergut, 'The theoretical core', p. 7.
45 Steinmo *et al.*, *Structuring politics*, p. 2.
46 Hay, 'Punctuated evolution', p. 5.
47 P. Hall and R. Taylor, 'The potential of historical institutionalism: a
   response to Hay and Wincott', *Political Studies*, 46: 5 (December 1998),
   pp. 958–62.
48 On this see Hall and Taylor, 'Political science', pp. 945–6.
49 The unreliability of the mediating factor can cause problems. It can create
   mediation which is less than effective thus resulting in expectations not
   being met and, consequently, a loss of efficiency or, worse, problems of
   institutional legitimacy.
50 R. Scott, 'Institutions and organizations: towards a theoretical synthesis',
   in Scott *et al.*, eds, *Institutional Environments* (California: Sage
   Publications, 1994), pp. 57–71.
51 Hay, 'Punctuated evolution', p. 5.
52 Immergut 'The theoretical core', p. 21.
53 Jack Knight, *Institutions and Social Conflict* (Cambridge: Cambridge
   University Press, 1992), p. 171.
54 In this proposed model, the mediation between political institutions and
   individuals involved in institutional exchanges can essentially be perceived
   as effected by rival, normative ideas about mediation itself, politics and the
   practice of politics. It is important to note that in this model, the recognition that the relationship between institutions and individuals is dependent on a mediating mechanism creating links between the two, is, in part,
   what accounts for its originality. Where in the other two models mediation is either negated or, in the case of rational-choice institutionalism,
   based on an exclusively exogenous mediating factor, here the mediation,
   and the recognition of there being a space reserved for the construction
   of a symbiotic and dynamic relationship, is part of the model's defining
   features.
55 M. Freeden, 'Political concepts and ideological morphology', *Journal of
   Political Philosophy*, 2 (1994), 140–64; M. Freeden, *Ideologies and
   Political Theory: A Conceptual Approach* (Oxford: Oxford University
   Press, 1998).
56 Freeden, *Ideologies*, p. 76.
57 On another level Freeden's work is mainly concerned with constructing a
   theory of ideologies capable of overcoming both the traditional episte-
   mology approach to the study of ideology (preoccupied with certainty and
   objectivity) as well as the strictly hermeneutic approach (unable to overcome its own doubts about meaning and understanding). Freeden's
   approach goes beyond this quandary while recognising the pluralistic
   aspect of the answer to the question 'what is an ideology?'.
58 Freeden, *Ideologies*, pp. 76–7.
59 Language is constitutive of ideologies as it determines the concepts themselves constitutive of ideologies. At the same time however, language

could also be understood as a constant challenge to the stability of any given ideology as a system of related concepts. This is at the root of the difficulty in understanding ideologies: ideologies invite and withstand the elaboration and description of their core theoretical precepts but, in practice, tend to behave as entities in a constant state of flux and evolution.

60 For a short, clear discussion of Freeden's theory see R. Griffin, 'The "post-Fascism" of the *Alleanza Nazionale*: a case study in ideological morphology', *Journal of Political Ideologies*, 1: 2 (1996), 123–45. Especially pp. 126–7. See also, S. Hazareesingh, *Political Traditions in Modern France* (Oxford: Oxford University Press, 1994), pp. 8–11.

61 Freeden, *Ideologies*, p. 78.

62 The notion of core concepts is not an unproblematic one with its echoes of platonic essences, but, Freeden stresses time and again that the term 'core' to which he refers can only be 'employed as a flexible and empirically ascertainable collection of ideas, fashioned by social conventions' (Freeden, *Ideologies*, p. 84). These cores only exist insofar as 'an empirically ascertainable cultural consensus ascribes to them some minimal element or elements'. Freeden, 'Political concepts', p. 147.

63 It is not within the scope of this research to discuss the nature of ideologies in a more in depth manner, but it might be useful to add for the reader, Freeden's analogy of the 'table/concept': 'Ideologies may be likened to rooms that contain various units of furniture in proximity to each other. Two important, if obvious, observations need to be kept in mind: (1) rooms may be distinguished by the kinds and combinations of units of furniture they accommodate (kitchens will have sinks and cookers; studies will have desks and bookshelves); (2) the same type of room will appear in an infinite variety of furniture combinations (there are hundreds of different don's studies in Oxford). This is precisely the position with regard to ideologies. Though it is impossible to give a clear-cut definition of liberalism, it is empirically ascertainable that liberalism has always contained units such as liberty, human rationality and individualism ... If we find liberty, rationality and individualism at its centre, while equality – though in evidence – decorates the wall, we are looking at an exemplar of liberalism. If order, authority and tradition catch our eye upon opening the door, while equality is shoved under the bed or, at best, one of its weaker specimens is displayed only when guests arrive, we are looking at a version of conservatism. Core adjacent and peripheral units pattern the room and permit its categorisation'. Freeden, *Ideologies*, pp. 86–7

64 Griffin, 'The "post-Fascism"', p. 127.

65 As underscored by March and Olsen this has dramatic consequences for the understanding of political leadership. It means that political leadership need no longer be conceived of as an exogenous force coming to the fore at crucial moments of bargaining or brokerage, but rather as a process shaping – and itself shaped by – institutions, experience and practice over time. For March and Olsen, historical institutionalism allows for a conception of leadership which "emphasises the transformation of preferences, both those of the leader and those of the followers ... Leaders interact with other leaders and are coopted into new beliefs and commitments. The leadership role is that of an educator, stimulating and accepting

changing worldviews, redefining meanings, stimulating commitments."
March and Olsen, 'The new institutionalism', p. 739.

66 M. Weir 'Ideas and the politics of bounded innovation', in Steinmo *et al.*,
Structuring Politics, pp. 188–216.

67 Weir, 'Ideas', p. 189.

68 Weir, 'Ideas', p. 189.

Chapter 3

Presidentialism and the new institutionalism

This study of the French *Front national* will demonstrate that the presidentialisation of French politics from the 1960s onwards is one of the major explanatory variables in the party's success. This book seeks to establish that the presidency and its effects (presidentialism) have profoundly affected the structure of political opportunities in France. Thus, of interest here, in terms of the structure of political opportunities framework, are three particular elements: the presidency, presidentialism and the party system. The hypothesis is that, in France, the changes imparted on the first two have had a dramatic impact on the third. This, in turn, explains the modification of the ideological stance of the FN and its consequent success.

From the perspective of the modified political opportunity structure introduced in the last chapter, the presidency and presidentialism constitute a formal institution and a set of informal procedures and dominant strategies or formal institutions. Both the presidency and presidentialism will be examined in this chapter. Indeed much of the aim of this chapter is to discuss the literature on presidential regimes in light of what has been established about institutions and bring to the fore the limitations of this literature which fails to treat the presidency and presidentialism as distinct but related instances of formally and informally institutionalised power.

Chapter 2 established that while institutions are a set of formal and informal rules and practices over time, they are also the nodal point at which structure and agency come together in a dialectical relationship. As noted by Elgie and others, however, institutions are 'heterogeneous entities … which may set in train certain conflicting institutional logics'.[1] In other words, institutional logic is not necessarily logical and a web of interdependent institutions will produce unforeseen results.

The argument here is that the creation of a strong semi-presidential or presidentialised system in France in 1958 (and re-inforced in 1962) has produced unforeseen results in the French party system, on the nature of leadership in France and on the currency of certain ideas. It is important first and foremost to spend some time on the literature surrounding presidentialism: this literature is plentiful but, despite its institutional focus, fails overall to take into account some of the issues raised in Chapter 2 regarding institutions: it does not look at unintended consequences, it seldom takes on board the dynamic contextual causal links between institutions and thus, ultimately, does not succeed in painting an accurate picture of the way the presidencies work or what their effects are.

In a presidential system the president is the head of government or head of state (e.g. Finland and France). Certain regimes have popularly elected presidents who are heads of state but not necessarily heads of government (for example Austria, Iceland or Ireland or, of course, France). Another feature of a presidential system is that the president is generally popularly elected. Executive power is thus not determined by legislative elections alone. In an attempt to assess which types of constitutional arrangements are most conducive to democratic consolidation and democratic government in the long run, Skach and Stepan define a presidential regime as 'a system of mutual independence'[2] (as opposed to a pure parliamentary regime which they define as a system of mutual interdependence); mutual independence because legislative power has a fixed electoral mandate that is its own source of legitimacy while the executive power also has a fixed electoral mandate that is its own source of legitimacy. This definition of a presidential regime is very close to that adopted by Lijphart who (aside from stipulating that the president is a one-person executive) also adds two other points to his three-point minimal definition: presidents are popularly elected and have a fixed mandate.[3]

The notion of a fixed mandate shall be taken up again below, but two points are important here. First, while authors easily define the presidency, there is a consensus that presidentialism is a more flexible concept. Few presidential systems have presidents whose powers are only those and exactly those which are strictly stipulated by the constitution. In other words, a number of variants of presidentialism are hidden behind the concept of the presidency.

Second, most of the literature on presidential regimes is structured by the opposition between presidential versus parliamentary regimes. This contrast stems from the normative concern to delineate the type of regime which best guarantees a democratic order and often – particularly in the case of a presidential regime – the regime most likely to promote political stability. As such the literature on presidentialism often takes the form of a debate 'for or against a presidential regime'.

Presidentialism: definition and theoretical observations

In presidential regimes legislative elections do not determine executive power. Put in another manner, in presidential regimes the executive is kept separate from the legislative branch of government. In most parliamentary regimes, the parliament is the only democratically sanctioned, popularly elected governmental body. In a presidential system both the legislators and the president can draw on popular legitimacy. Whether or not the president is popularly elected, he or she can often rely on a strong plebiscitary element conducive to a form of democratic legitimacy.

The complexity of what Linz has termed 'dual democratic legitimacy' is, in fact, what has often accounted for the negative attitude to presidential regimes, as authors focus on the possible democratic deficit which seems to be constitutionally built into the concept of presidentialism. Presidents are often perceived to be above parties, the legislature (as the legitimate representative body) is seen as weakened by the strength of the executive and, finally, the personalisation of politics entailed by the presidency is viewed as both undesirable as well as suspect by political scientists precisely because the president or presidential candidate can rely on a form of plebiscitary politics to achieve a legitimacy not necessarily constitutionally granted to him or her.

For Linz, the main difference between presidentialism and parliamentarism – and the source of his dislike for presidential regimes – is presidentialism's fundamental rigidity[4] compared with the flexibility inherent in parliamentarism. He first points to the fact that presidents are usually elected for a fixed term of office and argues that this has a very real impact on the political process

> [I]t [the political process] therefore becomes broken into discontinuous rigidly determined periods without the possibility of continuous readjustments as political, social and economic events might require. The duration of the mandate of a president becomes an essential political factor to which all actors in the political process have to adjust ...[5]

Where a parliamentary system would allow for flexibility (defined as the possibility for negotiation and compromise) and any adjustments deemed to be required by the situation, a presidential regime offers no such leeway. This in turn, argues Linz, leads to a polarisation of politics which, in particular circumstances such as during a transition to democratic politics, might imperil the process.

Presidentialism also sets a high threshold to executive change. Here Linz points to the fact that a vote of no confidence is a much easier and speedy procedure than the impeachment which is constitutionally required to 'get rid of' a president. Finally, Linz points to the third rigidifying factor: what he refers to as the 'winner take all' aspect of presidential politics.[6]

Linz refers to the fact that a presidential candidate needs a mere plurality to take over the whole of the executive in contrast with the possibility of power sharing in a divided parliament. As in the words of Adam Przeworski cited by Linz:

> In presidential systems, the winner takes all: he or she can form a government without including any of the losers in the coalition. In fact, the defeated candidate has no political status, as in parliamentary systems where he or she becomes the leader of the opposition. Hence ... in ceteris paribus conditions ... the value of victory, W, is greater and the value of defeat, L, is smaller under presidential than under parliamentary systems.[7]

Lijphart objects to presidential systems on slightly different grounds.[8] For him a presidential system's major flaw is the fact that it always tends toward majoritarian democracy. Lijphart argues that in many countries in which there is no natural consensus (countries divided along racial, ethnic, religious or even linguistic cleavages), a presidential government removes any chance of consensual politics by forcing the system into majoritarian rule. 'Presidentialism entails the concentration of executive power at the extreme majoritarian end of the range: power is concentrated not just in one party but in one person.'[9]

So, for these authors, the main argument in favour of a parliamentary regime is the flexibility embedded in parliamentary procedures and, therefore, institutions. This is contrasted with a presidential regime's tendency to polarise political issues due to its institutional bias toward 'winner take all' politics.

But Linz and Lijphart are not the only authors whose evaluation of presidential regimes is less than positive. Scott Mainwaring for example points to presidential regimes' poor record in terms of sustaining and promoting democracy over long periods of time.[10] In his 1993 article, Mainwaring argues that presidential systems do not cope well with severe political crisis.[11]

Generally, it can be argued that the criticisms levelled at presidentialism are structured around the opposition of parliamentary and presidential regimes. In other words the disadvantages of presidential systems are only delineated through comparison with parliamentary regimes. This is in itself questionable since as Shugart and Carey point out: 'Regimes with elected presidents vary in the ways in which the president may check, cajole, confront or simply submit to the assembly majority.'[12] They usefully conclude that presidential regimes need not be understood as the polar opposite of parliamentary regimes. The authors also point to the discrepancy between what they refer to as the 'virtual academic consensus' on the homogeneity and the ease with which presidential regimes are classified and the actual political practice concerning the implementation and workings of various presidential regimes.[13]

These points, in turn, enable one to evaluate presidential regimes outside the narrowly defined opposition within which most authors confine themselves. It is precisely this step away from the opposition which provides the analytical opening needed for a more realistic, but also richer, understanding of presidentialism.

Distinguishing between the presidency and presidentialism

Most of the authors we have examined criticise presidentialism's rigidity. In one way or another these scholars are concerned with a presidential regime's lack of flexibility, its propensity to transform conflict into crisis and, conversely, its inability to diffuse conflict and promote compromise. In a word, parliamentary regimes bring about some form of consensus politics and are more apt to resolve conflict, whereas presidential systems bring conflict to a head, often in a constitutional and institutional setting which itself makes no provision for the resolution of conflict.

These criticisms, however, are more paradoxical than they at first appear: indeed, Mainwaring's argument mixes accusations of rigidity with arguments that the rigidity causes presidential regimes to have recourse to non-constitutional solutions. Shugart and Carey's remark about the variations in presidential regimes points to the fact that much of presidentialism's power resides in the president's use of potential powers, his/her capacity to use the institution and the institution's leadership potential in various ways.

In other words presidentialism is not just too rigid it is also too flexible, i.e. subject to leadership bids, overly dependent on personality traits and charismatic appeals. It is this second, largely undefined – yet constantly alluded to – aspect of presidentialism which, in conjunction with its constitutionally stipulated powers, makes for its interest as an institutional effect which, in turn, affects the presidency itself. This is not to say that this perception of presidentialism is accurate; nevertheless it hints – however clumsily – at the complexity of the phenomenon. Neither of these interpretations is entirely satisfactory but the criticisms levelled at presidentialism underscore the problematic aspects of the institution of the presidency and of presidentialism.

The presidency's political power lies in part in its ability to legitimate its institutional and ideological spin-off effects; in other words all that which we have subsumed under the term 'presidentialism'. It is thus the possibilities and the potential contained in this move from the formality of the constitution to the practice of presidentialism which grants presidentialism its importance, an importance consistently misrepresented by most authors. One of the reasons the power and potential of presidentialism are misrepresented is that most authors refuse properly to address what is entailed both symbolically and practically by this move. Given the definition of institutions in the previous chapter it is important to stress that a presidential regime should not be understood as a formal institution on the one hand and more or less informal political practice on the other. Such an understanding would reinstate the old, dualistic and more static conception of institutions and would do little to further an understanding of presidential regimes. This 'tandem' is made up of the institution of the presidency and of presidentialism – taken as a set of gradually institutionalised emanations of the presidency, which encompass emerging political practice on the one hand and the concepts and values associated with the presidency's role on the other. The presidency and presidentialism are thus closely related but it is presidentialism which binds the institution of the presidency to a broader institutional and public context.

Most often the distinction between presidentialism and the presidency is not formally acknowledged in the vocabulary used by students of presidentialism. The conflating of 'presidentialism' and 'the presidency' is itself an indication of how misunderstood the two concepts really are, for it is in distinguishing them one from the other that their real significance and therefore their real, and potential, effects can be appreciated. More particularly, the conflation of presidentialism with the presidency leads to a confusion of cause and effect.

The presidency is an institution, presidentialism is a political effect of the presidency upon practice and, therefore, over time, an institutionalisation of the effects of the presidency. In other words, presidentialism encapsulates effects such as the personalisation of power, the effects on the party system of a popularly elected president, the effects on each party and its organisation as a consequence of having to contest mass, popular presidential elections and therefore the increased role played by image, style and national myths. The actions and political practice which result from the structuring of politics by a presidential regime, combined with national myths and existing political practice, result in presidentialism according to a given polity.

None of these authors make any subsequent effort to explain how a president makes use of non-institutional powers, nor where the 'aura' to which Linz refers comes from,[14] nor why popular expectations created by presidents are different from those created by a prime minister. Most importantly the issue of how – i.e. by what mechanism, political, emotional, psychological or other – any of these acts acquire democratic legitimacy is not addressed. For in many ways this is the crucial question: the constitutional basis of the presidency legitimates political acts but also presidential claims to legitimacy itself.

Much of the legitimacy is derived by the sort of relationship which a president is able to build with the nation, in other words the legitimacy is derived in near-plebiscitary manner. Presidents are seen as attempting to rely 'upon a state-people political style and discourse that marginalises organised groups in political society and civil society'.[15] The dividing line between popular support and legitimacy is therefore thin, thinner than in a parliamentary regime. Conversely the dividing line between a legitimate and an illegitimate act is also thinner. This means that support and legitimacy are linked in a particular manner in a presidential regime because the two are mediated via the simultaneous personal relationship of the president to the nation and to the state.[16]

The issue of the personalisation of power that goes with presidentialism, the almost palpable personal relationship of the president to the nation, the notion that this relationship is both institutional and at the same time 'extra-institutional', is an issue from which those seeking to address presidentialism and its effects generally shy away, yet these powers are often only implicitly granted by the constitution.

A historical-institutionalist analysis of the presidency would explicitly cater to the 'ideational' spin offs of the institution. In other words, historical institutionalism leads us toward the decoupling of the institution from its effects, while allowing us to analyse the relationship between the two. Presidentialism – i.e. some of the presidency's effects – are 'unintended consequences' of the presidency: opening up the gap between the two allows us to look at the ideas, myths, personalities that mediate the relationship between the presidency and other institutions.

Paradox: the presidential regime as crisis solution

Before going any further in a theoretical evaluation of presidentialism, let us look at what types of advantages scholars and politicians can see in presidentialism. The advantages are the proverbial flip-side of the coin: the rigidity might be seen merely as the consequence of strong government, the popular appeals as symptomatic of an attempt to mobilise democratic legitimacy through popular elections, the propensity to stretch constitutional meaning a necessary result of attempted efficiency and expediency, and executive/legislative deadlock the price of efficient checks and balances.

Presidential government is usually brought in at a time of transition and crisis resolution. Much of the recent literature on presidentialism focuses on Latin America; references to France and the United States abound, but the concern is primarily presidentialism's democratic potential, or rather the potential for democratic stability – or a transition toward it – contained in presidentialism.

In other words presidential regimes are seen as efficient enough to bring about strong democratic government in situations where weak legislatures were at the mercy of the military, or again where weak legislatures were seen as unable to usher people into partisan political choices, which would lead to a more structured – if potentially polarised – political process. At the risk of oversimplifying: presidential politics and presidential regimes have been seen as providing a catalyst for structured democratic politics in places where political preferences and cleavages had either been 'frozen' by a period of authoritarian/military rule, or where these preferences were no longer expressed efficiently enough for politics and policy to take shape (France in the Fourth Republic for example).

A presidential regime's appeal lies therefore in three main attributes: efficiency, democratic legitimacy and the capacity of the president through that democratic legitimacy to bridge fundamental political divisions, to reconcile the nation – at least symbolically – over divisive

issues by appearing to be both the person who draws the lines of partisanship and yet reassures the people that these lines are not so deep
that s/he cannot bring the nation together. Viewed in this fashion, the
presidency is not divisive, but an acknowledgement of existing divisions and an attempt at proclaiming that while differences exist, these
differences are not a threat to the integrity of the nation.

What complicates the practices of presidentialism is that the president is both partisan and non-partisan, part of a party and above
parties, part of the people and above the people.[17] Presidentialism
derives both its power and its negative press from the fact that this
awkward position means that presidents must be able to maintain these
two relationships – which are in large measure contradictory – simultaneously. In essence, if they fail to do so, they loose the legitimacy
associated with the presidency and that which constitutes presidentialism. On the other hand if they are able to sustain these two relationships, they are easily perceived as a demagogues or 'wily'.

The dilemma illustrates why presidential politics are so difficult to
define and why authors are often reluctant to examine the ambiguities
of the presidential role: the maintenance of the dual relationship which
is so crucial to a democratic and stable presidency depends almost
entirely on a leader's capacity to juggle the relationships, make use of
the constitution and adapt the existing presidential framework to
his/her needs in order to fulfil the dual expectations. Hence an appropriate examination of presidentialism necessarily leads to the examination of personal traits, characteristics, capacities and personality of a
single individual, much of which has escaped traditional political
science. One way of getting around this (while remaining in the realm
of social science) is to examine the institutionalised instance of that
personality. This avoids the pitfalls of political psychology by focusing
on actions: acts of speech, acts of political decision making and policy
making within the framework of the presidency as an institution.

The French presidential system defined and assessed

The French system has been described as a bi-polar executive, a divided
executive, a parliamentary presidential republic, a quasi-parliamentary
and a semi-presidential government and finally as a premier-presiden-
tial system.

For the purposes of this analysis, authors examining France's presidential regime can be classified into two camps. There are on the one

hand those authors – like Duverger – who believe that France's president has quite considerable powers which go far beyond those outlined by the formal set of rules in the constitution. And there are those who – like Suleiman – believe that the powers of the president are in fact derived from the constitution itself, in other words that those powers contained within the constitution are quite sufficient to grant the president of the French Republic very significant powers. In others words, there is no disagreement as to the fact that the president is extremely powerful in France. The disagreement is over the nature and source of this power and whether it is coherent within a republican framework.

Suleiman's main point is that the French president derives his power from the fact that he is constitutionally entitled to dissolve the Assembly. According to Suleiman, this constitutionally granted power is at the root of the transformation of the executive and then of the parliament and finally of the role of the deputy. For Suleiman, then, it is quite clear that the possibility of dissolving the Assembly is the catalyst in a long chain of transformations which make the Fifth Republic distinctive. As such the power resting within the president's hands is the key to an understanding of contemporary French politics, and this power stems directly from the formal constitutional framework within which the president has to act.

By depicting the changing role of the deputy as caused by the changing role of parliament (itself altered by an executive powerful enough to polarise the party system and therefore transform the organisation of the parties themselves), Suleiman traces the roots of the Fifth Republic straight back to article 12 of the 1958 constitution. The 1962 amendment, by legitimising the executive in the way that it does, triggers the possibility of the use of the article to ends never properly envisaged before. As Suleiman writes:

> The chief reason the dissolution of the Assembly becomes conceivable and feasible, is that the Fifth Republic's party structure is characterized by a bi-polarization that can insure a majority for one side or the other.[18]

In other words the personalisation of politics through the strengthening of the executive, and the increased legitimacy acquired by the office of the president lends increased political and tactical relevance to article 12. This in turn contributes to the far-reaching transformation of the parties' organisation, to changes in the nature of their leadership and in turn to what parliamentarians can expect to be able to do as they become increasingly tied to the party and ever less so to their constituents. While the consequences are not clearly spelled out it is nevertheless quite clear that this reduction in the scope of the role of parliamentarians can only be interpreted as a reduction in the scope of parliament in general.

In another article,[19] Suleiman underscores the scarcely debatable point that presidential politics has brought a measure of stability to French politics, and goes on to add that despite this undeniably positive contribution, the presidential regime has also had an unforeseen impact on a host of other political institutions. It is worthwhile underlining here Suleiman's worried '*constat*' that the presidential system has reduced the legitimacy of the legislature by reducing the role of parliamentarians. Suleiman's conclusion is mixed, but it points in the direction of the perennial questioning of the legitimacy of a presidential system within a republican framework.

The second category of authors is best exemplified by Duverger's contribution to the field of presidential politics. Here we refer to Duverger's 1980 article in which he puts forth a model for a semi-presidential regime: 'The purpose of the concept of semi-presidential government is to explain why relatively homogeneous constitutions are applied in radically different ways.'[20] Duverger groups under the heading 'semi-presidential' polities where 'a President of the republic, elected by universal suffrage and given personal powers, co-exists with a government resting on the confidence placed in it by parliament'.[21] This of course applies to the French presidential system. Nevertheless the main interest of the article lies in his conclusion that tradition and practice greatly exceed constitutional provisions in terms of their impact on the political process.

The four essential variables on which the model is based are:

1. constitutional rules
2. the make up of the parliamentary majority
3. the position of the president with respect to this majority
4. national and contingent factors.

Having examined the case of France, Duverger concludes that it is one of the most paradoxical cases of presidential politics in that it has a constitution which grants very few powers to the president and yet, in practice, the French president is one of the most powerful in Europe. Indeed, in his grid France is sixth out of seven in terms of levels or degrees of constitutional powers granted to the president and yet first with respect to the power the president wields in practice. Duverger thus concludes that practice and tradition outweigh constitutional parameters in shaping the presidency and its powers. This point is important in various respects. Firstly – and on this Duverger and Suleiman can be seen to agree – constitutional rules can have unforeseen consequences, for example they can have more or less of an impact than thought at the time of the establishment of the constitutional framework.[22] Secondly, Duverger's point links practice and tradition to presidentialism in a way which allows for the constant assertion and reassertion of the legitimacy of presidential powers in republican France.

The main difference between the two authors seems to lie in their different evaluations of the regime's legitimate republican credentials. Where for Suleiman presidentialism is seen as quasi-abusive of the natural link between republicanism and parliamentarianism; for Duverger presidentialism is the embodiment of the republican tradition. In his argument Duverger refers to de Gaulle's controversial interpretation of the constitution in 1964. De Gaulle proclaimed that

> the indivisible authority of the state is entrusted completely to the president by the people who elected him, that there is existed no other authority, either ministerial, civil, military or judiciary which has not yet been conferred and was not being maintained by him, and finally that it was his duty to adapt the supreme domain, which is his alone to fit in with those, the control of which he delegates to others.[23]

As Duverger points out, 'these fine phrases fail to take into account that the National Assembly is elected by the people, like the President and that like him it is a repository of national sovereignty'.[24] This remark however does not lead Duverger to question the legitimacy of de Gaulle's power. In fact, he underscores the idea that the presidency in France has never involved the violation of the constitution.[25] What is notable, therefore, is this argument's implicit concern with the fact that the constitution remains inviolate, but that in fact it remains so because it plays a subsidiary role to that of the president within a republican tradition and therefore is extended, adapted, stretched and interpreted in order to avoid conflict popular consent. In such an argument, therefore, the constitution can be seen as process more than as framework. Regarding it strictly as framework serves no analytical purpose whatsoever in that it is reduced to a weak, discountable instrument. Regarding it as process subsumed under tradition and practice serves the purpose of reconciling the practice of presidentialism with that of republicanism.

What is noteworthy then, is that both Suleiman and Duverger are reconciled with the presidentialisation of politics in France, but for different reasons: Suleiman because the Fifth Republic has brought stability and efficiency to French politics and because presidential power is only efficient when the president has majority backing in the assembly (as such, the Fifth Republic is seen as presenting an effective, if somewhat unforeseen, system of checks and balances) and Duverger because he draws his confidence in the legitimacy of the Fifth Republic from the compatibility between a presidential system on the one hand and the French Republican tradition on the other.

These positions are particularly interesting to note as they under-score the fact that the literature on presidentialism has moved away from the 'tension' which once defined it and which Gaffney identifies:

> The theoretical approach which explicitly or implicitly informs the great body of analysis of Fifth Republican politics in all periods is a simple one which we can call the tension theory, that is to say, an approach which sees the dynamic of politics and political change as a tension or conflict between two conceptions of the organisation of power, the one involving a drive toward democracy (and reliance on parties and parliament) and the other a drive away from it (towards the presidential or other executive office and the practice of presidential rule).[26]

What is characteristic of the more recent literature on presidentialism in France is a move away from the reversion principle – i.e. the notion proper to the very early years of the Fifth Republic, that presidential-ism was a measure adopted only temporarily as a crisis remedy which would be abandoned once the crisis was resolved – and a move away from the tension theory described by Gaffney.

What works such as Suleiman's and Duverger's do not do is to account for the reasons why this tension is transcended. The following section in this chapter – on the French party system – suggests that the tension in French politics (reflected in the early literature on presiden-tialism) can be understood as the manifestation of two opposing polit-ical drives present in all contemporary liberal democratic polities. In the French case Fifth Republican presidentialism reconciled these opposing tendencies and thus has profoundly modified the structure of political opportunities available to political actors.

The two faces of presidentialism in a democratic context: rally politics revisited

Let us now turn to an examination of the party system as shaped by France's political system. The FN can only be understood as a political force if it is studied within the context of the French party system and if that system is understood as having been shaped and altered by the presidentialism characteristic of the Fifth Republic. Yet French party politics have generally been studied without enough reference to presidentialisation. What this section shows is that the study of party systems and political parties (and, more specifically, the French party system and French political parties) has largely ignored two contradictory drives which animate most party politics in an era of mass political participation: the 'party' and the 'rally' drive. The argument here is that the French Fifth Republic, by strengthening the executive and creating a strong presidency, allowed for the rally drive to become institutionalised. The institutionalisation of this drive accounts for the structure of political opportunity in Fifth Republican France which in turn offers an explanation for the emergence and success of the FN.

The impact of presidential politics: parties and rallies

John Gaffney sums up the impact of presidentialism by evoking two levels of effects. According to Gaffney, presidentialism can be said to have both contingent and systemic effects. Two systemic effects are that presidentialism forces the parties into bi-polar alliances and encourages the personalisation of politics. This intensification of the divide between Left and Right is nevertheless simultaneously countered by the fact that the personalisation of politics and the popular election of the president entail that the president should represent more than his or her own party given that they must be able to capture the political centre. This in turn means that the bi-polarisation of the party system is inherently contrary to presidentialism's (and majoritarian politics') need to capture the median voter. Finally presidentialism in a democratic context encourages both the need for control by leadership as well as leadership rivalries.[27]

Two contingent effects are also of great significance to this study. The first is the asymmetry (the 2002 presidential and legislative elections were the first to have been held under the new system which reduced the presidential mandate from seven to five years to coincide with the legislative cycle) of the legislative and presidential political cycles. This asymmetry highlights the personalisation of French politics, in that it underscored the importance of who was in office at a given time as well as where – in time – they were in their term of office. Both of these issues affected the nature of possible alliances.

Most importantly, however, the asymmetry put the parties under excruciating pressure as electoral machines which needed to produce alliances every five years while producing rival '*présidentiables*' (those seen as potential presidential candidates) every seven. All this in the light of a highly personalised presidential race in which parties, regardless of asymmetrical cycles, need to come across as unified, disciplined electoral machines whose function is to produce a candidate who must look sufficiently disconnected from the party machine in order to take on the role of president of all the French.

This slightly schizophrenic tendency in French politics is best understood as the reason behind the presidentialisation of politics and as the reason for the heightened importance of political leadership under the Fifth Republic. Only the heroic political leader can be seen as acquitting him/herself of this dual task which, seemingly, requires him/her to be two people at once.

While these transformations of parties and of the attitudes of their leaders are rooted in the Constitution of 1958 and subsequent reforms, much of the inspiration for the constitution came from de Gaulle's conception of politics which was itself rooted in his military experience and his conception of the army.[28] De Gaulle's idea expressed in 1942 that 'in order to seize victory and to rediscover her greatness, France must form a rally'[29] never ceased to be the organising framework of his conception of French politics and his relationship to it. As Graham writes:

> Just as he [de Gaulle] had conceived of the French army as a variable mixture of hierarchy and warrior band, so he saw the Republic as a mixture of party and rally drives. His notion of the exceptional leader in the context of the army had been translated into the more complex idea of the individual who becomes a symbol, issuing a call for the nation to gather together and preserve its unity until the ordeal is over.[30]

This has echoes of what Hoffmann termed 'heroic leadership'[31] (so as to avoid Weber's more problematic and ill defined 'charismatic leadership'). Hoffmann appealed to the Bonapartist tendency in French culture, which, according to him, is ever present alongside the republican tradition in France and provides the French with the blueprint for the preservation of the integrity of the French state in times of crisis.

The notion that France enjoyed a Bonapartist disposition ('*un tempérament Bonapartiste*') is also present in the writings of André Siegfried:[32]

There is in France a Bonapartist disposition whose seed has never been destroyed by democracy. It persists in a latent form in certain circles ... The situation in which a Bonaparte meets his destiny is that of anarchy in government and the disrepute of parliament. At certain times, elective assemblies seem to lose touch with the real world; they become absorbed and entangled in artificial quarrels which seem important to them but which are of no interest to the public; the official representatives of opinion are no longer its real representatives, and the country ceases to feel itself governed. This is when a man who has the makings of a Caesar acquires his full stature. Over the heads of the parties (which he affects to see them as nothing but cliques), he speaks directly to the mass, not only to the active and organised electors but also to the crowd of the indifferent, the abstentionists, citizens who have not taken sides, those whom the committees have not recruited and whom he is going to make into the foundations of his whole system.[33]

For Siegfried, as for Graham, the two traditions are 'mutually dependent forces'.[34] This is of particular interest, but it is Graham's notion that the co-existence of the two traditions are symptomatic of two fields of political power in liberal democracies which is of relevance for this part of our argument. Indeed, Graham writes:

The existence of these contrasting styles of leadership is the outward sign that the free play of representative institutions generates two quite different fields of political power which we may term the party drive and the rally drive.[35]

For Graham, the party drive is the result of the demands of groups whose expectation is shaped by the idea that political associations aggregate their demands and further their interests as a group. The rally drive is produced by the 'diffuse anxieties of groups and individuals who look to prominent personalities to accept a form of moral responsibility for the welfare of the community as a whole'.[36] For the purposes of this analysis, rally politics are the style, rhetoric and practice of politics resulting from the rally drive. As such, rally politics are heavily reliant on a rhetoric of unity and cohesion and will resort to mass gatherings most often around a prominent leader chosen to coordinate and organise the rally. Party politics will privilege representational politics and thus a rhetoric of delegation and access to resources coupled with a more hierarchical, less centralised and more delegational form of participation.

The author points out that the two drives are not ascribable to different sectors of society; rather, they co-exist at all times within individuals and groups and represent two contradictory demands made on politics and politicians in particular: to meet the demands of specific interests on the one hand while preserving the integrity of the community (or the nation) on the other. Political parties in representative democracies are subject to these two contradictory drives and are required to represent the interests of a particular section of the population while preserving the integrity of the polity as a whole, sometimes, as Graham stresses, by having recourse to exceptional or heroic leadership.

Graham's understanding is rooted in liberal democratic politics and a conception of political parties within those polities rather than in a version of French exceptionalism. The rally drive thus acquires its usefulness as a concept in comparative politics because it allows the researcher to account for the management of stress in democratic systems, for the emergence and disappearance of different types of parties and for the transformation of existing ones. Rally politics can therefore be said to be a characteristic of polities which occasionally deviate from liberal democratic practices without necessarily rejoining the extremes of the political spectrum or mutating into fully developed authoritarian regimes. The existing and perennial drive toward rally politics in every political party and within every polity can – in political studies at large – partly account for the crisis[37] remedies in liberal democracies under stress. For as long as the crisis lasts, a successful rally both transcends and encloses the parties which comprise its community, only to release them to resume their full representational role once the situation has returned to normal.[38] To put this in terms more congruent with the rest of my argument: I would argue that the rally and party drives – which are the two sets of contradictory demands made on politicians – find an echo in two types of political responses (in leadership, rhetorical and political terms). The party drive is exploited by representative politics (party politics), while the relentless exploitation of the rally drive over the party drive leads to populist politics. As Graham points out, the rhetoric which goes hand in hand with this type of rally politics can be most effective. It can depict the nation as surrounded by enemies who are both outside and inside and can insinuate more or less explicitly that the governing politicians are not able to deal with the crisis or, worse, are responsible for it. While Graham does not use the term, what he have is a classic definition of populist politics. We will return to the issue of populism in a subsequent chapter, but it is important to highlight, even at this stage of the argument, that the two components of politics identified by Graham are roughly similar to the components identified by Canovan who draws on the work of Oakeshott to argue that populism fits within one of the two styles of modern politics (which Canovan refers to as redemptive and pragmatic) and that 'despite the tension between them, the two styles are inseparable in modern politics'.[39]

The fact that the Bonapartist phenomenon can be seen as an archetypal example of rally politics should not obscure the fact that while Bonapartism can be seen as a foundational (or path-determining) moment in how France would enact rally politics from then on, Bonapartism is only one instance of rally politics. Furthermore, the rally drive is shaped by political institutions and by the ideological and ideational context in which it emerges.

Most importantly, the following sections will demonstrate that in the case of France, presidentialism fundamentally transforms the impact and thrust of the rally drive by granting institutional legitimacy to rally politics and, therefore, gradually institutionalising them. Rally politics which are associated with crisis in the Second, Third and Fourth Republics, become subsumed under presidential politics and thus emancipated from the context of crisis. This means that rally politics are no longer confined to periods of crisis but, rather, become internalised by French political parties who are forced to resort to rally politics for presidential elections while maintaining a party political outlook crucial for legislative contests. The Fifth Republic as a structure of political opportunity thus allows access to parties who contain a particularly strong rally element. In twentieth century France, rally politics benefit also from the presence of ideological constructs and concepts which promote a particular understanding of leadership and its relationship to power. As such, rally politics as we will see in the following chapters are shaped, in great part, by the legacies of a French proto-fascism of which one key characteristic was the relentless exploitation of the rally drive in the form of populist politics.

One of the notable problems in the literature on France and on French parties is its failure to take the existence of this dual drive into account and the effects of the advent of the Fifth Republic on parties (and therefore the party system) through the institutionalisation of rally politics in the form of presidentialism. As such the literature surrounding political parties in France is always unable to account for change (if and when change is detected) and, therefore, unable to account for the emergence, success and transformation of parties such as the FN.

France in comparative perspective

Our understanding of party systems is marked first and foremost by the works of writers such as Duverger[40] and Kircheimmer[41] whose analyses are the first to address contemporary party systems and their development and evolution. The post-war party systems of Western Europe have been understood as 'frozen',[42] and then more recently as buoyant.[43] By the late 1960s and early 1970s, the thesis whereby distinctive parties would be gradually replaced by bland catch-all parties was increasingly challenged as competition and mobilisation resurfaced on a variety of issues and new parties and movements emerged.

As underscored by P. Mair,[44] the literature on radical transformations and accelerated evolution of European party systems has since then been so plentiful, that it has almost completely drowned out the few dissenting voices who sought to discern elements of continuity and stability in a few countries. Yet it is crucial to emphasise the different patterns exhibited by a nation such as France and its different pace of change.

France emerged as the notable stable exception amidst its wildly fluctuating European counterparts. Studies at the time seemed rather prone to exaggerate either the quiescence or the changes within parties and across party systems. The explanations that underscored the freezing and then possible elimination of cleavages, just as much as those which emphasised major change or deep transformations, tended to overstate the case. Two reasons can be offered in explanation. First of all, parties tended to be studied as one-dimensional institutions. More often than not parties were examined on the basis of a simple (perhaps simplistic) model of voting choices. Parties aggregated preferences based on a set of cleavages and then transmitted these preferences to sites of decision making via representative institutions. To some extent this understanding is, of course, quite accurate: parties do those things. Where this approach reveals shortcomings however, is by not taking into account that parties do not do just those things but may, in fact, be doing other things. By ignoring the fact that parties were often involved in other activities, most explanations were unable to detect change in parties or party systems (Italy is a good example here: the complete crumbling of Italy's party system took most analysts by surprise in the late 1980s and 1990s), in part because they were not looking at the relevant area of party or partisan activity.

Secondly, by not looking at the relationship between parties and other institutions, the literature on political parties long ignored the manner in which change or transformations affected political parties or party systems. The neo-institutionalist literature, therefore, by positing links between institutions, allows the analyst to look at what else parties might be doing given their links with other institutions. This means that by looking at these other relationships, and by accepting that parties are multi-dimensional organisations, a fuller picture of changes in voter attitudes and preferences, of changes within parties and of political change in general emerges.

Finally, most understandings of parties obfuscate an essential characteristic of parties, which is their inherently dual nature that was underscored in this chapter's first section. More specifically, it could be argued that the study of political parties has not given itself the tools necessary to track and explain change. The study of parties and party systems has been unable to account for change within representative democracies and has forced researchers to choose between two equally unsatisfactory options: authoritarian regimes (with no parties or a single party) or liberal democracies (with a plurality of liberal democratic parties). The emergence of a non-liberal party or a party with illiberal tendencies within a liberal democracy has been granted little scope for study. Yet, while as pointed out earlier, liberal democracies come under various types of stress, most existing studies of parties and party systems do not account for the emergence of parties or transformation of existing parties under conditions of stress without also inferring that the liberal democratic framework is itself threatened. An understanding of the dual nature of parties – as combining party politics and rally politics – could do much to allow for middle-range explanatory options.

The case of the French party system and French political parties more specifically is a case in point: given the literature's inability to isolate the two competing drives within parties and the transformations which were affecting them, the quiescence of the French party system (the fact that voters were still tied to one party and that by and large most parties occupied a solid niche within the system) was often overstated. Some of the quiescence – as well as some of the transformations detected – can be said to have been largely illusory.

But France emerged as an anomaly in the midst of Western European party systems in the late 1960s. Whereas in most other countries a fragmentation of the party system and a de/re-alignment of the electorate had begun to occur as early as the 1970s, France exhibited uncharacteristic stability on both these counts throughout the 1960s and 1970s.

Discussion in the remainder of this chapter will show, however, that deep transformations were taking place in France at much the same time as anywhere else but these were not easily observable given the focus of the literature. It is also worth noting here that such an approach points, in part at least, to a solution to neo-institutionalism's 'creational bias' – its focus on institutional creation at the expense of subsequent institutional development and evolution despite the emphasis placed on path dependence in areas of the literature. Shifting the focus to gradual institutional transformations through an analysis of the impact of institutions on one another as well as the impact of ideas and ideologies on institutions (and vice versa) is a first step in this direction.

Institutionalising the rally: the drive toward presidential politics

Commentators disagree on when changes are seen to begin to occur in the French party system. David Cameron's influential thesis posits a first transformation away from the Fourth Republic's notorious instability and weak government toward what he has termed it a 'swing into partisanship' with the beginnings of the Fifth Republic.[45] But often those same commentators (including Cameron) are at a loss to explain France's subsequent immobility amidst a Europe characterised by rapid electoral change. Some evidence however tends to lend credence to Michael Lewis-Beck's thesis that partisan attachments were stronger than often thought toward the end of the Fourth Republic and that Gaullism, though it ushered in major changes, might also have capitalised on already-existing ties of partisan attachment.[46]

What is unquestionable is the fact that, regardless of origins and causes, partisan attachment remained high and stable throughout the 1960s and 1970s while changes in voter behaviour and in parties began to be detected by the mid-1980s and early 1990s.

Several points need to be made here. The first is that voter behaviour and party transformation must not be conflated. It is clear that parties can exhibit stability while alienating some voters and gaining others, just as – and the French mainstream Right is a good illustration of this in recent years – parties might be able to rely on a pool of voters but undergo internal crises of such proportions so as to self-destruct.

Again, while these events have an impact on one another they should neither be seen as synonymous nor as simultaneous.

Secondly, it might be plausible to explain the quiescence of the French party system through a combination of two claims: that partisan attachments were stronger in the Fourth Republic than once thought and that, regardless of whether or not this last proposition is true, Gaullism was indeed a hegemonic force which more than any other present in Europe at the time contributed to the relative stability of the political parties and the party system by institutionalising the rally drive in French politics.

Gaullism should be perceived as a force which threw most parties into such internal turmoil that their active participation in the political system was delayed as they each went through the throes of the transformation necessary for the new type of political participation, activism and organisation required by the new framework of the Fifth Republic. The period between 1962 and the early 1980s (or at the very least the late 1970s) should be conceived of as a period of radical transformation within all the other, non-Gaullist, parties, a period of frantic adaptation in the light of the new political opportunities offered by the Fifth Republic:

> The developing presidentialism of the Fifth Republic saw the parties regaining their strength, but this according to the manner in which they adapted to the presidential contests. More fundamentally the parties themselves were changing in their organisation, orientation, and eventually their ideologies, and were responding to the exigencies both of the presidential contests, as they perceived them, and of the wider political culture.[47]

The transformation of the party system, regardless of the reasons for its earlier quiescence, can and should be seen as a direct result of the forces unleashed by the presidentialisation of politics by de Gaulle.

As we shall illustrate below, the story of the transformation of the French party system is the story of the transformation of French parties. This, in turn, is the story of the presidentialisation of politics in France and the gradual institutionalisation of rally politics. From 1962 onwards, the changes occurring within the various parties in terms of strategy and programme can easily be detected and directly traced to the parties' attitudes toward the new system in place which required much more on their part than a simple rallying to the constitution or an acceptance of de Gaulle's authority. Before turning to the Fifth Republic, however, the problems faced by its principal institutional predecessors, and the gradual emergence of a strong presidency option shall be briefly outlined.

The emergence of a presidential logic

From mistrust to necessity

Though the revolution contributed to a mistrust in heads of state – monarchical or other – which only subsided with the Fifth Republic's entrenchment in French political life, the aftermath of the 1789 revolution was placed under the sign of various republican experiments; what most of these experiments had in common was their clearly expressed desire to make no single individual powerful enough to usurp popular sovereignty. The period from 1793–94 to the beginning of the Second Republic can therefore be understood in part – in terms of the locus of political power – as a vigorous swinging between attempts at weak constitutional monarchies/assembly government and political coups designed to restore power within the hands of a single individual. The Convention concentrated power within the hands of a twelve-member *Comité du Salut Public* which was then wrenched from them by the Liberal government which followed. The First Empire concentrated power in the most absolute way in the hands of an emperor and, while the restoration of 1815 attempted to emulate a British-style constitutional monarchy, the attempt was short lived and came to an abrupt halt with the 1830 revolution. Louis Philippe's July Monarchy (1830–48) was as close as the French ever came to the British model, but the Second Republic – by allowing for the election of the president and then using a popular vote to elect Louis Napoléon to the presidency – ushered in a renewed period of mistrust toward personalised forms of power and presidential power more particularly.

As pointed out by historians, the *coup d'état* of 1851 determined much of the attitudes of the public and politicians alike toward direct popular elections of the president, and paved the way for France's subsequent political experiments. The rally drive became associated with the actions of Louis Napoléon who, after having been elected President of the Second Republic in December 1848, staged a coup in December 1851, and used a referendum to legitimate his usurpation of power and as a springboard for the overhaul of the Constitution. By 1852 Louis Napoléon, now Napoléon III, had established a new constitutional order: the Second Empire which was to last until the end of the Franco-Prussian war in 1870 and the establishment of the Third

Republic. Rally politics and a strong executive in the form of a strong president were from then on to be associated with the Bonapartist episode. As Graham writes:

> ... the rally drive was associated with Bonapartism that is with a set of circumstances in which a strong man appeals to the broad mass of society, uses the technique of plebiscite to obtain approval for his actions, reduces parliament to a subordinate status, and finally re-establishes order within a democratic framework.[48]

The Third Republic's weak, parliament-centred government should thus be understood as the reaction of a much traumatised nation seeking to avoid the personalisation of power and popular elections which were seen as leading inevitably to coups and dictatorships.

Most presidents, even the forceful ones such as Poincaré, were invariably confronted with the fact that the prime minister wielded all of the power and, while it was the president's prerogative to appoint the prime minister, it was nevertheless in the latter's hands that the real power resided. The president's power was almost exclusively concentrated in that one act of appointing or withholding the appointment of the prime minister. Popularly elected, the parliament and it's head – the prime minister – were virtually all-powerful: the president's selection by the assembly did not (could not) grant him the legitimacy necessary to over-rule a prime-ministerial decision for more than a 'cosmetic' time span and, eventually, no matter what the issue, the presidents were forced to back down and play by the rules of the game set out in the constitution.[49] The Fourth Republic, far from taking into account the disaster brought about by generations of weak presidents, drew its lesson strictly from the Vichy experience and president Lebrun's disregard for the advice of the representatives of the sovereign people. The republican model was, more than ever, seen as unable to provide strong government from the elected bodies, while at the same time strong, personalised leadership was feared and rejected as antithetical to republican precepts.[50]

The sequence of political (but also social and diplomatic) crises which befell France from 1940 onwards created a series of contexts which provided ideal conditions for rally politics. The next section will illustrate the manner in which institutional arrangements affected rally politics and will shed light on the Fourth Republic as an instance of institutional tension, transformation and development.

Institutional patterns of the Fourth Republic

If the Third Republic is remembered for stalemate government, the Fourth is remembered for its pervasive *immobilisme* leading to weakness and crises.[51] The received view is that in the Third Republic the Radicals used their considerable influence to resist rather than to enact policy. Their actions thus often tended to promote inactivity which over time weakened the institutions of government. According to Williams, the main difficulties plaguing the Third Republic were, therefore, not only the institutional devices which had been set up in the cabinets' path (committees of specialists, procedural rules destined to leave the ministries weakened and ineffective, a powerful senate shielded from the demands and checks of universal suffrage), but, rather, a failure to rally public opinion around a political objective which would in turn yield a clear majority for action of one form or another. Only on extremely narrow political programmes was there any consensus: the political cleavages at work otherwise maintained the country in a state of policy limbo which was preferred by all to the chaos foreseen as the only other option in the political game.

Almost all sectors of the population (small farmers, businessmen, workers) seemed to prefer the social stability sired by stalemate to the potential gains of a riskier strategy of political and economic modernisation. As summed up by Williams:

The basic reason for the weakness of French government was thus the contentedness of the dominant section of opinion. This middle block … was wholly negative in outlook, equally opposed to clerical reaction and to socialist experiment, neither wanting nor expecting advantage from positive governmental policies. Its aim was to prevent action, of which it was almost sure to disapprove.[52]

The makers of the Fourth Republic were adamant that France should not return to the weak, unstable governments of the 1930s. While the rejection of the Third Republic was clear (96 per cent of voters voted against returning to the Third Republican regime in the 1945 constitutional referendum)[53] the bases (institutional and otherwise) upon which the Fourth Republic was to be established were less so. The constitutional debates spawned by the Fourth Republic produced governments whose instability and weaknesses were easily to surpass those of the Third and, despite a series of reforms destined to strengthen the administrative machinery of the state and avoid the Third Republic's slowness and stalemate, the Fourth Republic seemed unable to command more legitimate authority over its citizens.

The solution to governmental weaknesses lay in reforms which were opposed by various segments of the population. Based on a suspicion of parties and any factional interests which might overpower it, the Right refused the Left's demand for a powerful assembly in line with the revolutionary tradition. On the other hand the Left refused the idea of a powerful executive too reminiscent of a painful past. The agents of the Fourth Republic were as unwilling as those of the Third Republic to accommodate institutionally the rally drive in French politics.[54]

The constitution, approved in October 1946, was based on socialist principles and designed to force the parties to play a powerful role in organising and disciplining public opinion. A lack of coherence and sense of purpose had been identified as the disease of the Third Republic: the men of the Fourth thus counted on political parties to structure public opinion and ideological currents into something sufficiently coherent and expressible so as to create majorities; political parties were made into the cornerstone of the new constitution. The prime minister was to be elected by the legislature and reflect the majority view, as for the executive he would be, in the words of Williams 'a projection of the legislature'.[55]

The Fourth Republic president can be seen as having even less power than his Third Republic counterpart.[56] What this rescinding of powers illustrates is the national elite's incapacity to combine democratic Republican government through parties with strong and effective government.[57] As the Fourth Republic proved itself incapable of resolving, or even weathering, the Algerian crisis, the conception of the executive as it had emerged since 1877 was increasingly challenged by the need for a stronger executive capable of imposing a stability which the parties, hostages to their sectional interests, could not impose. While Conservative forces were concerned with strengthening the executive in order to control the Assembly, the Left tried to keep the executive as dependent as possible on the latter. Paul Coste-Floret, an MRP member and rapporteur of the second constitutional draft warned that 'In France presidential government would mean dictatorship and Convention government like that of 1793 would lead to revolution. Democracy [would] work only in a compromise system where parliament and executive were balanced.'[58]

The system sired by the new constitution, however, was not so much balanced as stuck: the '*tripartisme*' implemented by the constitution did nothing more than grant constitutional legitimacy to what was already an '*état de fait*'.[59] This resulted in a situation whereby the

constitution of 1946 was attacked by everyone before it was even ratified. Rather than produce consensus its first effect was to provoke
dissatisfaction, hostility and suspicion from all sides as the major parties
participated in politics on the basis of a political strategy dictated by the
need to remain within the system rather than through commitment to
the new constitutional deal.[60]

Yet the parties that had held power in 1940 were no longer able
to lead by 1950, while the strong leaders who had emerged to replace
them were consistently opposed to the regime and thus relentlessly
prevented from making an impact on government. By 1954 it was
acknowledged that 'the Third Republic had replaced the Fourth' and
'*immobilisme*' characterised the Fourth as did 'the System', i.e. 'the
men and customs embodying this "*immobilisme*" in the assembly'.[61]

Rally politics, path dependency and bounded innovation

It is most useful to understand the Fourth Republic as evolving into
the Fifth thanks to a combination of factors: path dependence and
bounded innovation on the one hand, persistent ideological tendencies
on the other. The three are interconnected: path dependence stipulates
that the order in which things happen has an effect on what happens
and how it happens and that, therefore, the trajectory of change up to
point X constrains the trajectory of change from point X onwards[62] is
ultimately connected to notions of bounded innovation which also
imply that ideas and actions may be channelled by earlier politics and
policies.[63] Clearly both approaches draw on the concept of temporal
paths which are shaped by past policies and ideas. But where path
dependence underscores the fact that 'the final pattern depends on the
particular choices that happen to be made'[64] in a sequence of several if
not many possible choices (and is not dependent on certain initial
conditions), bounded innovation emphasises the gradual elimination
of possibilities each time a choice is made.

Broadly, of course, the institutional development of the Third,
Fourth and Fifth Republics can be seen as constrained by the form of
revolutionary upheaval which created the Republican framework and a
host of attitudes toward leadership, order, hierarchy and social and
political change. But, to avoid the problem of infinite regress posed by
theories of bounded innovation and path dependency, let us simply
state that one could usefully view the transition from the Fourth to the
Fifth Republic through two theoretical lenses.

The first is a combination of bounded innovation and path dependency; the second, is achieved through the tracing of persistent ideological constructs woven together by – and together helping to shape – the various institutional frameworks. Path dependency and bounded innovation are of relevance here because they allow for an analytical account of the transformation of French politics from 1946 to the present. Path dependency can in part account for the gradual institutionalisation of the rally drive and the party drive in French politics by providing an argument as to the nature and the parameters of the evolution of institutions in France.

The fact that France and French political life were deeply marked by the Bonapartist experiment and that France was striving to achieve a stable democratic order within a republican framework, means that the hundred or so years between the mid-nineteenth and twentieth centuries are dominated by tension between the drive toward the strengthening of representative politics, i.e. a privileging of the legislative and party politics over the executive; and a fear of the dismemberment and annihilation of the republic. Each political crisis heightened this tension and led to a revival of heroic leadership and its attendant rally politics.[65]

The path to presidentialism and the limits of innovation

De Gaulle's ideas, which he had set out in his 1946 Bayeux speech, called for a stronger presidency, a reduction in the role of political parties and for an assembly with diminished powers. The constitution of 1958 (ratified by 79 per cent of the electorate via national referendum on 21 December 1958) established the Fifth Republic; 1958, therefore, marks the beginning of stronger executive government in France but, until 1962, the regime should be seen as a compromise between assembly government and presidential government.

In 1958, the presidency, and more particularly the presidency's power and legitimacy, were not linked to universal suffrage, indeed the source of either of these remained unspecified and unclear,[66] but the early months of 1961 saw the issue of universal suffrage raised once again. In a strange and poorly managed series of announcements and counter-announcements de Gaulle finally conceded in April 1961, that the matter of a universally elected president was being given serious consideration:

I know that many people consider that the manner in which the president is currently elected, by a limited electoral college – composed as the current text stipulates – would not grant he who might succeed me the popular national mandate which befits this office and which has been conferred upon me, outside of any electoral arena, by exceptional circumstances … I do, for my part, recognise that there would be something rather inadequate in this mode of designation of any head of state who might come after me. In order to remedy this, and by re-enforcing what I might refer to as the future president's personal factor, one might think that he should be elected by universal suffrage. This could be envisaged.[67]

Though de Gaulle made no further moves until the end of the Algerian war, his contemporaries testified as to the number of conversations, meetings and discussions surrounding this theme throughout 1961. In June 1962, a few short weeks before the referendum on Algerian independence, de Gaulle finally declared that according to him 'a direct agreement between a people and he who is in charge of leading it has become, in these modern times, essential to the Republic'.[68]

The dominant explanation for de Gaulle's insistence on the adoption of this measure is that by 1962, with the Algerian war over, the political parties seemed once again to engage in the sort of perpetual political harassment of the government which had characterised the previous two republics. De Gaulle seems to have been convinced that the government and the party system were on a collision course and that the issue of a universally elected presidency provided good ground for the battle to come: it would be difficult for the parties to accuse de Gaulle of authoritarian government as he prepared to consult the sovereign people on whether they felt they should be allowed to elect their president.[69]

From 1962 onwards France's political history is that of a Republic's gradual coming to terms with the institution of the presidency, of that presidency's effect on political life and of the institutionalisation of the rally drive in French politics: in a word with what we have referred to as presidentialism. In many ways the Fifth Republic – often presented as a break with the previous four republics – can be depicted quite convincingly as the next logical step in the political life of France as a republic. Rather than simply an instance, in neo-institutionalist terms of regime change, the Fifth Republic can be seen as an experiment in bounded innovation as well as path-dependent regime consolidation.

French historiography and political analysis is a historiography of crisis; revolutionary periods are followed by apparent periods of calm (*acalmie*) only to be broken by violent and much expected turmoil.

This historiography of crisis is, paradoxically, rooted in a firm belief in a classical conception of politics as tending toward homeostasis, the much sought after 'point of equilibrium' toward which all politics should strive and tend. The literature on democratic transitions has done well to remind us that a stable democratic regime, or simply the conduct of democratic politics, is essentially the reverse of that, not the imposition of homeostasis – which often lends to authoritarianism for the sake of democratic ends – but, the capacity to deal with its opposite, uncertainty.[70]

In the case of France and as underscored before, dealing with uncertainty had often meant resorting to a form of rally politics not unlike authoritarian forms of populism. The advent of the Fifth Republic marks France's institutionalisation of the means to deal with uncertainty within a democratic framework (rather than without). The advent of the Fifth Republic thus signifies the taming – through institutional innovation in the guise of a strengthened and popularly elected executive – of the two opposing drives of party and rally politics which become necessarily subsumed to the necessities and exigencies of presidentialism, the latter allowing for the expression of both.

Converting to presidential politics: bounded innovation in the Fifth Republic

The period from 1958 to 1962 should therefore be seen as a phase during which the crystallisation of the republicanism versus presidentialism dilemma occurs poignantly, once again against the backdrop of a crisis and yet more constitutionally enshrined than ever before. The adoption of a strong presidentialism – or in this case presidency – was seen as a crisis remedy, a necessary measure which would allow for a re-affirmation of the principles of republicanism – and of France's inherently republican identity – once the Algerian crisis was resolved. The period from 1962 onwards heralds the reconciliation between the two drives. 1962 marks this passage as de Gaulle called for the referendum on the introduction of universal suffrage for the election of the president. The 'republican parties' were defeated in their opposition to de Gaulle and the referendum was approved by 61.7 per cent of the population; the parties opposing de Gaulle were also defeated shortly afterwards in the general elections of November 1962 when de Gaulle's party (*Union pour la Nouvelle République* (UNR) backed by the small Independent Republican party), won a majority of seats. For the first time in France, the 1965 presidential elections were held under universal suffrage.

After a period during which the debate was dominated by the resolution of the Algerian crisis and the likelihood of de Gaulle reverting to another form of rule,[71] the debate – particularly that internal to the parties – became focused on how best to adapt to the Gaullist Republic. The answer to that question lay in each party's capacity to re-create itself both programmatically and as an electoral machine in order to cope with the pressures of the presidential elections and the pressures of the different electoral cycles of the presidential and the legislative elections.

Despite some of the frantic opposition to de Gaulle – an opposition which became all the more strident once it became quite clear that de Gaulle had no intention of quietly retiring to Colombey after resolving the Algerian crisis – the period during which the opposition believed or attempted to believe that de Gaulle would revert to orthodox governance was relatively short lived. It is essentially defined by the opposition of such men as Pierre Mendès France whose convictions would not allow him to support what he referred to as a system in which the people surrender their sovereignty as they 'are required to choose a man, even if he is the best man, instead of choosing a form of politics'.[72] This opposition, however, waned as it became apparent that '*alternance*' (the alternating between the Left and the Right in power) would no longer come about as a result of a change of regime; the Fifth Republic looked as though it was going to last and most parties began to plan accordingly.

The interesting point to note is that, while the regime was still young and contested, the first presidential election had the effect of rallying around de Gaulle all those who had been his enemies. This is exemplified by the (abortive) candidacy of Gaston Defferre. Defferre, who had opposed the constitution of 1958 and the 1962 reform, nevertheless can be said to have run in conformity with the new regime and, particularly, in conformity with the 1962 revision. In the manner of a man who had internalised the main tenets of the new regime, Defferre presented himself as having the right to define a political programme while putting himself forth as the guarantor of its subsequent application.

Another point of significance with respect to the Defferre candidacy is that, having begun his campaign as 'Monsieur X', he did so outside the *Section Française de l'Internationale Ouvrière* (SFIO). What is noteworthy here is that this new regime, with its emphasis on a '*présidentiable*', encouraged a sort of heroic leadership from the wings. While Defferre eventually backed down in favour of a non-SFIO candidate acceptable to both the SFIO and the Communists (François Mitterrand), it is nevertheless important to note his willingness to come forth as a candidate as if outside his party and thus to force his party subsequently into the contest. This illustration of the influence of one man upon the party as an electoral machine remains one of the hallmarks of elections in the Fifth Republic.

Defferre's abandoning of the race is just as important in terms of illustrating the converse set of forces at play in the presidential contests. While he was able to force his party's hand and drag it into the presidential election by standing alone and unexpectedly, he nevertheless was himself the victim of the party's rallying presidential politics (and thus a victim of the assertion of the party drive), its embracing of '*une grande fédération*' and the ensuing conflicts amongst the parties of the Left which spelt the end of his candidacy. As such, what was emerging here in the early days of the 1965 election were the dual, rival constituent forces of presidential politics: the increased power of the *présidentiable* over the party but, concomitantly, the party's growing importance in the backing of the candidate. Coupled with the strain of the diverging political logics of the legislative and the presidential elections, these four poles constitute the parameters of presidential politics.

The attitudes of the two other candidates in the same year serves as a further illustration of the gradual presidentialisation of the regime. Like Defferre's, François Mitterrand's candidacy was initiated outside the parties: while he ran as the sole Left candidate ('*candidat unique*') he simply solicited the advice of each of their leaders (Guy Mollet, Pierre Mendès France and Waldeck Rochet). Again, it is quite obvious that this sort of procedure places a premium on leadership and reinforces the impression that the *présidentiable* is so independently of any party. During the campaign, despite his overt criticism of the presidential election, Mitterrand called for the abrogation of article 16 but went no further in proposing any institutional or constitutional reform. More importantly, his campaign was placed under the sign of a presidential discourse: for example, he put forth seven options and twenty-eight propositions which – despite his refusal to admit it – constituted something very close to a programme of government. Further into the campaign he declared that he would, once elected, make use of all the rights which the constitution confers upon the head of state and would immediately dissolve the national assembly. As for the other candidate, Jean Lecanuet, his campaign can be interpreted as having been well in line with the constitution. Remarking on television on the evening of 3 December 1965 'we are ready for the changing of the guard ... you no longer fear the aftermath of Gaullism ... do not postpone this ineluctable event',[74] Lecanuet was acknowledging that as early as 1965 the interpretation of the constitution had become presidential.

The 1974 presidential elections confirm the trend and highlight the effect of the presidential forces on the parties themselves. The 1974 election ushered in the emergence of the two political blocs (on the Left and on the Right) as it saw the *Union de la Gauche* play a key role after the reconstitution of the Socialist party under Mitterrand in 1971 and the elaboration of the Common programme (in June 1972) between the Socialists and the Communists. Despite the fact that Mitterrand was supported by four parties (the Socialist party he had just 'renovated', the Communist party, the *Mouvement des radicaux de gauche* (MRG) and Michel Rocard's *Parti socialiste unifié* (PSU)) he was not actually designated as candidate by any of them and it was he who put himself forth as candidate and announced his own candidacy. Would de Gaulle have dared to dream of such a bypassing of the political parties?

Mitterrand's attitude was again that of a president in the wings; referring to 'his' economic programme and promising such precisely defined measures as an increase in the minimum wage and the lowering of the age of retirement to sixty. While none of these measures or promises was revolutionary they were interesting when seen as those proposed by a politician whose 1964 book *Le coup d'état permanent* was an indictment of de Gaulle's reform and vision of politics. Ten years later Mitterrand seemed to have reformed a party and personally rallied to the very form of politics he once denounced. Further, the candidate who eventually won the election was not a Left-winger, but he was nevertheless not a Gaullist. Valéry Giscard d'Estaing's election was the first sign that the Fifth Republic need not be a Gaullist Republic and that its institutions could stand to harbour a candidate from another political party.

It would be interesting to speculate how Poujade might have fared under Fifth Republican institutions. His fortune would have depended on whether or not Poujade himself had the political acumen to learn to exploit the institutions of the republic and the particular structure of political opportunity they offered, as other politicians did. It is nevertheless conceivable that given the similarities between the appeal made by Poujade and the rhetoric and discourse adopted twenty years or so later by Le Pen, that Poujade and the *Union de Défense des*

Commerçants et des Artisans (UDCA) might have mutated into much the sort of party which the FN was able to become.

The appeal of Le Pen's FN – as will be shown in coming chapters – resided in the same populism used by Poujade and, more importantly, his anti-party stance and his anti-system bias would have been given, much as they were given to Le Pen, a space into which to expand. In 1956 when Poujade and his MPs were elected to the National Assembly, French politics existed almost exclusively in that arena. Ten years later the political arena had been considerably enlarged as the presidential cycle shaped a party system – and, more broadly, a political system – in which parties such as the UDCA could maintain their rally identity rather than attempt a full transformation into parties. In other words, the newly shaped French political arena allowed rallies to capitalise on their anti-systemic stance because politics could also legitimately be carried out outside traditional parties; or so it seemed.

To conclude on rally politics one point is of great importance given the remainder of this book, namely the relationship between rally politics and populism. For Graham, whose definition of rally politics has been adopted here, the notion of rally politics seems to replace the concept of 'populism'. Yet it is maintained here that the two are distinct and are in a complex relationship to one another. The idea that politics and in particular party politics are conducted on the basis of two contradictory but inseparable drives is of great use for the study of the organisation of parties and for the examination of the role of leadership within parties. As underscored earlier, such an approach allows for the detection of change and offers explanations as to why change is taking place within a particular party or across a party system as a whole.

Nevertheless, given the definition of institutions adopted for this book, the argument depends on the interaction between ideas and institutions and the recognition that ideologies evolve alongside institutions as much as they are shaped by them. Graham's definition of rally politics downplays the effect of the ideational and ideological on institutions and remains too narrowly organisational. The identification of the clusters of ideas which shape institutions is a key aspect of this project and the emphasis on the interdependence between the two, a crucial step in our analysis of the FN and its success in France.

It could be argued that all populism is based on a form of rally politics but not all rally politics are a version of populism. From rally politics to populism there is but a step, and it may be slight, but it exists. Populism and rally politics differ in that where rally politics is essentially a facet of all politics corresponding to demands for unity and cohesion over demands for democratic representation, populism is more prescriptive or, rather, goes further down the prescriptive road: the rally is necessary but not sufficient. What is needed and prescribed in most versions of populism is a purge of the negative elements (hence the use of so much organicist vocabulary in populist rhetoric). The difference with fascism in this respect is the much smaller role assigned to elitism and violence in populism – at least in theory. Populism, therefore, is closer to exhibiting the qualities of a system of thought made up of clusters of concepts, or ideology loosely defined.

Rally politics on the other hand is more identifiable as a series of political devices (rhetorical and other) which reflect a diffuse – though no less imperative for that – set of demands placed on politics and politicians (and characteristic of all mass politics) rather than a prescriptive and definitive *Weltanschaüng*. The differences between de Gaulle on the one hand and Poujade and Le Pen on the other are rooted in this distinction. De Gaulle uses rally politics principally for the purposes of the rally; Poujade and Le Pen use rally politics in order to advance what might be termed a populist agenda. While rally politics perceive the fragmentation of the polity as dangerous, there is no fundamental resentment of elites *per se*. Elites are only resented if they are seen as having contributed to the fragmentation and weakening. Populism on the other hand creates and exacerbates the dividing line between people and elites in order to create conflict; here the creation and exploitation of the divide is ultimately more important than the unity of the nation.

The next two chapters will illustrate how concepts pertaining to ideologies such as fascism, nationalism and populism found themselves 'dragged along' from one context to the next, drawing strength from one aspect of the institutional framework, losing force through another, mutating and surviving much like organisms in an evolving but not necessarily hostile host. Chapters 6 and 7 will also illustrate how rally politics and their institutionalisation allows for certain combinations of ideas to gain renewed appeal and increased institutional tolerance.

Notes

1 R. Elgie, *Electing the French President: The 1995 Presidential Election* (London: Macmillan, 1996), p. 52.

2 A. Stepan and C. Skach, 'Constitutional frameworks and democratic consolidation', *World Politics*, 46 (October 1993), 4.

3 A. Lijphart, in J. Linz and A. Valenzuela, eds, *The Failure of Presidential Democracy* (London: The Johns Hopkins University Press, 1994), p. 93.

4 J. Linz, 'Presidential or parliamentary democracy: does it make a difference?' in J. Linz and A. Valenzuela, eds, *The Failure*, pp. 8–16.

5 J. Linz, 'Presidential', p. 8.

6 J. Linz, 'Presidential', pp. 14–16.

7 A. Przewoski, *Democracy and the Market: Political and Economic Reforms in Eastern Europe and Latin America* (Cambridge: Cambridge University Press, 1991), cited in Linz 'Presidential', pp. 14–15.

8 A. Lijpart, *Democracies: Patterns of Majoritarian and Consensus Government in Twenty One Countries* (New Haven, CT: Yale University Press, 1984).

9 Lijpart, 'Presidentialism', p. 97.

10 Scott Mainwaring, 'Presidentialism, multipartism and democracy: the difficult combination', *Comparative Political Studies*, 26: 2 (July 1993), 198–228.

11 Mainwaring, 'Presidentialism', p. 207.

12 M. Shugart and J. Carey, *Presidents and Assemblies: Constitutional Design and Electoral Dynamics* (New York, NY: Cambridge University Press, 1992), pp. 1–2.

13 Shugart and Carey, *Presidents*, p. 3.

14 J. Linz, 'Presidential', pp. 6–7.

15 Stepan and Skach, 'Constitutional', drawing on Guillermo O'Donnell 'Democracia delegativa?' *Novos Estudios CEBRAP*, 31 (October 1991), 19.

16 Here legitimacy is defined along the lines of a skeletal version of David Beetham's definition. In a defense of his influential 1991 work (D. Beetham, *The Legitimation of Power* (London: Macmillan, 1991), Beetham writes 'I started from the simple proposition that what the powerful can get the subordinates to do is not only a matter of the resources they can command, but also a question of their moral authority, normative standing or "legitimacy"' (D. Beetham, 'In defence of legitimacy', *Political Studies*, XLI: 3 (1993), 488–91). In fact Beetham's definition of legitimate power rests on three simple criteria: conformity to rules, justifiability of rules in terms of shared beliefs and legitimation through expressed consent (Beetham, *The Legitimation*, p. 20) (non-legitimate power is thus to be understood as in breach of rules, creating a legitimacy deficit – discrepancy between the rules and supporting beliefs-and withdrawal of consent or 'delegitimation').

17 Juan Linz addresses this dual allegiance: 'The symbolic and deferential dimension of power – (...) – is difficult to combine with the role of partisan politician fighting to implement his program. (...) Many voters and key elites are likely to see the second role as a betrayal of the role of head of state, who is somewhat above party and a symbol of the continuity of the state and the nation that is associated with the presidency'. J. Linz, 'Presidential', pp. 24–5.

18 E.Suleiman, 'Toward the disciplining of parties and legislators: the French parliament in the Fifth Republic', in E. Suleiman, ed., *Parties and Parliaments in Democratic Politics* (New York, NY: Holmer and Meier, 1986), p. 85.

19 E. Suleiman, 'Presidentialism and political stability in France', in Linz and Valenzuela, eds, *The Failure*, pp. 137–62

20 M. Duverger, 'A new political system model: semi-presidential government', *European Journal of Political Research*, 8 (1980), 165–87.

21 Duverger, 'New political system', p. 165.

22 Suleiman writes, 'Political stability in France as well as the functioning of the presidential system since 1958 have been conditioned as much by the transformation of the party system as by the constitutional changes, that is to say, as much by the unforeseen consequences of the constitution as by the constitution itself'. 'Toward the disciplining', p. 145.

23 De Gaulle in Duverger, 'New political system', p. 171.

24 Duverger, 'New political system', p. 171.

25 Duverger, 'New political system', p. 172.

26 J. Gaffney, *The French Left and the Fifth Republic: The Discourses of Communism and Socialism in Contemporary France* (London: Macmillan, 1989), p. 6.

27 J. Gaffney, in J. Gaffney and L. Milne, eds, *French Presidentialism and the Election of 1995* (Aldershot: Dartmouth, 1997), pp. 273–4.

28 For a discussion of de Gaulle's conception of the army and the transposition of these ideas to the world of politics see B. D. Graham, *Representation and Party Politics* (Oxford: Blackwell, 1993), pp. 11–20.

29 De Gaulle, radio broadcast in Brazzaville, 21 September, 1942, cited in Graham, *Representation*, p. 117.

30 Graham, *Representation*, p. 117.

31 S. Hoffmann, 'Heroic leadership: the case of modern France', in L. J. Edinger, ed., *Political Leadership in Industrial Societies: Studies in Comparative Analysis* (New York, NY: Wiley, 1967), pp. 253–74; see also the French version 'Le héros politique: Pétain, de Gaulle, Mendès-France' – part I, *Preuves* (June 1967), 25–45; Part II, *Preuves* (July 1957), 286–93. *Le Mouvement Poujade, Cahiers de la fondation nationale des sciences politiques* (Paris: Presses de la fondation nationale des sciences politiques, 1956).

32 A. Siegfried, *Tableau politique de la France de l'Ouest sous la Troisième République* (Paris: Armand Colin, 1964), p. 473.

33 Siegfried, *Tableau*, pp. 473–4.

34 Graham, *Representation*, p. 83.

35 Graham, *Representation*, p. 83.

36 Graham, *Representation*, p. 84.

37 Whether crises are real or perceived is always a matter of some debate. For the purposes at hand the perception of crisis is a sufficient condition.

38 Graham, *Representation*, p. 85.

39 M. Canovan, 'Trust the people! Populism and the two faces of democracy', *Political Studies*, 47: 1 (March 1999), 9.

40 M. Duverger, *Les partis politiques* (Paris: Armand Colin, 1951). Translated into English and published by Methuen, London, 1954.

41 O. Kirchheimer, 'The transformation of Western European party systems', in J. LaPalombara and M. Weiner, eds, *Political Parties and Political Development* (Princeton, NJ: Princeton University Press, 1966), pp. 177–200. See also, S. Wolinetz, 'The transformation of the Western European party system revisited', *West European Politics*, 2: 2 (1979), 5.

42 S. M. Lipset and S. Rokkan, ' Introduction' to *Party Systems and Voter Alignments* (New York, NY: Free Press, 1967), p. 51.

43 On party system change and stability see: H. Daalder, 'The comparative study of European party systems: an overview', in H. Daalder and P. Mair, eds, *Western European Party Systems, Continuity and Change* (London: Sage, 1983); S. Bartolini and P. Mair, *Identity, Competition and Electoral Availability: The Stabilisation of European Electorates, 1885: 1985* (Cambridge: Cambridge University Press, 1990).

44 P. Mair, 'La trasformazione del partito di massa in Europa', in M. Calise, ed., *Come cambiano i partiti* (Bologna: Il Mulino, 1992), pp. 99–120.

45 D. Cameron and R. Hofferbert, 'Continuity and change in Gaullism: the General's legacy', *American Journal of Political Science*, 17: 1 (1973), 78–83; see also D. Cameron, 'Stability and change in patterns of French partisanship', *Public Opinion Quarterly*, 36 (Spring 1972), 19–30.

46 M. Lewis-Beck, 'France: the stalled electorate', in R. Dalton, S. Flanagan and P. A. Beck, eds, *Electoral Change in Advanced Industrial Democracies: Realignment or Dealignment?* (Princeton, NJ: Princeton University Press, 1984), pp. 428–33.

47 J. Gaffney, 'Introduction: French presidentialism and the Fifth Republic,' in J. Gaffney, ed., *The French Presidential Elections of 1988* (Aldershot: Dartmouth, 1989), p. 10.

48 Graham, *Representation*, p. 88.

49 Both Millerand and Doumergue tried to play a role in policy making and attempted to bypass ministers, and therefore parliament; both of them were unsuccessful.

50 For broad discussions of the Presidency from the revolution see J. Hayward, 'From republican sovereign to partisan statesman', in J. Hayward, ed., *De Gaulle to Mitterrand: Presidential Power in France* (London: Hurst and Company, 1993), pp. 1–35; P. Morris, 'Presidentialism in France: a historical overview', in J. Gaffney and L. Milne, eds, *French Presidentialism*, pp. 5–21; J. Gaffney, 'Introduction', pp. 2–36; J-L.Seurin, *La présidence de la République en France et aux Etats-Unis* (Paris: Economica, 1986); J. Massot, *L'arbitre et le capitaine. Essai sur la responsabilité présidentielle* (Paris: Flammarion, 1987).

51 It is worth noting in passing that this view of the Fourth Republic as a dreadful political experiment has come under a series of challenges. The Fourth Republic was indeed problematic and ineffectual on many fronts, however, scholars have repeatedly underscored the mythification and exaggeration of the Fourth's inadequacies by de Gaulle.

52 P. Williams, *Crisis and Compromise: Politics in the Fourth Republic* (London: Longman's, 1958), p. 9. The American Catholic economist Michael Novak makes an interesting parallel between the immobilistic tendencies of the radicals and anti-clericals on the one hand and those involved in the elaboration of a Catholic social doctrine in the years following the Second World War on the other. According to Nowak both movements failed due to their inability to construct solid ideals connected to reality. The attempt to devise a doctrine which neither supported communist or socialism while at the same time refusing to embrace capitalism with any conviction was the death warrant of the post-war Catholics. The radicals' failure to embrace an economic or social doctrine based either on socialism or on liberalism signaled their failure. M. Nowak, *Une éthique économique* (Paris: Ed. du Cerf, 1987), p. 296.

53 P. Morris, 'Presidentialism', p. 13. On the referendum and the events leading up to it see also, J. P. Rioux, *La France de la quatrième République, I. L'ardeur et la nécéssité 1944–1952* (Paris: Seuil, 1980), pp. 6896. For another analysis see also D. Pickles, *French Politics: The First Years of the Fourth Republic* (London: Methuen and Co. Ltd., 1953).

54 As underscored by a host of authors then, the Fourth Republic was an attempt to reach compromise while implementing change. A creation of the Centre-Left, it came under assault from the Gaullists as well as from the communists. The communists (with the support of the socialists and inspired by the Convention of 1793) tried to establish an all-powerful assembly as the central governing principle of the new constitution, but the proposal was rejected in the referendum of May 1946. The Left was then faced with the necessity of compromising with more moderate groups and in particular with the increasingly influential MRP.

55 Williams, *Crisis and Compromise*, p. 190

56 The most important curtailment of the president's power was the stipulation in the constitution that the appointment of the prime minister was now conditional on the national assembly's approval. Further, the president was no longer allowed to communicate to the Assembly by message and he was stripped of his title and function of commander of the armed forces.

57 Morris, 'Presidentialism', p. 16.

58 Coste-Floret in *Journal Officiel*, 20 August 1946, p. 3185. Cited in Williams, *Crisis and Compromise*, p. 191.

59 As underscored by Rioux, *tripartisme* appeared comfortable: it allowed the men who were involved in it to seal their hold on an unprecedentedly large electorate (they controlled three quarters of the voters) and an assembly stacked in their favour. The constitution of 1946 thus institutionalised what Rioux referred to as '*les facilités du moments*' (momentarily available easy options). Rioux, *La France*, p. 145.

60 Over the next decade, and from the outset, the constitution would be in a perpetual state of renovation: in 1950, for example, it was decided that eleven articles should be amended, then, a few months later, it was decided that twenty-eight articles needed to be amended. Most of the grievances centred around a parliament at the mercy of parties which had the powers to overthrow a government every six months, while excluding any strong personality from power.

61 These are Duncan MacRae's words and his definition of 'the system', but de Gaulle was the first to refer to the customs of the parties and assembly as such. D. MacRae, *Parliament, Parties and Society in France 1946–1958* (New York, NY: St. Martin's Press, 1967), p. 2.

62 C. Hay, '"Punctuated evolution" and the uneven temporality of institu-
    tional change: the "crisis" of Keynesianism and the rise of neo-liberalism
    in Britain,' paper presented to the *Eleventh Conference of Europeanists*
    (Baltimore, 26–28 February 1998), p. 17; C. Tilly, 'The time of states',
    Social Research, 61: 2 (1994), 269–95; Paul Pierson, 'When effects
    become cause: policy feedback and political change', *World Politics*, 45
    (1993) 595–628.
63 M. Weir, 'Ideas and the politics of bounded innovation', S. Steinmo, K.
    Thelen and F. Longstreth, eds, *Structuring politics: Historical institution-
    alism in Comparative Analysis* (Cambridge: Cambridge University Press,
    1992), p. 192.
64 J. Goldstone, 'Initial conditions, general laws, path dependence, and
    explanation in historical sociology', *American Journal of Sociology*, 104: 3
    (1998), 834.
65 Two clusters of events yield a useful picture of he manner in which parties
    whose tactics were those of rally politics behaved and how they failed
    under Third and Fourth Republican institutions. These are De Gaulle's
    wartime rally and his creation of the *Rassemblement du Peuple Français*
    (RPF) in 1947 and Poujade's *Union des Commerçants et Artisans*
    (UDCA) in 1956–58 on the other. For this, see C. Fieschi, 'Rally politics
    and political organisation: an institutionalist perspective on the French far
    right', *Modern and Contemporary France*, 8 (February 2000), 71–89.
66 In his 1946 Bayeux speech, de Gaulle did not support the idea of a univer-
    sally elected president of the republic. At the time, he declared that the
    head of state should be elected by a '*college qui englobe le parlement, mais
    beaucoup plus large et composé de manière à faire de lui le président de
    l'Union Française en même temps que celui de la République*' (a college
    which includes parliament but which is far broader and compsed so as to
    make him into both the President of the French Union and that of the
    French Republic) (Ch. De Gaulle, 'Discours de Bayeux', in *Discours et
    messages, Vol. 1. Pendant la guerre, juin 1940–janvier 1946* (Paris: Plon,
    1970). Still seeped in classical nineteenth-century republicanism and
    ready to resuscitate the ghost of Bonaparte, Michel Debré – de Gaulle's
    Prime Minister at the time – had voiced his hostility to the idea of a
    universally elected president and likened it to government by 'pronuncia-
    mentos'. On 27 August 1958, Debré had reiterated his disapproval but
    this time through new arguments: the election of the president of the
    pepublic via universal suffrage was incompatible with his role as national
    arbiter. Furthermore, Debré invoked the nineteen million voters in
    Algeria (40 per cent of the total voting population at the time), whose
    preference could lead to the election of a president elected against the
    majority of the voters based in metropolitan France (on this see Jean
    Touchard, *Le Gaullisme, 1940–1969* (Paris: Seuil, Points Histoire, 1978),
    pp. 238–41). Debré insisted once again upon this risk in a 1958 speech
    before the Conseil d'Etat.
67 De Gaulle in Touchard, *Le Gaullisme*, p. 241.
68 De Gaulle in Touchard, *Le Gaullisme*, p. 241.
69 Michel Debré makes the following points concerning national defense and
    institutions: 'One of the elements of deterrence is the credibility of an

authority who would carry out the terrible threat should the need arise. This credibility assumes that the head of state has legitimacy in his own right, independent of the legitimacy of institutions. He therefore had to have the support of universal suffrage. The second idea has to do with institutions. France is still a country where it is difficult to picture the formation of two parties which alternate in power and thus ensure the democratic functioning of the state. Extreme groups in France contest the legitimacy of the republican form of government. Because of this, the Republic still lives under the threat, despite the merit of institutions, of once more falling into the system of coalitions of various parties which dominate government. Basing the authority of the head of state on universal suffrage is a safeguard against this eventuality'. M. Debré, 'The constitution of 1958: its *raison d'etre* and how it evolved,' in W. G. Andrews and S. Hoffmann, eds, *The Impact of the Fifth Republic on France* (New York, NY: SUNY Press, 1981).

70 F. Hagopian, 'Democracy by undemocratic means? Elites, political pacts and regime transitions in Brazil', *Comparative Political Studies*, 23: 2 (1990), 144–70; A. Przeworski, 'Some problems in the study of transitions to democracy,' in G. O'Donnel, P. Schmitter and L. Whitehead, eds, *Transitions From Authoritarian Rule: Comparative Perspectives* (Vol. 3) (Baltimore, MD: Johns Hopkins University Press, 1986.), pp. 47–63; A. Mac Ewan, 'Transitions from authoritarian rule', *Latin American Perspectives*, 58: 15: 3 (1988), 115–30; G. O'Donnel, P. Schmitter and L. Whitehead, *Transitions from Authoritarian Rule: Latin America* (Vol.2); *Transitions* (Vol.3); *Transitions from Authoritarian Rule: Tentative Conclusions about Uncertain Democracies* (Vol.4) (Baltimore, MD: Johns Hopkins University Press, 1986).

71 As pointed out by Gaffney there is quite a significant gap between the understanding of presidential power and presidentialism between 1958 and 1962, and the understanding of the same concepts in post-1962 France. The difference lies in a shift in understanding of the principles of republicanism and an abandoning, after 1962, of the reversion principle, i.e. the idea that the regime once the crisis resolved would revert to real; or 'effective' republicanism. J. Gaffney, *The French Left*, see especially Ch. 1 'Presidentialism and the Fifth Republic', pp. 1–11.

72 P. M. France, *La vérité guidait leur pas* (Paris: Gallimard, 1976), p. 38.

73 O. Duhamel, *La gauche et la Vème République* (Paris: PUF, 1980), Ch. 2, pp. 247–73.

74 J. Massot and G. Vedel, 'Alternance et cohabitation sous la Vème République', special issue of *Notes et Etudes Documentaires*, 5058 (August 1997), 50.

Chapter 4

Fascism and populism

The argument of this book is that the FN's success is based on a new ideological synthesis and doctrinal body of thought rooted in fascism but adapted to the exigencies of a new institutional and constitutional regime of the Fifth Republic. Institutional change in the Fifth Republic heightened the relevance of one of the core concepts of fascism – populism – thereby transforming proto-fascism into a national-populist movement and party: the FN. The aim of this chapter is to consider fascism as an ideology and to illustrate that ideologies are in a symbiotic relationship with institutions.

The argument is that the far Right in France has adapted to prevalent institutions. Looking at the nature of ideologies allows us to track the evolution of ideas as they come into contact with institutions and institutional settings. Ideologies[1] are particularly relevant here as a distinct and discrete phenomenon because they offer an insight on how ideas and actions mesh and as such have much to tell us about the workings of institutions.

For the purposes of this project a definition of ideologies has been adopted that focuses not on what ideologies do but rather on what ideologies are. The work of Michael Freeden enables the researcher to isolate core concepts of an ideology and enables him or her to track the evolution of a particular cluster of concepts over time and thus detect ideological transformations and conceptual shifts. In this book ideologies are thus taken to be constituted by a set of concepts (core, adjacent and peripheral). This morphological approach, introduced in Chapter 2, allows for the proper contextualisation of ideas as it places a premium on the fact that ideologies evolve, change and mutate under various pressures, including institutional ones. Conversely, this conception of ideologies also allows for the proper valorisation of context (historical and political). What follows is a brief definition of the possible core concepts of fascism. The following chapter will examine how fascism's ideological morphology has been shaped and altered as political practice and the institutionalisation of political practice has evolved over time.

The matrix[2] of fascism: a synthetic morphology

The argument here fits within the broad school of 'generic fascism'.[3] The premise in much of the work in this field is that fascism can be treated as a body of doctrine and political action/practice which despite potential contradictions is, nevertheless, largely coherent and can be reduced to basic tenets. The goal is to specify the core, adjacent and peripheral concepts of fascism as an ideology. This accomplished, it will be possible to see which of these have had to be substituted, removed or added for a populism to emerge from what was once a French version of fascism. The elements which form the matrix of fascism have been selected after an extensive review of the literature and have been deemed to be the most relevant.

For the purposes of this analysis we have elaborated our own micro-version of a morphological model of fascism based on the following potentially constitutive elements. I have chosen the elements below as they are the recurrent ones in the seemingly endless literature on fascism:

- (ultra-)nationalism
- a philosophy of rebirth (palyngenesis)
- revolutionary values
- a reliance on violence
- extreme elitism
- populism
- holism/collectivism
- the *führerprinzip* or the importance of the strong leader

To this list shall be added the idea of 'syncretism' which, while not a core concept in Freeden's sense, needs to be examined in light of the relationship of these concepts to one another.

In order to isolate core concepts the elements listed must be further reduced and ordered. As the upcoming discussion will show the list is further reducible as many of these can be usefully 'collapsed' into one another. More importantly it is worth underscoring that the concepts isolated are themselves in a particular relationship to one another. In other words Freeden's insistence that the relationship between the concepts constitutive of an ideology is itself crucial and part of the morphology of a particular ideology is illustrated in the relationship between the core concepts which we have isolated as constitutive of fascism.

Nationalism

Nationalism is one of the main components of fascism. The fascist society is always depicted as founded on the nation, whether one reads Gentile:

> Let us pay [tribute] to generous memories, to raise our consciousness of being free citizens of a great nation. For where Nation is understood in this way, even liberty is less a right than a duty: a prize which is only achieved through the self denial of the citizen prepared to give everything to his Fatherland without asking for anything in return. Even this concept of the nation, which we see as central to, is not a Fascist invention. It is the soul of the new Italy which slowly but surely will prevail over the old.[4]

or José Streel:

> The community of the people [*communauté populaire*] – which in the present stage of historical development is fundamentally confused with the nation – is the nation considered as a complete social environment in which man can blossom. It pre-exists the individual and is not dependent on an unstable set of conditions. It is above all conflicts of interests which can manifest themselves within it; it imposes on all its members links powerful enough, and a solidarity effective enough, to transcend all ideological and economic differences.[5]

As for Maurice Barrès, he can be seen as one of the foremost theoreticians of nationalism (and as we shall see later on as one the earliest advocates of a proto-fascism). While Barrès' nationalism evolves significantly from an organicist nationalism to a conservative one, sentiments of belonging always hold a prominent place in his writings. Nationality is the essential characteristic of any human group and one of the main themes in Barrès' writings is the idea that one should do everything to preserve and maintain the cohesion of the nation and of national characters. Barrès' nationalism emerges alongside the loss of Alsace-Lorraine, is shaped by the Dreyfus affair (a period during which it acquires the most significant elements of its biological determinism) and finally turns into a nationalism which owes much to Taine. As pointed out by Sternhell, Taine's 'context' and 'race' become Barrès' ' Earth' and 'Dead'.[6]

While it is true that some writers associated with fascism espoused a pan-European stance (for example Degrelle, Drieu la Rochelle, Mosley or Bardèche), it is quite clear that this pan-Europeanism is based essentially on the same restrictive notion of community as garden-variety nationalism. It is simply a pan-European nationalism whose theoretical core is more directly influenced by theories of Aryan, or pan-European biological superiority and dominance. It nevertheless bestows upon Europe the characteristics with which the national community is normally endowed.

Emerging alongside the rise of mass politics and growing interdependence between nations, fascism posits the nation as the community whose existence has been endangered by cosmopolitan ideals, whose strength has been sapped by the decadence of Enlightenment goals and which ultimately needs to be regenerated by violent upheaval. It is essentially because of the centrality of the nation as primeval community that nationalism plays such an important role in the pantheon of fascist ideas and at the core of fascist ideology. The words of Charles Maurras are particularly illuminating:

> The fatherland is a natural society, or (much the same) a historical one. Its defining character is birth. One no more chooses one's fatherland – the land of one's fathers – than chooses one's father or one's mother.[7]

Or:

> A fatherland is a union of families composed by history and geography; its principle excludes the principle of liberty of individuals, of their equality, but it, does however, imply a real, profound and organic brotherhood.[8]

The notion that the nation is a natural order as distinct from those social pacts symbolising liberal, egalitarian, post-enlightenment, contractual societies has several important facets.

Firstly, it posits the centrality of community over and above individual choices and emanations of the individual will. It therefore creates the image of an individual whose value as such is negated by the conditions of his or her very existence, his or her birth in a particular community. Interestingly, however, which community matters little at this stage: the nation, the fatherland pre-exists its conception in the

mind of its member. Its worth as a distinct community is only emphasised after the value of community *per se* has been clearly revealed as
pre-dating the individual who shall, in time, be required to know and
praise its unique characteristics.[9]

Secondly, the notion of community as nation – or vice versa – can
be understood as the main spring for the triggering of the discourse of
decadence so central (as shall be shown) to fascism. It is, above all, the
collective body of the nation which is seen as endangered by the forces
of decadence. The concept of palyngenesis is ultimately connected to
the belief that violence and destruction will be undergone as a collective experience just as the chosen ones will be reborn as a new nation
together. As such the concept of palyngenesis cannot be divorced from
the body undergoing it, i.e. the body of the nation.[10]

Palyngenesis: the rebirth of the people

The idea of rebirth, or palyngenesis, can easily incorporate in one
semantic and symbolic swoop notions of radicalism, revolution and
violence. While the concept of violence is not etymologically contained
in the word palyngenesis (literally to create anew), there is nevertheless
no palyngenesis without violence of some sort. The myth of palyngenesis is used when periods of decay are seen to be reaching their climax
and are expected to yield a new, renewed social and political order. As
Griffin further points out, against notions of New World Orders 'the
"palyngenetic myth" comes to denote the vision of a revolutionary
new order … At the heart of the palyngenetic political myth lies the
belief that contemporaries are living through a "sea-change", a "watershed"'.[11]

In other words, palyngenesis is irrevocably linked to notions of
violence. It is also linked to notions of progress – albeit violent
progress – thus giving fascism its radical, revolutionary quality rather
than a conservative, nostalgic quality.

Klaus Theweleit shows how the concept of palyngenesis encompasses violence, revolution, progress and radicalism:

> What the texts cited have most clearly demonstrated is a refusal by fascism
> to relinquish desire – desire in the form of a demand that 'blood must
> flow', desire in its most profound distortion. In the German Communist
> Party (KPD) desire was never seen as the producer of a better reality: that
> party never so much as intimated that there might be pleasure in libera-
> tion, pleasure in new connections, pleasure in the unleashing of new

streams. Instead desire was channeled into plotting and scheming tactics and strategies – literary ones included – while fascism screamed 'Germany awaken!' What was sleeping had ears to hear its call as a bell-peal of immediate resurrection: 'the dead' could now return from the entrails. *Fascism's most significant achievement was to organize the resurrection and rebirth of dead life in the masses – 'strange as it may sound to men who have never struggled for existence'. In the contemporary context, dead life can hardly be called a rarity; and its resurrection remains an important political process – perhaps the most important political process of all.*[12] [My emphasis]

It seems therefore that for the sake of economy and classification the reliance on violence, the radicalism, the military values and the revolutionary spirit can all be subsumed within the concept of palyngenesis.

The idea of palyngenesis is in a particular relationship to nationalism. Well aware of the mobilising powers of myths, Griffin defines fascism as dependent on two main elements: the myth of palyngenesis on the one hand and what he calls 'populist ultra-nationalism' on the other.

After a lengthy discussion devoted to the various uses of the palyngenetic myth in most religious or political traditions, Griffin sets out the parameters within which he intends to use the term: 'I intend to employ it,' he writes, 'as a generic term for the vision of a radically new beginning which follows a period of destruction or perceived dissolution.'[13] To this, Griffin adds that while only the most nostalgic and backward-looking ideologies do not include an element of palyngenesis, the use of the term becomes fully relevant when combined with his other core element, namely populist ultra-nationalism. Here, again, Griffin recognises the fact that this is an element that is found in many ideologies, more or less prominently and adds that 'nationalism' as a term has been a victim of its own success. He does however point out that he uses the term quite specifically:

> To refine the term so that it becomes useful for the investigation of fascism I propose to use the more specialised sub-category 'populist ultra-nationalism.' I follow Eley (1990. p. 281) in using 'populist' not to refer to a specific historical experience (for example late nineteenth century American or Russian Populism) but as a generic term for political forces which, even if led by a small elite cadres or self-appointed 'vanguards', in practice or principle (and not merely for show) depend on people-power as the basis for their legitimacy.[14]

It is precisely because the 'ethical' community of ultra-nationalism is perceived by those who belong to it as representing a microcosm of a natural order that this organicist version of community is seen as sometimes falling prey to degeneration, corruption, decadence and 'ill'-being of various forms. It follows, therefore, that the community's well-being hinges on periods of rebirth and regeneration that follow those of decadence and degeneration.

The combination of the two terms in order to create the dual conceptual core of 'palyngenetic populist ultra-nationalism' thus appears to yield an analytic category greater than the sum of its parts, and one particularly useful for the understanding of fascism as an ideology. 'Just as the combination of two lenses in a telescope,' writes Griffin, 'can bring a distinct object suddenly into focus.'[15] The two concepts thus bring into focus an ideology whose defining mobilising element is the vision of a national community which after a period of degenerative decadence rises from its ashes and escapes destruction through violent renewal.

The role of an instrument such as populism plays a crucial role here. More than the chivalric underpinnings of fascism, the main rhetorical, symbolic (and often institutional) device used by fascists is that of populism.

Populism

Populism is what, in effect, provides a bridge (both in practice and in discourse) between the – seemingly contradictory – elitism and the egalitarian collectivism of much fascist thought.[16] This is essentially because populism allows the people to imagine themselves as an elite. What gives this elite its specificity is the belonging to a nation which is itself seen as superior to others by its traditions, folklore, people etc. Populism, therefore, allows fascism to depict society as naturally and 'organically' ordered, but incorporates the concept of elitism through the notion that the people are chosen to be a great nation.[17]

These words by Giovanni Giurati illustrate the synthesis of elitism and collectivism achieved by a populist discourse:

> The Fascist party must be aristocratic in the sense that it must embrace the flower of the race in terms of moral purity, intellectual training, discipline, devotion to the Fatherland. But it must also be a mass party if it wants to provide tens of thousands of Blackshirts able to hold the supreme offices of the State, run the local councils and provinces, regiment the working masses, instruct the youth, in a word bear the enormous burden of constructing a modern State.[18]

The words of the Romanian leader Codreanu place an even greater emphasis on the sacrality of the concept of a people:

> A people only achieves true consciousness of itself if deep in its soul it is alive not only to its personal interest, but to its great unity and inner bonds. The people has:
> 1. a physical and biological heritage: flesh and blood;
> 2. a material heritage: the soil of the fatherland and its treasures;
> 3. a spiritual heritage. ...
> There will come a time when all the peoples of the earth will fight their way through to this final resurrection, all the peoples with their dead leaders. Then each people will be given a special place before the throne of God. This final act, this overwhelming moment, this resurrection of the dead, is the highest and most sublime goal which a people can aspire to. A people is thus an entity whose life continues beyond the earth![19]

This quotation is particularly interesting in its mixing first of all of the physical, bodily aspect of a people with the sacred; and secondly in its ambiguity with respect to the place of the nations which, on the one hand, are evoked as all being chosen as the nations of God and on the other seem to have to expect a hierarchy 'before the throne of God'. To some extent it can be argued that this is the same ambiguity which lies at the core of fascism within the notion of a populism based on all of the people (the whole nation) and at the same time on an elite of the people.

While the word has been widely used and applied to different contexts (nineteenth-century Russian populism, nineteenth-century American populism, the Thatcher years in Britain and, of course, to many twentieth-century Latin American regimes) the scholarship on populism is remarkably sparse and the term still falls short of encompassing something very precise.

For the purposes of this book I have looked at three of the main theoretical texts on populism. Ionescu and Gellner's 1969 edited volume entitled *Populism: Its Meanings and National Characteristics*; Ernesto Laclau's 'Toward a theory of populism' in the book by the same author entitled *Politics and Ideology in Marxist Theory: Capitalism – Fascism – Populism* and, finally Margaret Canovan's 1981 work *Populism*.[20] While I do refer to other works, these three books are the best attempts at achieving theoretical consensus on the term.

The edited volume by Ionescu and Gellner – now a little dated – was a first attempt at theorising a widely used yet curiously ill-defined concept. The collection's main contribution to the field is that it stands as an illustration of the number of ways in which the term was being used. Some of the participants to the conference from which the volume is drawn appear to have even given up on the possibility of using the term in any meaningful manner.

More useful for our purposes is the work by Ernesto Laclau. Laclau's work is the main attempt to establish a Marxist theory of populism. His central argument is that there are many different types of populism. What they share is not that they all arise out of the same class or at a particular stage of development but rather that they all use 'popular democratic interpellations'.[21] 'Populisms' therefore differ radically from one another, however, they are all related to one another given that they are all dependent on socio-economic conditions. Populisms emerge as a result of a 'crisis of the dominant ideological discourse, which is in turn part of a more general social crisis'.[22] Secondly, the specific form that populism takes is dependent on the class through which 'popular democratic interpellations are adopted'.[23] Laclau's main appeal is that while he is willing to recognise the many strands of populism he is nevertheless not put off by this diversity and soldiers on trying to define its main components. This Marxist theory of populism is useful insofar as he isolates a crucial aspect of populism and that is its anti-elitist stance and mode of discourse. The stress placed upon the anti-elitist rhetoric allows Laclau to pinpoint one of populism's most powerful springs: its capacity to create a gap (rhetorical or otherwise) between the people and a dominant power bloc. 'Populism', writes Laclau, 'starts at the point where popular-democratic elements are presented as an antagonistic option against the ideology of the dominant bloc.'[24]

As shall be demonstrated in the next few pages, Laclau identified the key aspect of populism. Whether the gap he identifies is dependent on objective contradictions or class contradictions, as he argues, is largely irrelevant – at least for the purposes of understanding populism; what matters is the identification of the rhetorical power and political appeal of the gap between elite and people identified and exploited by populist politics.

Margaret Canovan's understanding of populism – an understanding not dependent upon a Marxist teleology – moves populism away from class structures, and stresses that, according to her, making populism independent from Marxist class distinctions reveals its true complexity and its perennial power. In her work Canovan divides populism into two families: agrarian populism which she defines as a kind of rural syndicalism, and political populism.

The latter's emphasis, she writes, 'is much less upon any particular socio-economic base or setting, and much more upon political characteristics'.[25] Within the second category we find the following, further differentiation:

- populist dictatorships (e.g. Peròn)
- populist democracy (e.g. calls for referendums and 'participation')
- reactionary populism (e.g. George Wallace and his followers)
- Politicians' populism (a broad, non-ideological coalition building that draws on the unificatory appeal of the people)

Canovan draws the following conclusions from her survey of populist phenomena: first and foremost it would appear that most populisms share characteristics across categories; on the other hand the author also notes that the overlapping does have its limits: 'No movement has ever been populist in all the senses identified, and ... indeed none could ever satisfy all the conditions at once.'[26]

Canovan's conclusion is that at its heart, aside from there being an assumption that sovereignty lies with the people, populism relies on the capacity to draw a line between people and elite, a line which is not dependent on class but, perhaps more perversely, is drawn between the people and those who claim to, or are supposed to represent these very same people. This is where the power of populism lies: in its ability to create conflict, or at the very least create the perception of distance between the people and those whose role should normally be to work for the people. Populism assumes that 'the ordinary voter is more trustworthy than the average politician'.[27]

Reactionary populism provides us with a political paradox which sheds much light on the nature of fascism as hinging on a variety of ultra-nationalism, and as dependent on syncretising capacities while remaining rhetorically and ideologically dependent on the twin myths of decadence and rebirth. Populism adds to this the necessary, paradoxical reactionary tendencies of those little people who feel betrayed by that elite which is seen as having usurped the right to govern the great body of the nation, their great body.

The reactionary populism identified by Canovan

> is an appeal to the people which deliberately opens up the embarrassing gap between 'the people' and their supposedly democratic and representative elite by stressing popular values that conflict with those of the elite: typically it involves a clash between reactionary, authoritarian, racist or chauvinist views at the grass roots and the progressive, liberal, tolerant

cosmopolitanism characteristic of the elite ... The strength of reactionary populism and the reason it creates so much heartburning among its analysts, is that the problem to which it gives rise in a democracy are not just practical ones of managing political dissent, but problems of legitimacy.[28]

In her more recent work, Canovan underscores an aspect of populism which complements Graham's argument about party drives and rally drives very well. In an article published in 1999, Canovan suggests that there might be a more effective way of looking at populist politics in order to understand its occurrence in established democracies. Her suggestion is that the reasons for these occurrences lie not only in the context in which populist grievances emerge, but are to be understood as tensions inherent to democracy itself – as she puts it 'populism is a shadow cast by democracy itself'.[29] Drawing on the work of Oakeshott, Canovan argues that we should understand democracy as the 'meeting point for two contrasting styles of politics'[30] namely 'redemptive' politics and 'pragmatic' politics. Her argument is that the pragmatic face of democracy is essentially a series of coping mechanisms designed to endure stability and ensuring the peaceful resolution of conflicts. The redemptive face of democracy, is more entwined with notions of salvation, democracy's appeal to the ideal of the people and a set of other ideas designed to, as she writes 'lubricate the machinery of pragmatic politics'.[31] Where Graham argues that the two drives are to be found as co-existing in parties and all democratic organisations so too does Canovan argue that these two facets of democracy are inseparable from one another and from democratic politics. In both cases the forces are seen to be in tension, yet in both cases we also find an argument that highlights the ambiguity of democracy, and thus a sense in which populism is not inherently undemocratic, but rather that it is a necessary part of those contexts which we perceive as vulnerable to it.

The crucial point for us is that populism, this sort of populism, is the democratic paradox which lies at the heart of fascism: populism is that core element of fascism which reconciles fascism's elitist outlook on the one hand with its collectivist needs and its emergence within the political space opened up by mass politics on the other. Populism is the manner in which the elitism often apparent in fascist thought and practice and the authoritarianism of the practice become reconciled with – and dependent upon – mass political participation. This is particularly relevant in the case of France, given the country's advanced form of liberal democratic politics at the turn of the nineteenth and twentieth centuries. Populism also reconciles fascism's progressive radical character embedded in palyngenesis with the reactionary impetus from which it draws its perception of decadence.

Canovan's analysis of the tactical use of populism as a political style (politicians' populism) which draws on the hazy but rhetorically appealing concept of 'the people' is also extremely important for the purposes at hand. Referring to this category of populism as a style of politics does not seem to do it justice, as the notion of style implies something frivolous or at the very least inessential or superficial. Nothing could be further from the truth as the power of the appeal to the people – however ambiguous – should never be under-estimated. This sort of populism posits a party that will act in accordance to principles higher than those of ordinary politicians, a party which shall not succumb to ordinary, political selfishness and put the people first. Aside from the exaltation of a community's entitlement to representation much of the power of this sort of appeal lies in its ability to create an entity called the people and more importantly in the capacity to claim that the divisions within this people are unreal and artificially created by the selfish interests and mismanagement of the elite currently in power.

The solution is put to the people: let one party and one leader stamp out these artificial divisions, unite the people and represent them all. Where populism reconciled the tensions between palyngenesis and reaction, elitism and community; so the concept of leadership provides the ultimate element into which the constituent core concepts of fascism can be synthesised. The embodiment – in one man – of salvation and rebirth, of community and individualism and of decisive action in the face of corruption and decadence becomes a logical, emotional and ideological imperative.

Leadership and führerprinzip

No matter which political tradition one chooses to focus on, the concept of leadership is a murky one. By declaring that man was a political animal, Aristotle in effect put man at the heart of the practice of politics granting some individuals a capacity to lead others by virtue of an added quality 'phronesis' (prudence or practical wisdom). The western tradition of politics is thus bound up with the story of exemplary leaders seen as possessing a capacity not available to all mortals.[32]

The notion of a charismatic leader is particularly difficult to evaluate with respect to fascism. Although an even cursory knowledge of the phenomenon would lead an observer to believe that strong leaders play a crucial role in the fascist morphology, the acknowledgement by fascist authors and thinkers of the role of the leader is far more ambiguous. The centrality of the role of the leader, although visible to the naked eye, cannot for a number of reasons be straightforwardly incorporated into the fascist doctrine.

The first reason is to do with modern conceptions of democratic politics which, while placing the people rather than an elite or a particular person at the heart of politics, simultaneously underscore the accentuated need for leadership given the numbers involved. As such it might even be fair to argue that revolutionary mass politics are therefore necessarily prone to leadership cults. In other words the democratisation of politics creates a pressure to evacuate the notion of the charismatic and sole leader from the theory of politics while at the same time creating an even more pressing practical need for the selection or emergence of that leader. Fascism, by relying on mass politics and mass support, cannot therefore internally promote the 'selection' of a great leader, the emergence of a leader has to be perceived as just that: an emergence which is seen as disconnected from the ideology of fascism. The leader emerges because the people have discerned in him special qualities that are themselves 'super-human' and yet at the same time essentially human (i.e. which are an essence of admirable humanity) by virtue of their being 'of' the people not of a doctrine. The emergence of the one who leads is thus to be seen as necessary but accidental.

Fascism fetishises the necessity (yet accidental nature) of the emergence of the leader. In other words, it mythologises the inevitability of the emergence of a leader amongst the ranks of ordinary people. Because of the tension between elitism and collectivism present at the heart of fascism and given the role of populism in reconciling this tension, the role of the leader is refracted and expressed through the core concept of populism. This is not to suggest that the concept of leadership is subsumed within that of populism, but rather that the articulation of the role of the leader is rhetorically dependent on the populist aspects of fascism.

It is quite striking for example that while as Wolfgang Sauer writes[33] 'Fascist regimes are almost identical with their leaders; no fascist regime has so far survived its leader' the direct references to the role of the leader in fascism are few and far between. The role and emergence of the leader are largely under-theorised by fascists while at the same time perceived as mythological inevitabilities. It is as though the nationalism inherent to fascism would preclude the further theorisation of the emergence of the leader since the superiority of the national community is both dependent on, and the result of, its capacity to sire individuals with extraordinary qualities destined to redeem the decadent nation.

Fascism's cyclical conception of time also partly explains the simultaneous under-theorisation (or rhetorical under-evaluation) of leadership with its concomitant inevitability and necessity by tying this conception of leadership the cycle of decadence and rebirth: the rebirth is tacitly linked to the emergence of the leader and the new man. The new man, while he is in the future, is also incarnate in the presence (and present) of a living man who will be able to break the hold of decadence, regenerate time and create the utopias. The fascist conception of time, by fusing present and future – as most utopias – is therefore crucial in explaining the under-specification of the role of the living, political leader while at the same glorifying the new man, the embodiment of regenerated time and reborn community.

Marinetti's text on physiological patriotism illustrates the game of substitution played by fascist ideologues and prefigures the cult of the *Duce*. It glorifies Mussolini yet stresses the essentially futuristic aspects of fascism:

> Prophets and harbingers of the great Italy of today, we Futurists are delighted to salute in the Prime Minister, not yet 40, a marvelous Futurist temperament ... Mussolini has a formidable Futurist temperament, but is not an ideologue. If he was an ideologue he would be a prisoner of ideas. Instead he is free, untrammelled ... he had to end up obeying his special brand of patriotism, which I call physiological. Physiological patriotism, because it is physically constructed in the best Italian tradition, fashioned out of the craggy rocks of our peninsula into dressed blocks of stone. Lips made prominent, contemptuous by an audacity, a pugnFaciousness, which spits on everything which is vain, slow, cumbersome, useless. Massive head but ultra-dynamic eyes which vie with the speed of the cars racing across the plains of Lombardy ... A baton in his pocket like an ever-ready sword. Bent over his writing desk with elbows wide, his arms poised like levers to strike out at someone who is bothering him – or his enemy ... A Futurist orator, who prunes, cuts down, drills through, ties back the opposition's argument, methodically shearing away all the tangled weeds of objections, cutting through the crowd like a torpedo-boat, like a torpedo.[34]

This fusion of present and future highlights another manner in which leadership and time are inextricably intertwined in fascist thought. The centrality of the notion of leadership is quite understandable in cultures imbued with Christian notions of, on the one hand, redemption through physical death and spiritual resurrection, and on the other, salvation of the happy few against a backdrop of apocalypse. But fascism presents the particularity of fusing these Christian myths with more pagan versions of utopia, utopias which are not necessarily dependent on the bodily sacrifice and then resurrection of a chosen one. Without going into detail, fascism can be also seen as an ideology which superimposes, upon Christian myths, more pagan versions of community, often reminiscent of a sort of perverted Rousseauan State of nature. In many ways the fusion of these utopias, Christian and pagan, explains in some measure the theoretical ambiguity and under-theorisation of the concept of leadership coupled with its practical, lived inevitability and glorification.

Ambiguities of the fascist doctrinaires aside, the role of leadership in fascist thought is striking. As mentioned earlier on the chapter, given the types of tensions inherent in fascist ideology the translation of these tensions to the level of an individual who will both bear them and reconcile them is essential. More particular to fascist thought, the centrality of the figure of the 'new man' gives sheer physicality a place in fascist thought which it cannot claim in other secular systems of thought. Finally, the glorification of action over thought means that leadership, the ability to make decisions and the capacity to act on them, is a defining aspect of fascism.

Synthesis

Fascism's syncretic capacity also seems relevant to its adequate defini-tion. Some of what is evoked by the idea of synthesis is, in part, covered by the concept of palyngenesis which points to a new path – a radically different one from the ashes of the old order – but it is important to specify what this particular aspect of fascism covers. Synthesis appears last in this list. The reason is that it is not a concept constitutive of fascism along the same lines as the other ones included here. However, it is nevertheless an essential element of fascism as an ideology since it can be understood as what grants fascism its capacity to exist as an ideology in practice. To be clearer: one of the reasons for which fascism has often been denied the status of an ideology is that it does not seem to present a coherent body of doctrine, a set of texts or references. It was thus argued that there was no ideological corpus coherent enough to serve as the basis of an ideology. The argument here is that this 'eclecticism' and apparent incoherence and the overcoming of these is one of the defining features of fascism.

The incoherences are reconciled through fascism's syncretic capacity. Further, and related to the first objection, fascism has been seen as promoting action over thought, deeds over theories: But action, in the fascist mode, should be seen as mythical, endowed with the capacity of bringing everything together through a physicality which escapes theorising and, thus, the possibility of incoherence. As such the element of synthesis should be included and discussed here as essential to fascism.

For Eatwell fascism is fundamentally anti-conservative (hence the insistence placed in fascist thought on rebirth). The synthesising of policies, ideas, critiques and so on is crucial to achieving a fascist doctrine whose elements are taken from very diverse and often contradictory bodies of pre-fascist thought. This process, which Eatwell calls 'syncretism',[35] explains how fascism is able to draw on varied support. Eatwell therefore dismisses on the one hand Soucy's argument that fascism was a 'new variety of authoritarian conservatism and Right wing nationalism which sought to defeat Marxist thought'.[36] This view according to Eatwell simply fails to take into account fascism's obvious radical outlook. On the other hand, Eatwell also dismisses Sternhell's view that fascism was neither Left nor Right on the grounds that this fails to take into account fascism's distinctly Right-wing credentials. It is useful here to add a point to this: this project does indeed draw on the notion that fascism was able to draw from Left and Right, however this bicephalous tendency is reflected essentially in the sections of the population from which fascism draws its support and on the synthesis which fascist leaders are forced to effect in order to appeal to that support. The ideology of fascism, on the other hand, should not be seen as 'hesitating' between the Left and the Right.[37] Further, and as stressed by Eatwell, the Left/Right synthesis is only one of the many syntheses which fascism seeks to operate.

Despite the fact that Robert Paxton would certainly disagree with a concept of generic fascism defined first and foremost by its ideas, it is necessary to refer to him here in this context of a discussion of synthesis. To Paxton, fascism can be judged, analysed and understood only through its actions. Its contradictions are resolved only in action.[38] That may be true, but, first, a movement's action should be interpreted in the context of its expounded and adopted doctrine and, second, action is seldom, if ever, divorced from discourse – the two make up political practice – and a particular discourse can be juxtaposed with a particular action to make for ambiguous political practice. This is nowhere more true than in the case of fascism where the contradictions are a profoundly defining feature of an ideology that seeks to appease sections of society all the while inflaming others. The differences in the actions of small syndicalist groups such as those studied by Sternhell and the mass party of 1920s Italy are not so much accidents, neither are they the result of a action/thought dichotomy but, rather, the manifest expression of a synthesising, adaptative capacity proper to fascism.

Eatwell's arguments on the matter of synthesis are convincing: drawing on the idea of a crisis of civilisation – masterfully expounded in the writings of Sternhell – it follows that fascism as an ideology would try to reconcile and synthesise elements from existing if decaying bodies of doctrine before being allowed to make *tabula rasa*. In other words, fascism's syncretism is underscored by its aim which is to regenerate the political world by regenerating humankind. Such aims do much to validate an intrinsic syncretism. Further, the concept of synthesis or fascism's 'syncretic capacity' complements Freeden's notion of ideological morphology well.

In conclusion, one could argue that 'syncretism' is a cognitive strategy by which intellectuals fashion fascism, but a strategy without which fascism would not be able to mobilise and as such would no longer qualify as an ideology. Ideologies' essential mobilisational role thus indicates that all ideologies must exhibit a version of this cognitive strategy. To some extent, the importance of syncretism to fascism is arguably a demonstration of a weakness in Freeden's work: ideologies are also more than clusters of concepts, however malleable, they are also constructed.

The next section demonstrates why this matrix of fascism must be put in historical context. Fascism as an ideology can be seen as having been dependent both in meaning and in practice on the institutions of liberal democracy. These institutions give rise to practices which allow for the development of fascism, they open up a political space within which fascism can flourish while at the same time providing a newly enfranchised electorate with the instruments for the political expression of a discontent born of the ideals of liberal parliamentary democracy. Secondly, and more immediately for the purposes of this chapter, the concepts which make up the core of fascism, because they are linguistic and political conventions, evolve, unravel and sometimes, disappear as a result of institutional change.

French fascism?

There are several reasons why the scholarship on the far Right in France takes fascism as a point of departure or, at the very least, as an important point of reference. The first of these reasons is that – somewhat logically – movements and parties taken to be situated on the extremes of the Right of the political spectrum are compared, contrasted and evaluated against past manifestations of far-Right activism most of which in the modern period are instances of – or related to – fascism (either as a regime form or as an ideology).

Secondly, French scholarship expends much energy attempting to refute the importance of fascism in France in the face of more sceptical – often foreign – scholars. Hence, much of French scholarship on the far Right exhibits a concern for fascism as a result of its drive to refutation.

With respect to the purposes of this book, taking fascism as a point of departure for the analysis of a far-Right party is congruent with the adoption of a historical institutionalist approach committed to illustrating the ideological nature of the mediated relationship between individuals and institutions.

Examining the scholarship on fascism as it relates to various episodes in French history or to the writings of certain French authors is a major undertaking as historiography on the matter continues to be inherently divided. For the purposes of this chapter the major historiographical strands of this debate shall be delineated and the discussion will end with a focus on Sternhell's understanding of the phenomenon of fascist thought and fascist movements in France. The next chapter will examine the components of fascism which are still present in the FN in order to examine the impact of Fifth Republican institutions on far-Right doctrines and the FN in particular.

Fascism in France: the elusive ideology

One of the main strands of Right-wing historiography is represented by the writings of René Rémond and in particular his exhaustive albeit contested *Les droites en France*.[39] Rémond's main task in his book is to divide the French Right into three main traditions: first, a reactionary and traditionalist strand descended from ultra-royalism; second, a liberal conservative tradition originating in the July Monarchy and, third, Bonapartism which Rémond sees as having achieved a synthesis, proper to France, between democracy and authority.[40] According to the author, one of the main achievements of this Bonapartist Right is to have neutralised or diffused movements and parties of the far Right. This, for Rémond, explains why France has always been hostile to fascism and accounts for the absence of a truly fascist episode in France.

The Bonapartist Right, again given Rémond's argument, inoculated France against movements and parties of the far Right. Rémond explains the 'failure' of fascism in France first of all through an examination of various factors such as France's international situation (a victorious and pacifist nation), France's relative stability after the First World War and during the Great Depression, and finally the country's demographic structure (an elderly population perhaps less prone to embarking on passionate political adventures). The mainstay of Rémond's argument however lies elsewhere. The factors which provide the bulwark for his argument are more strictly political ones involving the deeply rooted nature of French democracy, the Left's anti-fascist mobilisation and, perhaps most importantly for Rémond, the occupation of the Right of the political spectrum by strong, viable, mature political forces.[41]

Rémond's work presents a number of positive aspects which need to be underscored at this stage. His analysis spans such a significant amount of time that it yields a still unsurpassed understanding of the evolution of the French Right – in general – as a phenomenon spanning generations, regimes and revolutions. Rémond's approach also has other advantages. It is an approach which is both historically and culturally rich; but most importantly it points to the impossibility – or at least the difficulty – to reduce the far Right to a single characteristic or trait in any period.

As for the objections to Rémond's argument, they are plentiful and well known and they stem in part from the advantages which we have just highlighted. The most straightforward are, for example, that the boundaries between his three strands of the French Right are far more permeable than Rémond argues. As Passmore writes,

> the problem lies rather in the assumption that the traditions exist in the real world in a pure form and that they are internally coherent. It is more appropriate to regard them as useful abstractions; ideal types which serve as a means of illuminating the nature of movements which in practice constructed their identities from a great variety of material – not always French in origin.[42]

Secondly, it is problematic – from a methodological as well as from a logical point of view – to hive off fascism from the three 'indigenous' rights, particularly as this is achieved by eradicating fascism's links with the 'ultra-Right' and downplaying the similarities between fascism and Bonapartism.[43] Another interesting argument made by Passmore against Rémond is that,

> as chronological distance from the founding years increases, it becomes ever more difficult to fit individual movements into any of the three categories. In consequence Rémond's method becomes increasingly anti-contextual. The essential components of each tradition are regarded as constant in all periods, while other features of particular movements are dismissed as a product of historical contingency.[44]

Finally, Rémond's approach offers only a cursory examination of Vichy, an episode which might justly cause one to think that the mainstream Right did not occupy the ideological ground quite as solidly as Rémond argues. It does seem rather difficult to reduce the whole collaborationist episode to what Rémond refers to as '*un phénomène d'importation*'.[45] While Rémond clearly does not endow fascism with much historical importance in France, others have on the other hand, drawn very different conclusions.

France as the cradle of fascism

Rémond's analysis of the French Right has been attacked by many scholars who have drawn radically different conclusions regarding the nature of fascism in France and the importance of the fascist phenomenon in French history and society. Of those who disagree with Rémond the German historian Ernst Nolte was one of the most vocal. In a brilliant but highly controversial study, Nolte brought together Italian Fascism, national socialism and the *Action française*.[46] While Nolte made abundantly clear that he did not assimilate the *Action française* to fascism, he nevertheless insisted on seeing in *Action française* a precocious form of fascism.[47]

Robert Soucy, Zeev Sternhell, William Irvine and Kevin Passmore are other key figures whose studies have challenged Rémond's argument about the role of fascism and the nature of the far Right in France. Soucy's point is that Maurice Barrès can be read as proof of the existence of a fascist or rather proto-fascist stream in France.[48] The argument's merit lies in its delineating the difference between fascism and what the author refers to as the 'conservative Right'. By refusing the rigid distinctions set up by Rémond, Soucy insists on the permeability of the boundaries between the different sorts of Right and on the similarities of outlook often exhibited by groups which fall on either side of the boundaries. According to Soucy therefore, fascism and conservatism share a number of features and are more interconnected than often thought, particularly in the areas of social and economic reform where differences lie in the tactics advocated rather than the aims pursued.[49]

The study leads to an all encompassing conception of French fascism which incorporates a host of movements and leagues. Soucy underscores the similarities amongst them and points to the fact that they are all essentially anti-parliamentarian, anti-Semitic, anti-liberal, anti-Marxist, in league with the *petite bourgeoisie* against the working class, intensely nationalistic, staunch defenders of the army, imbued with military values and ready to resort to violence in order to attain their political objectives

For this author, the main defining feature of fascism is that it emerges as a movement in opposition to the Left and as such fascist movements can be interpreted as instances of a Right-wing backlash. This also means that the definitional net is cast very wide, as such the groups falling into it are plentiful and varied.

More recently, and building upon Soucy's work on the *Croix de Feu*, Kevin Passmore and William Irvine[50] have made worthwhile contributions to the debate by underscoring that French historians' dismissal of fascism as an important phenomenon in France rests on their successfully being able to argue that France's major far-Right movements of the 1930s (Colonel de la Rocque's *Croix de Feu* and its subsequent incarnation the *Parti social Français* (PSF)) were not fascist. If such movements can be excluded from a fascist typology – which is what most French historians labour to do[51] – then it can be claimed that fascism was indeed of little importance in France.

Irvine's article is therefore devoted to debunking the arguments regularly put forth by French historians. To counter this, Irvine puts forth a set of well-thought-out and convincing counter-arguments: La Rocque was not too bourgeois to be a fascist; the sociological composition of the movement – and then the party – was perfectly consistent with that of other fascist parties such as the Italian Fascists; the legalism and so called 'moderation' of the movement were also consistent with other versions of explicitly fascist movements (and were according to Irvine – in the case of the *Croix de Feu* and the PSF – more the result of the threat of dissolution rather than a programmatic stance). Finally, Irvine turns to the received view that the *Croix de Feu* and more particularly the PSF were simply Ceasarist-Bonapartist formations: for Irvine Bonapartism is to be taken as a code for 'conservative'. As such, the author proceeds to contrast the PSF with other conservative parties of the era in France. He concludes that they were dissimilar in every respect: in their concern for and scale of membership, in their rhetoric and symbolism, in their geographical implantation and, most strikingly, in their attitude to the Left (to which the PSF, unlike the conservative parties, was not hostile). The PSF according to Irvine looked nothing like a conservative party, rather in its 'neither Right nor Left' stance, it was more closely similar to Doriot's – explicitly fascist – PPF.

For Irvine then, this means that the definition of fascism adopted by French historians is one which either should include the *Croix de Feu* and the PSF or exclude the parties of Mussolini and Hitler. This thus leads to Irvine's statement that

> If the *Croix de Feu* can be shown to have been fascist ... It would no longer be possible to argue, in the tradition established by René Rémond forty years ago, that French fascism was the work of an isolated minority.[52]

Passmore's analysis of the *Croix de Feu* also concludes that it can be labelled fascist. He, however, bases his analysis on a definition of fascism as a sub-category of national populism which accounts for fascism's synthesis of radicalism and conservatism.[53] Passmore uses the remainder of his piece to illustrate the *Croix de Feu*'s blend of conservatism and reaction in order to argue that the movement, while arguably tailored to French conditions, was fascist. While neither Irvine nor Passmore fully endorse Sternhell's view that fascism was intrinsically French and that it was essentially the expression of a frustrated anti-Marxism, both of these authors' works should be read as the continuation of the debate surrounding the nature of French fascism sparked by Sternhell.

Zeev Sternhell's conclusions are in many respects quite similar to Soucy's, particularly with regard to the importance and the deep roots which both authors attribute to French fascism. Sternhell, however, arrives at his conclusions by means of a wide-ranging and highly original argument. One of the advantages of Sternhell's works, especially given our argument, is that it takes into account historical context as well as ideological production. Some of Sternhell's conclusions might be questionable, but his analysis is situated precisely at that confluence of historical circumstance and institutional development crucial to the study of political parties and mobilisation in general and to this project's general argument.

Briefly, Sternhell's position is that fascism is first and foremost a European response to what he sees as a crisis in civilisation:[54]

> At the end of the XIXth century, the intellectual climate in Europe under-goes a marked change which contributes to the creation of a new political option/orientation. France, Germany, Russia, Austro-Hungary, Italy witness the emergence of phenomena – which aside from their specific characteristics linked to local conditions – bear a great resemblance to one another. These countries seem to suffer from the same malaise. And despite the numerous forms it might have taken, its expression makes it easily recognisable: a questioning of the main ideas and institutions asso-ciated with industrial civilisation and a systematic negation of the values inherited from the XVIIIth century and the French Revolution.[55]

Sternhell sees the writings of Le Bon, Tarde, Freud and Jung, and the music of Wagner as evidence of a backlash against positivism which favours the emergence of anti-rationalist, anti-intellectualist and deter-ministic thought. The writings of Barrès are therefore interpreted not so much as a reaction to the French defeat of 1870 (which is never-theless seen as a very important contributing contextual factor)[56] but, rather, as the result of a revolt against the spirit of the Enlightenment, liberal-democratic values and the excesses of capitalism.[57]

Drawing on his assessment of France's liberal democratic creden-tials Sternhell arrives at conclusions which, while rooted in the same observations, are diametrically opposed to Rémond's: since France was the most advanced liberal-democratic regime in Europe at the time, any ideological and political doctrine fuelled by a resentment against liberal democratic values and aimed at destabilising the liberal demo-cratic order would be more likely to emerge there rather than in a place where the liberal democratic order was less developed or less well entrenched and where, therefore, it might have had less scope for soci-etal impact. This reasoning is what leads Sternhell to conclude that France was the laboratory of fascism: France was furthest down the road of liberal parliamentarianism and, therefore, the place where – on the one hand – the crisis of the liberal order would be most pronounced, and – on the other hand – where the necessary space for contestation would be available.[58]

> This is why French fascism, despite its political weakness, is the closest to an ideal-type fascism in the Weberian sense of the word. But it is also the

country in which the fascist ideology – in its essential aspects – emerges a
good twenty years before similar phenomena in the rest Europe, including in Italy.[59]

In his book *Ni droite, ni gauche* Sternhell pays great attention to the
institutional and, more precisely, to electoral assaults on liberal politics.
Anti-liberals could use liberal institutions to undermine liberalism.[60]

Further, Sternhell emphasises the fact that the doctrine which
emerges from this context is novel – a revolutionary Right, itself inseparable (both in terms of claims and tactics) from the liberal order it
wants to topple. For Sternhell the emergence of this new, revolutionary Right is of paramount importance, given its effects on the Left,
whose response to the new force is to become more and more integrated into the liberal order. This in turn has two major consequences:
on the one hand it turns the revolutionary Right into the only alternative to the system, on the other hand, and no less importantly, it radi-
calises the fringes of the Left – those who remain fundamentally hostile
to the liberal, democratic, parliamentary order – and pushes them into
the arms of the revolutionary Right. For Sternhell then, fascism is born
of the encounter, at regular intervals, between the opponents of the
liberal democratic order situated both on the Left and on the Right of
the political spectrum.[61]

The fascist ideology about which Sternhell writes is thus conceived
of as the synthesis of ideas coming from opposite horizons. It fuses
the political values of the Right with the social values of the Left,
Barrès' organic nationalism (culturally rooted in pessimism and anti-
Semitism) with a frustrated socialism.[62] Sternhell's work has been
highly polemical and many of his writings have sparked major political
and historical controversy (particularly *Ni droite, ni gauche*)[63] some
which has obscured the nature of both some well-founded criticisms as
well as the value and originality of his work despite some obvious flaws.
Sternhell's analysis has the great merit of offering not only an alternative to Rémond's interpretation but, in fact, a radically opposed view:
where Rémond sees fascism as a marginal (and imported) phenomenon
in France, Sternhell depicts it as a French invention, coming from the
Left and playing an essential role in French history and politics.

The main criticism one can level at Sternhell is that his analysis is,
in many respects, teleological. Fascism is posited as the necessary and
almost pre-determined outcome of the turn of the century's intellectual and cultural crisis. Along the same lines, Sternhell can also be
accused of turning anything slightly related to fascism within that
particular period of time and cultural epoch into an instance of fascism,

not taking into account the fact that fascism was itself borrowing from the era's cultural milieu. This leads Sternhell to turn partial affinities, selective borrowings, fractional and sometimes fortuitous agreements into instances of a latent fascism or embryonic fascistic thought. The more selective work of Irvine and Passmore is of greater use in this respect.

The main problem with Sternhell's work is that his interpretation of fascism in France or French fascism rests on a definition of fascism which is both too broad as well as too thin. By not actually setting a 'fascist minimum', Sternhell allows for an all-inclusive notion such that a minuscule populist gathering of obscure young writers often seems enough to be allowed into the not-so-exclusive club of fascist groups or movements.

But for the purposes of this research, Sternhell's approach is extremely useful in other ways. His work has been without a doubt a most useful catalyst in fascist studies that has led to the re-examination of the role of fascism in France and has served, as illustrated here, as a useful antidote to Rémond's complacent approach. By doing this, Sternhell has allowed for the emergence of a scholarship that takes fascism in France as a point of departure for the understanding of any movement right of the centre-Right such as the FN. It has also pointed to the fact that fascism must be understood as the result of institutional and cultural pressures and as the heir to an era of mass politics ushered in by liberalism and the practice of liberal democracy. Fascism is dependent on, and the result of, the political space created by liberalism and the politics of parliamentary democracy.

Thus, for the purposes of this book two main conclusions emerge regarding Sternhell. The first is the importance of a systematic approach to the ideological content of fascism, an approach such as the one presented earlier which distinguishes between core, peripheral and adjacent concepts. Secondly, Sternhell's main theoretical contribution is the attention paid to the momentum granted to fascism by political institutions.

Preliminary conclusions on fascism in France

The aim of this last section was to illustrate the complexity of the debate surrounding fascism in France or the incarnation of fascism in France. Given the scope of this debate – both within France and outside it – it is impossible to evaluate the FN ideologically or politically without reference to the long tradition of extreme right-wing thought in France, a part of which is distinctly fascist or proto-fascist. This is also important given the claim that the FN is an heir to fascist thought in France The FN began its life as many of the earlier movements with a distinctly fascist core, but gradually adapted to the exigencies of the new Fifth Republican regime and the political opportunities created by it. More specifically, the (fascist) concept of populism and its associated political practices have become the defining element of FN ideology. The FN also abandoned the notion of the revolutionary upheaval contained within the concept of rebirth.

By recalling the core concepts outlined earlier, one can argue that most of the movements evoked by the authors discussed above exhibited most of the core concepts: all of them were nationalist, some of them included a violent philosophy of rebirth, a few rallied around a leader whose qualities were perceived as intrinsic to their philosophy and many of them were populist in their outlook and their demands. Further, syncretism was a defining feature of most of these movements.

The role of fascist ideology stands, nevertheless, as a paradox in French political thought. While constituting the inescapable matrix from which one must begin when studying movements of the far Right in France, it is more difficult to pin-point fascist parties or fascist movements as such. Nevertheless, fascism constitutes a perennial intellectual option and it is this capacity that has had a profound impact not just on French political thought but also on French politics and French institutions. The impact of the fascist intellectual in structuring political options should not be under-estimated. And if, as was argued in Chapter 2, institutions are to be seen as instances of repeated political practice over time, the institutionalisation of the fascist intellectual and political option would keep France forever *en garde* but also forever enamoured – despite itself – with fascist thought. The reproduction, reconstitution and revival of many of the proto-fascist groups discussed earlier, and their capacity to mobilise a fringe of intellectuals across the past century does not amount to fascism in France but, rather, to a French fascism whose core concepts are those defined in the previous chapter.[64]

Finally, we will show in the next chapter that what shields France from experiencing the complete institutionalisation of fascism in the form of a fascist regime, is the relationship between populism and liberal democracy. Indeed while Sternhell may be right in identifying fascism's ties to a precocious liberal order; it is also the case that populism also has a strong connection with liberal politics and it is the strength of this connection – coupled with fascism's syncretic core – which eventually leads to the instability of the fascist option in French politics.

Fascism played, and continues to play, a more influential role in French politics and in French political thought than Rémond is ready to grant it.[65] It is important to retain from Sternhell's work the link between ideologies and institutions. For here one can turn to the fate of fascism when institutions undergo major transformations. Fascism can become the victim of its own syncretic capacities, as via the activities of its political leaders, it mutates into a presidentialised populism which is no longer fascist. Just as liberal democracy enabled the emergence of fascism, so the presidentialism of the Fifth Republic encouraged this mutation.

Notes

1   The notion of ideology has been understood in a variety of manners. From the initial use of the word by Antoine Destutt de Tracy when he used the term to capture the activity encompassed by the scientific study of ideas to the association of the term with Marxist thought, to the Parsonian, functionalist perception of the term and through to the current re-evaluation of the entire area of the study of ideology, no one has achieved a coherent, non-controversial view of what an ideology is. Most understandings of the concept are, now, however, able to integrate elements from previously separate schools of thought. It is often admitted for example that, as argued by many functionalist American political scientists, ideologies do perform integrative functions and that they do act as devices for mobilising mass political activity: but to these functions is added the recognition that ideologies have a dominating, or as Althusser argued, a 'dissimulative' role. This domination is no longer to be seen as the exclusive domain of the capitalist over the working class but that in fact it is a phenomenon produced by all classes. Whether the domination or dissimulation are conscious or unconscious is still very much a matter of debate. One thing is for sure, the concept has evolved and shed much of the negative connotations which the Marxist understanding had attached to it. The notion that an ideology is a 'trick' played on the mind, an illusion or as Marx argued an 'inversion of a distortion' has been counterbalanced by the quest for a theory of ideology which would enable scholars to separate ideas from say, the style of a regime; if only momentarily, if only in order to better integrate the two down the line. On the evolution of the term 'ideology' see in no particular order: T. Eagleton, *Ideology* (London: Verso, 1991); D. E. Apter, ed., *Ideology and Discontent* (New York, NY: Collier Macmillan, 1964); G. Sartori, 'Politics, ideology, and belief systems', *American Political Science Review*, 63 (1969), 398–411; P. Ricoeur, *Hermeneutics and the Human Sciences* (Cambridge:

Cambridge University Press, 1981), especially Part 1, Ch. 2; M.B. Hamilton, 'The elements of the concept of ideology', *Political Studies*, 35 (1987), 18–38.

2 The use of the word 'matrix' is particularly important as it seeks to under-score the distinction between our argument regarding fascism and notions of Weberian ideal-types. The Weberian ideal-type presents static charac-teristics from which we would like to distance this project. As Weber notes about his ideal-type, 'In its conceptual purity this mental construct cannot be found empirically anywhere in reality', Max Weber, *The Methodology of the Social Sciences*, p. 22, cited in A. Giddens, *Capitalism and Modern Social Theory: An Analysis of the Writings of Marx, Durkheim and Max Weber* (Cambridge: Cambridge University Press, 1971), p. 142. Echoing Weber and re-enforcing this point Giddens writes the following in his 1971 comparative analysis of Marx, Durkheim and Weber: 'An ideal type is constructed by the abstraction and combination of an indefinite number of elements which, although found in reality, are rarely or never discov-ered in specific form … An ideal type is a pure type in a logical and not exemplary sense.' (Giddens, *Capitalism*, p. 141). These ideal-types there-fore, are not in any manner dependent on context, nor are they meant to evolve since they are not meant to 'exist' in the real world. Indeed their static quality is part of what makes them useful. The notion of matrix on the other hand, implies possible evolution. A matrix is a mould or an object from which (or place in which) something develops. Geologically a matrix refers to a mass of rock within which gems are to be found. The matrix therefore encompasses the 'crucial' or most important elements as well as those objects which are less significant but nevertheless constitu-tive (such as context for example). While both words evoke a will to examine and specify constitutive elements, the main difference between them is that the ideal-type is a set, immobile and essentially reductive tool, whereas the matrix allows for an understanding of a particular object based on context and potential.

3 Proponents of this school of research on fascism include: R. Griffin, *The Nature of Fascism* (London: Routledge, 1993); J. Gregor, *Interpretations of Fascism* (Morristown, NJ: General Learning Press, 1974); R. de Felice, *Interpretations of Fascism* (Cambridge, MS: Harvard University Press, 1977); R. Eatwell, 'Toward a new model of generic fascism', *Journal of Theoretical Politics*, 4: 2 (1992), 174–85; G. Mosse, *International Fascism: New Thoughts and Approaches* (London: Sage, 1979); S. Payne, *A History of Fascism, 1914–1945* (Madison, WI: University of Wisconsin Press, 1995).

4 G. Gentile, *Che cosa è il fascismo* (Florence: Valecchi, 1925), p. 28.

5 J. Streel, *La révolution du vingtième siècle* (Brussels: Nouvelle société d'édition, 1942), p. 72.

6 Z. Sternhell, *Maurice Barrès et le nationalisme français* (Paris: Editions Complexes, 1985), pp. 290–305.

7 Ch. Maurras, *Oeuvres capitales* (Paris: Flammarion, 1954 [writings from 1897–1925]), p. 269.

8 Maurras, *Oeuvres*, p. 264.

9 This facet of the nationalism of Charles Maurras gives us an interesting clue as to the nature of time in far-Right thought. Here we have a conception of time which is anchored in the non-human, a form of divine time which escapes human consciousness and human measurement.

10 It is clear that fascism, as all ideologies, draws its strength in part from its reliance on metaphorical depictions of political and social reality, thus providing even more 'connections' (metaphorical ones) between the constitutive concepts. The use of a meta-language creates the opportunity for a second-level morphology which enables the relationship between concepts to be seen as double: logical and historical on the one hand and linguistic and metaphorical on the other.

11 For an excellent discussion of the nature of palyngenetic myths and their particular use in fascist ideology see R. Griffin, ed., *Fascism* (Oxford: Oxford University Press, 1995) , pp. 32–6.

12 K. Theweleit, *Male Fantasies, 2* (Cambridge: Polity Press, 1989), pp. 360–1 cited in Griffin, *Fascism*, pp. 292–3.

13 R. Griffin, 1993, *The Nature of Fascism* (London: Routledge, 1993), p. 33.

14 Griffin, *The Nature*, pp. 36–7.

15 Griffin, *The Nature*, p. 38.

16 With respect to elitism and collectivism/holism several things need to be said: the first is that the extreme elitism should be understood as a project of fascism; the elitism is to be obtained once palyngenesis occurs. The holism or collective outlook on the other hand is an instrument to attain a model, post-palyngenetic society. To this effect the words of Roger Griffin shed some light: 'Extensive study of the primary sources of Fascism or other fascisms convinced me that the core of its mentality was the idée fixe of devoting, and, if necessary sacrificing, individual existence to the struggle against the forces of degeneration which had seemingly brought the nation low, and of helping relaunch it towards greatness and glory. The fascist felt he (and it was generally a 'he') had been fatefully born at a watershed between national decline and national regeneration … He knew himself to be one of the chosen of an otherwise lost generation. His task was to prepare the ground for a new breed of man the homo fascistus …'. (Griffin, *Fascism*, pp. 3–4). Viewed in this way, collectivism and elitism are not contradictory: the two concepts occupy separate moments in the fascist agenda and the fascist mythology. Secondly, one needs to keep in mind the chivalric mythology that underpins much of fascist thought and symbolism. This chivalric mythology means, in part, that collectivism and elitism can cohabit – conceptually – because they can be seen as complementary according to the rules of a chivalric society: While the band of knights can be a rather ramshackle bunch, brought together by events and circumstance, they are drawn from the people; they only become a brotherhood once they have been anointed by a leader that turns the band into his followers. Fascism, in many ways, envisages the role of the people similarly. Collectivism and elitism can be reconciled because some of the people will be turned into an elite by the leader, nevertheless their being 'of the people' is an essential factor in their being chosen.

17 It is easy to see how the concepts of decadence and degeneration play a role here: the greatness of the nation can be seen as already having fallen prey to the forces of decadence, a fact which only reinforces the notion that the nation must be reborn.

18 G. Giurati, 'I giovani e il partito,' *Gioventù Fascista*, 1: 6 (1931), 3.

19 C. Codreanu, 'The programme of the iron guard', in *Die eiserne Garde* (Berlin: Brunnen Verlag, 1940), pp. 396. Cited in Griffin, *Fascism*, pp. 221–2.

20 G. Ionescu and E. Gellner, eds, Populism: *Its Meanings and National Characteristics* (London: Weidenfeld and Nicholson, 1969); E. Laclau, *Politics and Ideology in Marxist Theory: Capitalism – Fascism – Populism* (London: NLB, 1977); M. Canovan, *Populism* (London: Junction Books, 1981).

21 Laclau, *Politics and Ideology*, p. 172.

22 Laclau, *Politics and Ideology*, p. 175.

23 Laclau, *Politics and Ideology*, pp. 175–96.

24 Laclau, *Politics and Ideology*, p. 173.

25 Canovan, *Populism*, p. 11.

26 Canovan, *Populism*, p. 289.

27 Canovan, *Populism*, p. 176.

28 Canovan, *Populism*, p. 229.

29 Canovan, 'Trust the people! Populism and the two faces of democracy', *Political Studies*, 47: 1 (March 1999), 2–16, 3.

30 Canovan, 'Trust the people', 9.

31 Canovan, 'Trust the people', 11.

32 On theories of leadership see the classics: Aristotle, *The Politics* (London: Penguin Classics, 1962); Marx's *The Eighteenth Brumaire of Napoleon Bonaparte*, in Robert C. Tucker, ed., *The Marx-Engels Reader* (New York, NY: Norton, 1972); Max Weber, *On Charisma and Institution Building: Selected Papers*, ed. and with an introduction by S. N. Eisentstadt (Chicago, IL: University of Chicago Press, 1968).

33 Wolfgang Sauer, 'National socialism: totalitarianism or fascism?', *American Historical Review*, 73: 2 (December 1967), 420.

34 F. Marinetti, 'Benito Mussolini,' appendix to Antonio Beltramelli, *L'Uomo Nuovo* (Milan: Mondadori, 1973, originally 1924), pp. iii–vi.

35 Eatwell incorporates the notion of synthesis in his own four-point definition by linking synthesis to a concept of 'Third Way'. The Third Way relates to the idea that fascism is hostile to capitalism and to socialism but draws on elements of both in order to exist (we shall discuss this aspect more fully when we turn to Sternhell's work). The Third Way is connected to notions of palyngenesis and rebirth although it does not encapsulate the cathartic element of rebirth and allows for a more dogmatic, less myth-dominated version of fascism to surface. Roger Eatwell, 'Toward a new model', pp. 174–85, reproduced in Griffin, *Fascism*, p. 201.

36 R. Soucy, *French Fascism, the First Wave, 1924–33* (New Haven, CT: Yale University Press, 1991), p. 163.

37 See R. Eatwell, 'On defining the fascist minimum: the centrality of ideology', *Journal of Political Ideologies*, 1: 3 (1996), 303–19; R. Eatwell, 'The

drive toward synthesis', in R. Griffin, ed., *International Fascism* (London: Arnold, 1998) pp. 189–204; Eugen Weber, 'Nationalism, socialism and national-socialism in France', *French Historical Studies*, 2: 3 (1962), 273–307; A. J. McGregor, *Young Mussolini and the Intellectual Origins of Italian Fascism* (Berkeley, CA: Berkeley University Press, 1979).

38 R. Paxton, 'Les fascismes: Essai d'histoire comparée,' *XXème siècle*, 45 (March 1995), 3–13.

39 R. Rémond, *Les droites en France* (Paris: Aubier, 1982).

40 More specifically Rémond defines Bonapartism as a part of the French Right which reconciles popular sovereignty with strong executive power. Rémond, *Les droites*, pp. 200–14.

41 '*Comme il n'y avait pas en France d'espace où puisse se déployer librement une authentique droite révolutionnaire: tôt ou tard , d'elles mêmes ou sous la contrainte externe, elles se rangent au nombre des forces organisées dans le cadre des institutions légales. Il n'y a possibilité de rassembler des masses nombreuses que sur un programme respectueux des intérêts et des règles.*' (France did not provide a space in which an authentically revolutionary right could emerge sooner or later, therefore, whether spontaneously or through external constraint, these rights became institutionalised. Mobilising the multitudinous massess could only be undertaken within a programme respectful of interests and rules.) Rémond, *Les droites*, p. 168.

42 K. Passmore, *From Liberalism to Fascism: The Right in a French Province, 1928–1939* (Cambridge: Cambridge University Press, 1997), p. 4.

43 Burrin also makes the point that Bonapartism remains a problematic category as it encompasses Boulangism and antisemitic movements, La Rocque and Doriot, Gaullism and Poujadism, Chiraquism and Lepenism. P. Burrin, 'Le fascisme', in J. F. Sirinelli, ed., *Histoire des droites en France, Vol. 1* (Paris: Gallimard, 1992), p. 607.

44 Passmore, *From Liberalism*, pp. 3–4

45 Burrin, 'Le fascisme', p. 607.

46 E. Nolte, *Le fascisme dans son époque, Vol. I, L'Action française* (Paris: Julliard, 1970).

47 Nolte, *Le fascisme*, p. 88.

48 Soucy, *Fascism in France. The Case of Maurice Barrès* (Berkeley, CA: University of California Press, 1972).

49 Soucy, *French Fascism*.

50 K. Passmore, 'The French Third Republic: Stalemate Society or Cradle of Fascism', *French History*, 7: 4 (1993), 417–49; K. Passmore, 'The Croix de Feu: Bonapartism, national populism or fascism?', *French History*, 9: 1 (1995), 67–92; W. Irvine, 'Fascism in France and the strange case of the Croix de Feu', *Journal of Modern History*, 63 (1991), 271–95.

51 See for example, P. Milza, *Fascisme français. Passé et présent* (Paris: Flammarion, 1987); P. Milza, 'L'ultra droite des années trente' in M. Winock, ed., *Histoire de l'extrême droite en France* (Paris: Seuil, 1992), pp. 165–71; P. Burrin, *La dérive fasciste, Doriot, Déat, Bergery, 1933–1945* (Paris: Seuil, 1986).

52 Irvine, 'Fascism in France', p. 194.

53 This project adopts a different view and sees populism as a component of

fascism. The conclusions, however, are strikingly similar in that in both cases populism is used to reconcile aspects of fascism.

54 On this see also A. Lyttelton, 'The crisis of bourgeois society and the origins of Fascism', in R. Bessel, ed., *Fascist Italy and Nazi Germany* (Cambridge: Cambridge University Press, 1996), pp. 12–22.

55 Z. Sternhell, *Maurice Barrès et le nationalisme français* (Paris: Editions Complexes, 1985), p. 7.

56 Sternhell, *Maurice Barrès*, pp. 15–24.

57 Sternhell, *Maurice Barrès*, Introduction.

58 On this see also Paxton, 'Le fascisme peut paraître partout où la démocratie est suffisamment enracinée pour avoir engendré des désillusions. Voilà donc les limites temporelles du phénomène: aucun fascisme avant l'émergence d'une société politique massivement mobilisée. Pour donner naissance à un fascisme une société doit avoir connu la liberté politique – pour le bien ou pour le mal.' (Fascism can emerge wherever democracy is sufficiently embedded to have generated disillusionment. These are the phenomenon's temporal limits: there can be no fascism prior to the emergence of a massively mobilised polity. In order to sire a fascsim a society must have had a taste of freedom. For better or for worse.) 'Les fascismes', p. 9.

59 Sternhell, *Maurice Barrès*, p. 156. It is important to note that there is much disagreement on this. Authors such as Walter Adamson and Emilio Gentile have shown that a proto-fascism was being developed in Italy before the First World War. See Walter Adamson, *Avant-garde Florence* (Cambridge, MA: Harvard University Press, 1993); see also Emilio Gentile, *Le origini dell' ideologìa Fascista* (Roma: Laterza, 1975).

60 Z. Sternhell, *Ni droite, ni gauche: l'idéologie fasciste en France* (Paris: Seuil, 1983), pp. 33–76.

61 On the cross-cutting cleavages (religious, political and social) which create the 'crisis of representation', responsible for the emergence of a fascist movement such as the *Croix de Feu* see Passmore, 'The French Third Republic'.

62 It is important to note that Sternhell privileges the import from the Left over that of the Right.

63 Sternhell, *Ni droite, ni gauche*.

65 Such an understanding is also consistent with fascism's pragmatic outlook, what Passmore refers to as the 'prioritisation of action over programme', Passmore, 'The Croix de Feu', p. 74.

66 Recent work particularly on the *Nouvelle Droite* shows that many *Nouvelle Droite* thinkers – in particular Alain de Benoist – consider themselves to be in something which is no more than an 'interregnum' which will somehow yield further political options.

Chapter 5

The *Front national*: from heir to fascism to presidential hybrid

The FN owes a historical and ideological debt to fascism, but it is now distinct from it: it can be seen as ideologically and pragmatically distinct from fascism and as a hybrid containing some elements present in fascism but with other main elements absent. Present in the FN's doctrine are a few elements which are distinctly reminiscent of the fascist morphology. They are often subsumed within broader currents of ideas such as revisionism or counter-revolutionary principles but can still be identified – nationalism, the use of syncretism and a pervasive populism. The FN's hostility toward the political class (which Le Pen often refers to as 'the establishment') and its claim to be exhibiting a social, popular identity going against both a levelling egalitarianism and an undeserving political oligarchy echo some of those characteristics of fascism which we delineated earlier on. Also present in the discourse are a voiced will to create – or rather reconstitute – an elite, a marked preference – in terms of social organisation – for a national, virtually 'depoliticised' trade unionism and finally the exaltation of a strong but streamlined state. To this, one could add the cult of the leader or *führerprinzip* which is directly encouraged and stimulated within the party. Conspicuously absent are the elements connected to palyngenesis: violence and a philosophy of rebirth.

This chapter will illustrate that the FN should be seen as having a bipolar structure: on the one hand an ideological reliance on the traditional, ultra-nationalist, counter-revolutionary Right and on the other hand the practice of a version of populist rally politics.[1] To these commonalities which the FN shares with French proto-fascism, one needs to consider some major differences with fascist organisations or parties, particularly in political practice.

The counter-revolutionary tradition

In order to grant the elements of the fascist matrix their proper relevance in the case of the FN, it is necessary to contextualise, historically, the major themes upon which the FN relies to elaborate its ideological doctrine.

The counter-revolutionary tradition provides some of the ideological springs for the movements of the far Right in France. The theme of the upsetting of the structure of the political order – a crucial theme for the counter-revolutionaries – is a recurring one within the French Right and is often drawn on by Le Pen. It originates in the discourse of Barruel,[2] but order and hierarchy were later placed in the pantheon of classical French Right-wing political discourse by Charles Maurras and Maurice Barrès. Initially, as is pointed out by Ariane Chebel d'Appolonia,[3] there were various currents of thought supporting widely differing conceptions of 'order': proponents of a 'natural order' – a reflection of a superior celestial order – were clearly pitted against those who subscribed to the idea of a 'constructed social order'. Finally, the proponents of a more 'organicist' vision of society (a model drawn from the biological sciences) clearly denounced the non-scientific character and thus the erroneousness of the two other positions. It is clear that Le Pen has conflated the three positions. Although one could interpret this as leaving the responsibility of unravelling the strands to the interlocutor, in fact, they have been conflated in order to maximise support across different audiences.[4]

Another counter-revolutionary theme which originates in the late eighteenth century is that of a reaction against human rights. The reaction can be attributed to the French Enlightenment, as well as some of its critics such as Rousseau. All of them, however, by asserting the primacy of certain basic human rights over order and hierarchy, are portrayed by the far Right as enemies of the French nation as a community, and of the established social order. The traditional French Right considers the *Declaration of the Rights of Man and the Citizen* to be the embodiment of the French Enlightenment, hence its denunciation of both the Declaration and the spirit in which it was made. The Right's bias against human rights, which is picked up by Le Pen, is based on both the denial of the equality upon which the ideal is itself based, as well as a tendency to shy away from the abstract philosophical tendencies of the Enlightenment. The first part of this denial is connected to the idea of 'order' and 'hierarchy' founded either in nature or in society which precludes the notion of an inherent equality of rights (if not of duties): the second to that of valuing 'action' – and more specifically later on in the case of Maurras and Barrès of 'heroic action'[5] – over thought; of men of action over intellectuals; of spontaneity of sentiment over calculation and strategy. Instinct and the force of the unconscious are the hallmarks of Barrès' early work.[6] These tendencies fade in his later thought and his writings resemble more closely those of Maurras as he celebrates 'the vigorous realism'[7] of the French people.

This celebration of action and heroism proper to the counter-revolutionary tradition gives way to a tension, in the writings of Barrès and Maurras, between reason and emotion, between logic and spiritualism. This tension, proper to the traditional nineteenth century far Right produced by the counter-revolution, is discernible in Le Pen's discourse which often tries to appeal to both facts and instinct in the same sentence; for example his now famous claim that one is drawn to the far Right by a *biological* reaction to disorder, filth, laziness and vandalism.[8] This type of remark which justifies human emotions by seeing them as natural and understandable – if not laudable – rebellions against real, existing and disturbing 'facts' is present all through Le Pen's speeches and comments, and illustrates the usefulness of the tension between instinctive reaction (emotion) and facts, a tension already present in Right-wing thought at the turn of the century. Le Pen, in fact, takes the tension one step further by inviting the interlocutor to see the emotions as logical in themselves. In other words, the tension is no longer simply exploited to justify emotional behaviour. Rather, emotional behaviour is transformed into fact by being granted a biological, that is scientific basis and status.

Maurras and Barrès are crucial in the shaping of far-Right thought in France: a direct product of the counter-revolution, they nevertheless provide the French far Right with a bridge to modernity, and this essentially through their theorisation of nationalism on the one hand, and their perception of the role of the 'people' on the other. The latter can be seen as introducing populism to the ideological morphology of French proto-fascism.

Nationalism and populism

The concepts of nation and citizenship underwent a radical remodelling under the pen of Barrès. His work was the first system of thought to attempt to ground national values in a theoretical framework.

Indeed, his thought can be seen as founded on the belief and defence of national values. To this belief Le Pen is directly indebted and, as will be shown, his words and vocabulary very closely resemble Barrès' on the topic. Just as Barrès saw nationalist sentiment as alone capable of preserving and enhancing France's national grandeur against its growing cosmopolitan attitudes and the internal malaise characteristic of the inter-war years, so Le Pen depicted the FN as the only move-ment able to work against the external forces which had weakened France's position in the international arena, and as the only force capable of thwarting the enemies within.

The idea of a double conspiracy both external and internal is present in the writings of Maurras and Barrès: the internal conspiracy was pinned on the 'métèque' – the French person of foreign origin, or 'cross-breed' – and on the figure of the Jew, while the external threat was seen to be Germany and, more tellingly, the rest of Europe, both seen, ironically, as having been corrupted by French revolutionary ideals as well as, in turn, corrupting.[9]

The double conspiracy stemming from the enemies within and without is still central to the discourse of Le Pen.[10] Part of the reason for the centrality of the theme is its effective connection to that of the *real* people, the *real* Republic, the *real* gains of the Revolution which have been hijacked by the current political class to the detriment of the people. This allows for the concept of conspiracy[11] to be intimately connected with that of popular sovereignty and the possibility of direct democracy.

The tension between emotions and facts, to which we alluded earlier on, is the background to another element in the discourse of Le Pen, namely, an anti-intellectual streak. By accentuating the dual composition of the French mentality, both 'realistically vigorous' and 'instinctively heroic', both Maurras and Barrès set the stage for a discourse which privileges the instinct of the 'little people' over the traditional intellectualism of French political leadership, all the while intimating that the 'little people' have a firmer grasp of day-to-day reality than their bureaucratic counterparts who live sheltered lives of luxury in idle political scheming and chatter. Once again a tension appears: the '*petit peuple*' is both instinctive and seeped in a hard-facts knowledge of life, while bureaucrats and politicians are too 'polished' to be truly, instinctively French. Le Pen is an heir to this aspect of their thought and has made much play of the slighting of bureaucrats and bureaucracy in general – most specifically European bureaucracy, and deprecatory remarks about intellectuals both on the Left and on the Right of the political spectrum.[12]

The rally politics associated with populism described in the preceding chapter warrant further investigation in the case of Le Pen. Introduced in France essentially by Michel Winock and Pierre-André Taguieff,[13] the notion of national-populism allows for the re-insertion of a phenomenon such as Lepenism into the history of the French far Right. For Winock and Taguieff this serves as the basis for an argument which precludes any real comparison with other countries and with other versions of national populism. However, despite this tendency the effort to understand Lepenism and National Frontism as a part of French history, as the product of French developments rather than as an aberration or an unwelcome 'import', was commendable. Further, the analysis of national populism provided by these two authors contributed to distinguishing national populism from Bonapartism which – as a result of Rémond's work – had become the only label available for manifestations of Right-wing extremism in France. Rémond's analysis of the French Right (discussed earlier on) does not serve as the basis for this project as the latter rejects Rémond's conflating of fascism and Bonapartism. As outlined earlier on, however, there are traits common to Bonapartism and to fascism (but which can also be found in Boulangism and Poujadism) which are proper to what has been referred to here as populist rally politics.

The ideology of the FN, as it appears through its writings, the declarations of its leader and its main sources of propaganda, can be in part (in keeping with the populism and the nationalism present at the heart of fascism) convincingly traced to this current which should be interpreted as a mutated form of proto-fascism. What Taguieff and Winock fail to do is to account for why the FN achieves unprecedented electoral success as well as how institutional change affects the content of ideologies such as fascism and populism.

The national populism of the FN is related yet different from a pure form of counter-revolutionary thought. The difference lies first and foremost in the FN's acceptance of the French Revolution. Even in 1985 – long before the FN can be seen to have fully espoused the consensual populism of its later years – Le Pen declared

> Everyone is getting ready to celebrate the bicentennial of the revolution of 1789. Why not? France is 4000 years worth of European culture, 20 centuries worth of Christianity, 40 kings and two centuries of Republicanism. The FN is willing to accept all of France's past.[14]

As noted by Taguieff, nothing relating to the republic (note the 'revolution' with a small 'r' and seemingly treated as one amongst many others) is as significant as those things which are seen to be the founding instances of French nationalism. Nevertheless this selective acceptance (however lukewarm) of the French revolutionary heritage, is essential. Firstly, because it helps to differentiate the FN doctrine from the undiluted version of counter-revolutionary thought. Secondly, it places the FN squarely within the tradition of populist rally politics defined by the revolution and its foundational ambiguity toward leadership and representation in a liberal democracy.

Barrès himself is a product of this dual heritage. As described by Girardet:

> As a young bourgeois rebelling against his milieu and the conformism of his era, he joins until the very last years of the century, the ranks of those 'dictatorial patriots', of those 'Bonapartists of the restoration', 'democrats in love with glory' and 'grand-sons of the Grande Armée', that he, himself, cast in the role of the '*Déracinés*' and whose admiration for the 'holy wrath of the Marseillaise de Rude' he shares.[15]

Here one sees a Barrès who, rather than renege on the values of the French revolution, rather than deny its importance or its relevance, glorifies its heritage by attempting to reintegrate it into the pantheon of the *national* ideological heritage. Just as he exalts the virtues of the 'people' whose honesty and courage he opposes to the decadent mores of the parliamentary republic.

A century later, Le Pen draws on these very same springs and exploits that same plebeian register in contrast to the '*dictature des bavards*' (the dictatorship of the chatter-boxes). It is in great part within this tradition of populist rally politics (but institutionalised by the Fifth Republican regime) that Le Pen's discourse and rhetorical appeal should be understood from the 1990s onwards. Owing a debt to the nationalism of the counter-revolution, exhibiting traces of the populism of Barrès, having inherited the revolution's ambiguous relationship to rally politics and, hence, to leadership, the ideological morphology of the FN (and of Lepenism) is now that of a presidentialised populism.

Le Pen's discourse rests on a gross appropriation of a distorted reading of Pareto, Michels, Weber or Crozier which allows for the denunciation of a 'fat' liberal state, a vampire-like fiscal regime and the repudiation of the '*nouvelles féodalités*' (new fiefdoms) representing the new, post-revolutionary privileges. This discourse is then connected to a radicalised, Rousseauiste version of popular sovereignty linked to a glorification of the Swiss model.[16]

How is this enhanced democracy conceived? This real democracy would work for the citizens and not for what Le Pen refers to as the *'oligarchies politiques, syndicales, bureaucratiques ou médiatiques'* (political, trade union, bureaucratic or media oligarchies). This position goes a long way toward reaffirming the necessity for a strong state:

> The state must remain the ultimate arbiter of the national interest, the definition of which is not necessarily the sum of individual interests. It must preside over national unity and solidarity and regain its independence *vis-à-vis* all financial, religious, political, economic, philosophical, trade union and foreign oligarchies who would sacrifice the interest of the French people to their national interest or to the interests of their cast, clan or class.[17]

The restoration of true democracy hinges on the restoration of the true powers of the state. A strong state is thus seen as a prerequisite.

Palyngenesis

Crucial to the concept of palyngenesis is the notion of violent renewal. Firstly, it is obvious that whilst being a rigorously organised party, the FN is not an armed party. It is also important to note that the currently powerful elements within the FN are people who have been drawn from the activism of the 1970s. Most cadres are ex-UDF or RPR (Bruno Mégret, until recently second in position, Left the RPR to join the FN in 1982) who were disillusioned by the moderation characteristic of the parties to which they initially belonged and who were drawn to the FN in part because of Le Pen's comparatively more radical discourse. Other cadres have been drawn from the intellectual ultra-Right such as the GRECE (*Groupement de recherche et d'études sur la civilisation européenne*) and finally some have transited through the CNIP (*Centre national des indépendants et paysans*).

While there may be an active, perhaps more radical youth wing to the FN (in the form of Samuel Maréchal's *Front National de la Jeunesse* – FNJ), these people are an infinite minority and are kept well in check by the men and women of an older generation whose hold on the party is secure and will be secure – regardless of what happens to the party electorally – for some years to come by virtue of a simple generational effect.

The Left/Right synthesis which Sternhell evoked as characteristic of fascism was discernible in the early days of the FN. Aside from the well known '*ni droite, ni gauche*' slogan, Le Pen wrote things such as 'if being reactionary means reacting like a body reacts to illness, well then, yes, I am reactionary',[18] while at the same time – rather luke warmly – endorsing major change:

> while the term 'revolution' conjures up images of violence which I do not approve of, it is nevertheless true that in the future, France must undergo important changes in orientation and structures. In that sense one could say that it is a revolution.[19]

This is hardly inflammatory, revolutionary rhetoric. And even these declarations reminiscent of fascism's Left/Right synthesis have tended to disappear.

The main point to retain here, however, is that the party's credentials, while often purposely obscured by Le Pen in his speeches, are now quite straightforwardly Right wing. The party has evolved from its '*ni droite, ni gauche*' stance of the 1970s – a stance which, as mentioned earlier on, reflected to some extent its fascist inheritance in its attempt to define a third, synthesising way – to being a radical party of the Right. This belonging to the family of the Right is fully endorsed and upheld by Le Pen. It was upheld in 1984 when he wrote

> in the word Right, there is a notion of directness, of straightforwardness, there is the notion of frankness, which seems to me to be the principal quality of the Francs. The Right, or straight line, is the shortest distance between two points. There is an implication of directness, loyalty which seems to me to stem directly from the concept of Right and its corollaries.[20]

It continues to be upheld now through, on the one hand, a discursive 'rapprochement' with Gaullism and with the RPF. In May of 1998 for example Bruno Mégret (*Délégué Général* of the FN) declared in an interview published in *Le Monde*:

> I think the FN is predestined to progressively occupy all of the space abandoned ... by the Chiraquien politicians who have completely betrayed Gaullian ideals ... Many of the Gaullist values in 1940 at the time of the RPF and after 1962 are perennial values which, today, are embodied by the FN: the independence of France, the greatness of our country, the refusal of a regime dominated by political parties.[21]

The desire to be firmly established as a party of the Right is also reflected in the FN's increasing willingness to ally itself with mainstream Right-wing parties such as the UDF or the RPR (particularly in the *Mégretiste* faction of the FN). This was the case for example in the regional elections of March 1997. Though the public and the political world perceived these alliances as a sell-out on behalf of the two major parties of the Right, it needs to be underscored that the shift was also – if not more so – significant for the FN whose strategy of '*main tendue*' (extended hand) signalled an ever-growing desire to be perceived as part of the mainstream Right.

Much of this move toward the mainstream Right was attributable to Mégret – and we now know that his overtures to the mainstream Right did not always meet with unqualified approval and indeed fuelled the tension which eventually led to the split in the FN in 1998/99. However, in an interview with the author in July of 1998, Le Pen also commented that his dream had always been to create '*un grand rassemblement politique, un RPF*' (a great political rally, an RPF).[22] Whether this adjustment is partly rhetorical, whether it is tactical – which any such move necessarily is – it cannot be regarded as *only* that. The FN is a party far too aware of the need for a popular base and far too aware, also, of the dangers of alienating its mainstay.[23] As argued by Burrin whether the acceptance of the parliamentary regime was tactical or not, the point is that the FN can be seen to have become the victim of its tactics: Hitler and Mussolini may have participated initially in democratic politics but the avowed aim of the whole operation was to overthrow the regime, to renew politics violently. This is not, or is no longer, the aim of the FN. Whatever its hidden agenda or nostalgic longings might be or might have been, the FN is not (now) based on armed struggle nor is it directed toward the overthrow of the regime. Neither the ideology nor the programme nor the practice stemming from either, can be read as resting on a truly palyngenetic outlook or programme. While decadence is acknowledged, violent rebirth is not foreseen.[24]

This is only one of the ways in which the FN can be seen to have moved away from the initial, more stridently extremist, neo-fascism of its early years (including in its personnel, its tactics, its discourse, its aims, its style) to a national populism better suited to the exigencies of the Fifth Republic. The second way is its adaptation of leadership qualities to the exigencies of presidentialism.

Leadership

One of the core concepts identified as present in fascism was that of leadership. It is essential to note that much of the literature on the FN revolves around the analysis of the personality (sometimes referred to as authoritarian, sometimes as charismatic, sometimes simply as 'strong') of the party's leader since its creation in 1972.[25] Interestingly enough, however, few authors have adopted a fruitful manner in which to examine the role of Le Pen in the party.

Scholarship on Le Pen as a political leader falls into two main categories. One approach to the study of Jean-Marie Le Pen has been psychoanalytic. The book published in 1984 by Pierre Jouve and Ali Magoudi[26] was the first of its kind and shed a classic psychoanalytic light on the personality of the FN leader. The findings of these two authors essentially shed light on Le Pen's personality and his discourse by examining the transposition of an unresolved Oedipus complex into political language and political beliefs. Jean-Louis Maisonneuve[27] applies psychoanalysis to a whole gamut of far-Right politicians and yields interesting information on collective psychological phenomena in politics and political discourse more particularly.[28]

While both these books are interesting, in part because political psychology and the psychoanalysis of political leaders is still a budding discipline which has yet to be fully exploited, one nevertheless is struck by the banality of the diagnosis with which both of these books conclude. This is in part because the psychology of the far-Right mentality or personality is not contrasted with what might have been the results if the method had been applied to the Left, the far Left, the Christian democrats, or any other type of leader or movement. In other words the specificity of the conclusions – with respect to the far Right or Jean-Marie Le Pen – are not highlighted and as such the interest of the books tends to reside in the psychoanalytic approach and its merging with the political rather than in the conclusions reached on the subject of the study. This in itself remains of interest but the reader is left wondering whether, in fact, the diagnosis could not very easily apply to any individual sufficiently narcissistic to become involved in politics.

In the second category are authors who focus on Le Pen's personality as a media manipulator, as someone whose strength lies in his ability to speak in a particular manner and in effect to re-shape his audience's perception of particular concepts. One of the earliest works of this type was Edwy Plenel and Alain Rollat's book, *L'Effet Le Pen*[29] which came out in 1984 and can be seen as the first significant analysis of a movement – and particularly a leader – which many still had trouble taking seriously. The book was written immediately after the 1984 European elections in which Le Pen had succeeded in taking more than 10 per cent of the vote. One of the book's main points was that in an atmosphere in which the Left had converted to *realpolitik* and the mainstream Right stressed economic constraints, Le Pen was credited with single-handedly rehabilitating the role of the imagination in politics. As the authors stressed, Le Pen had no programme, no blueprint. He was 'all talk' and that was precisely what these analysts focused on. Their argument was that Le Pen was able to re-invent the meaning of certain concepts and therefore re-invent the context in which the public – and his potential voters – lived.

What was also new about Le Pen was his ability to draw on a stream of thought which has been present in France since at least the end of the nineteenth century, while tailoring it effectively to a political, liberal and social democratic order which had rendered the ideas and indeed the very words themselves taboo. This rehabilitation of a set of ideas could only have been achieved through a calculated response to those who effectively made the political decisions and shaped the political arena. In fact, the failures of the other post-war parliamentary Right-wing movements such as the *Mouvement Nationaliste du Progrès* or the *Rassemblement Européen de la Liberté*, resulted in part from the failure to examine the new political panorama and calculate what a public shaped by the experience of the Second World War would be willing to tolerate and subscribe to, even if opinion sympathised with the ideas put forth by the Right.

Le Pen can be seen as someone who had learnt his lesson well from the failures and successes of other political groups on both sides of the political spectrum. A hallmark of what has often been termed the New Right (Le Pen included) was its willingness to enter the debate on the terms forged by its opposition. The willingness to enter territory seen as belonging to the Left (such as culture, education, the media) signalled Le Pen's willingness to engage in political rhetoric and discourse which contained a recognised and recognisably social-democratic vocabulary. Once this had been done and its presence accepted in that debate, a rehabilitation of Right-wing vocabulary and themes began. We should add that it also signalled the failure of the Left properly to 'earmark' certain concepts, and incorporate a set of social democratic and inclusionary ideals into a theoretical framework strong enough to avoid recuperation by rival ideological movements and parties. For example, the disarray over the functioning and desirability of the welfare state, the implementation of immigration policy or the disagreement concerning guarantee of minority rights, particularly from the mid-1970s onwards, can be seen as having facilitated the recuperation of key concepts by the Right. With the emergence of a New Right, France was faced with a double and intrinsically strong ideological assault: the simultaneous rehabilitation of classical Right-wing French vocabulary and ideas, as well as the New Right/far Right's adoption of Left-wing issues and vocabulary. The rehabilitation of Right-wing discourse and ideas occurred through participation in a debate whose parameters were set by the Left. Under the cover of acceptable, respectable dialogue, issues and ideas particular to the Right in France were slowly re-absorbed into a debate from which they had been excluded.[30]

Other scholars who focused on Le Pen's discourse have dwelt on the coherence and reality of an 'ideological system'. The most recent (1997) and well-known work of this type is the collectively written book by Maryse Souchard, Stéphanie Wahnich, Isabelle Cuminal and Virginie Wathier, *Le Pen. Les mots*.[31] The aim of the book is to unveil the logic and coherence of Le Pen's discourse in the hope of under-scoring its ultimate cruelty and illiberality. Despite the impressive academic credentials of the authors and the unquestionably scientific methods and reasoning used, this is nevertheless very much what the French would refer to as a '*livre engagé*' (a book that takes a political stance). To a certain extent much of the literature on the FN suffers from this trait but, in this case, the problem with the analysis has to do with the authors' shared conception of politics. There is 'a truth' to be told in politics, they assume, thus, there are also many lies to be told. As such much of the volume is an analysis of the efficiency of Le Pen's lies and while this is interesting it nevertheless gives rise to a work which is more intent on demonstrating that Le Pen has elaborated a complex system of lies and deceit rather than explaining how and why this 'system' has served as the basis for his success. This would not be a problem if the authors did not consider their book to be a tool for the 'unmasking' of Le Pen and the weapon which would sound his death-knell. Such an approach reveals once again their own manichean approach to politics which is bound to fail to take into account the complexity of FN politics.

Another important and insightful analysis of this type is Pierre-André Taguieff's chapter entitled 'La métaphysique de Jean-Marie Le Pen' first published in 1989.[32] Taguieff analyses Le Pen's discourse as seeking to reconcile two opposing veins of nationalist discourse which posits simultaneously a natural order and hierarchy and an order constructed by the men of the 'real' Right. Taguieff then goes on to demonstrate that by engaging in contemporary competitive politics Le Pen has no choice but to fall on the side of the voluntarists, on the side of those who think they can shape society through politics. But, argues Taguieff, Le Pen's talent has been to be able to engage in politics while at the same time relying on an axiomatic discourse rooted in notions of a natural order and an immovable hierarchy and the enunciation of these facts in the face of an opposition whose discourse is entirely dependent on demagoguery, liberal illusions and Left-wing lies.

> Jean-Marie Le Pen himself, depicts the theme of the social order as a controversial one. But, he immediately offers the formulation of a solution, in the terms of a compromise or a synthesis: firmly right-wing convictions are defined by a compromise between belief in a 'Natural Order' and belief in a 'constructed Order' which implies a voluntary act.[33]

The underlying assumptions of this approach are more compelling than its conclusions. Ideologies may – and generally do – contain fundamentally contradictory propositions. These contradictions will be highlighted once an ideology gives rise to a movement which has to compete politically and devise a programme. The reconciliation of these contradictions at a political if not at an intellectual level will require a leader. Only through the synthesis operated by one voice and one body will the untenable become resolved, and this because appearances will allow one to believe that the contradictory ideas can and do cohabit in one being. This in turn has two major consequences aside from legitimating incoherence: the first is that it also grants currency and legitimacy to the contradictory beliefs which characterise most followers of political movements. The second is that it grants the leader a magical quality by endowing him with the appearance of being more than one, as he is able to embody such complexity as well as 'see coherently' where the others cannot do so on their own. In the case of the doctrines of the far Right it allows for the myth of the 'healer leader' who has given followers a vision of society based on the reconciliation of their beliefs which they could not have achieved without him.

While some of these works are interesting – chief amongst them Taguieff's chapter – they do not focus on what is most important, particularly in the case of Le Pen. Leadership is a core concept of fascist ideology, and it is at the core of the FN's ideology. Yet, what most of these works demonstrate – or attempt to demonstrate – is the importance of the leader or the leader's discourse for a specific type of politics or for a specific movement. What is more relevant in the case of Le Pen is not so much his personality but how his style of leadership has been moulded by institutional changes.

The transition from '*régime d'assemblée*' to '*régime presidentiel*', from the Fourth to the Fifth Republic, signals an acceptance of rally politics, an institutional espousal of political personalism, such as had been denied in the theory, if not in the practice, of French politics. The institutionalisation of the practice has major consequences for political parties. One of these consequences was to acknowledge the role and importance of the party leader and that of the *présidentiable*, a consequence which obviously facilitates the entry into politics of movements and parties which privilege the role of the leader in practice and the importance of leadership in theory.

In the next chapter we will show how the space opened in the Fifth Republic for the institutionalisation of leadership has presidentialised politics. More precisely we will show how the continuing presidentialisation of politics has transformed a party such as the FN. This in turn will help demonstrate that the FN has moved away significantly from a fascist core and that its ideology has been transformed by the presidentialisation of the French politics and the French party system more precisely.

Notes

1 Some authors have also argued quite convincingly that the FN owes a historical debt to Vichy. One of the main reasons is that Vichy – given its anti-Semitism – is a regime which the FN wishes to see rehabilitated. More precisely it should be rehabilitated in order to keep Vichyite political options open, at the very least in the discourse of the French extreme Right. Le Pen's discourse on the Second World War – in particular his references to the 'detail' of the gas chambers, various tasteless puns, or the referring to the 'historians' who are busy 'verifying' the facts about the holocaust – , his flirtation with the members of the German Republikaner and former SS officers, his attitude during the trials of former SS officers such as Klaus Barbie, all of these suggest that one of the main aims of the FN has been to try to contest the mainstream and accepted view of the Second World War in view of rehabilitating the Vichy regime and legitimating the political tradition of which it is a part. To rehabilitate a regime such as Vichy (a regime which in many ways could be considered to have seconded the Nazi regime), those associated with that regime needed to become not only historically tolerable, but historically useful. This meant constructing an argumentation which gradually denied the existence of

the Nazi atrocities and called into question the good faith, historical accuracy and scientific credibility of the scholarship on Nazism and fascism. As remarked by Burrin (P. Burrin, 'Le fascisme', in J. F. Sirinelli, ed., *Histoire des droites en France, Vol. 1* (Paris: Gallimard, 1992, p. 170). Le Pen's strategy has been to follow, in muted fashion, the advice provided by Maurice Bardèche as early as 1948: it needed to be established that the death camps and the holocaust as a whole were a falsification of history, an orchestrated coup set up by the Jews in the victorious nations (for a complete account of Bardèche's revisionist advice see Maurice Bardèche, *Nuremberg ou la terre promise* (Paris: Sept couleurs, 1948). Le Pen's revisionism is clearly a 'soft' revisionism: his tactics consist in either playing up the need for a 'reconciliation' amongst the French (when asked about Bousquet, a well-known collaborationist and former treasurer of the FN, Le Pen said *'Monsieur Bousquet à peut-être eu les responsabilités que vous dîtes, il a peut-être été un ancien SS, mais moi je suis pour la réconciliation des Français'* (Mr. Bousquet may well bear the responsibilities you outline, he might have been a former SS officer, but I am in favour of the reconciliation of the French people on this matter), Le Pen, *L'Heure de vérité* (Antenne 2, 13 February 1984.) or, more often than not, in attacking the 'received' consensus on the holocaust and then deriding those who subsequently attack him for holding revisionist views (the latter done by using – as trump card – his own links to the resistance, or the fact that his father was killed in service). Le Pen's period in the resistance is poorly documented. Although he claims to have been a *'maquisard'* at the age of sixteen, most people cannot remember him taking part in any such activities for longer than a few short weeks. His activities during those few short weeks are also poorly documented.

2 For whom the revolution was fate punishing France for having given Europe the image and the example of decadence.

3 A. Chebel d'Appolonia, *L' extrême droite en France de Maurras à Le Pen* (Paris: Editions Complexes, 1988). pp. 33–6.

4 R. Monzat discusses Le Pen's varied audience in detail in *Enquêtes sur la Droite Extrême* (Paris: Le Monde Editions, 1992), Ch. 21, especially pp. 292–304.

5 See for example Barrès' *Du sang, de la volupté et de la mort* (Paris: Plon, 1959, originally 1894). But also more specifically his *Cahiers* in which he writes: *'Tout au long de l'histoire, il y a la force qui se développe sans autre règle qu'elle même. A l'usage on entend par actions justes et glorieuses celles qui agissent dans le sens de la plus grande force du moment et qui, par conséquent, réussissent'* (Throughout history strength grows and develops without any rules other than its own. In practice, by just and glorious action, what is meant is those actions which exist in accordance with a moment's greatest strength and thus, by definition, succeed). *Mes Cahiers, Vol. II* (Paris: Plon, 1930), p. 58.

6 See 'Le jardin de Bérénice' in *Le culte du moi* (Paris: Livre de Poche, 1966, originally 1891) in which he writes *'c'est l'instinct, bien supérieur à l'analyse, qui fait l'avenir'* (It is instinct, far superior to analysis, which creates the future), p. 291.

7 M. Barrès, *Mes cahiers, Vol. XI* (Paris: Plon, 1938), p. 329.

8 Jean-Marie Le Pen, *Les Français d'abord* (Paris: Carrère, 1984), p. 70.
9 As Ariane Chebel d'Appolonia writes, '*Les coupables sont, comme Maurras les appelera, les "quatres états confédérés" … les Juifs, les Francs-maçons, les protestants et les métèques*' (the culprits are as Maurras will call them 'the four confederated states' Jews, free-masons, protestants and foreigners). Chebel d'Appolonia, *L'extrême droite*, p. 70.
10 This point is well documented and underscored by R. Monzat, *Enquête*, especially Ch. 21.
11 Le Pen's belief in the efficiency of a discourse drawing on a Malthusian fear of being annihilated from without and from within is clear in his verbal brandishing of the fate reserved for the enemies of the French nation. The enemies have changed less than one would expect over a period of fifty to a hundred years. The enemies within are still the foreigner, the Jew (often depicted as half foreign given his alleged non-allegiance to French traditions and values) '*les Juifs n'ont pas de patrie au sens où nous l'entendons. Pour nous la patrie c'est le sol et les ancêtres, c'est la terre de nos morts. Pour eux c'est l'endroit où ils trouvent le plus grand intérêt*' (Jews do not have a homeland in the sense in which we understand it. For us a homeland is the land of our ancestors, it is the soil of our dead. For them it is the place which is in their best interest) wrote Barrès in *Scènes et doctrines du nationalisme* (Paris: Plon, 1925, originally 1902), p. 63. The enemies without are still Europe, and most particularly Germany, the United States, the developing world and all the countries included in the former Soviet orbit. The latter were abandoned as a rhetorical target in the 1990s but the others are still resources in the galvanising of a nationalist sentiment drawn from the idea that all political strategy is based on the fear of threats.
12 For an analysis of Le Pen's discourse see Catherine Fieschi, 'Jean-Marie Le Pen and the discourse of ambiguity', in H. Drake and J. Gaffney, eds, *The Language of Leadership in Contemporary France* (Aldershot: Dartmouth, 1996), pp. 107–32.
13 M. Winock, *Nationalisme, anti-sémitisme et fascisme en France* (Paris: Seuil, 1990); P.-A. Taguieff, 'La doctrine du national-populisme en France', *Etudes*, 364: 1 (1986), 27–46.
14 J. M. Le Pen, 'Pour une vraie révolution française', *National Hebdo*, 62 (1985). This declaration is in fact rather restrictive: the Republic is reduced to its temporal aspects and weighs little in comparison to the 4000 years which have created the nation.
15 R. Girardet, *Le nationalisme Français. Anthologie, 1871–1914* (Paris: Seuil, 1983), p. 20.
16 The Swiss model, with its use of the popular referendum, is hailed as the perfect form of democracy. It is adapted and twisted in much of the FN discourse to be equated with an anti-parliamentary stance, weary of mediating, representative institutions and rooted in the fantasy of a perfect adequation and undistorted communication between the people and its leader. Here we find an element of the populism we identified at the heart of fascism.Yvan Blot, *Les racines de la liberté* (Paris: Albin Michel, 1985: Ch. VII, 'Le modèle suisse,' pp. 167–87; Ch. IX, 'Le recours: la démocratie authentique,' pp. 217–32.)

17 Le Pen, *Français d'abord*, p. 68.

18 Le Pen, *Français d'abord*, p. 176.

19 Le Pen, *Français d'abord*, p. 174.

20 Le Pen, *Français d'abord*, p. 70.

21 Mégret accentue sa tentative de récuperation du gaullisme par le Front national', *Le Monde* (12 May 1998). Also, when asked whether the FN did not originally emerge as an anti-Gaullist force Mégret added that while he did not agree with everything that de Gaulle had done he did feel that some Gaullist values were basic French values which the FN was the only party in a position to defend. Mégret concluded by adding 'The FN is the only movement in which Gaullist voters can once again find the values they hold dear.' 'Mégret: "créer une force politique nouvelle"', *Le Figaro* (8 May 1998).

22 Jean-Marie Le Pen interview with the author, Brussels, 1 July 1998.

23 It also interesting to note that when asked whether appealing so vocally to Gaullist values was not a bit of a gamble in terms of the 'Algérie française' voters, Carl Lang (then vice-president of the FN) answered quite candidly that those voters were either dead or almost dead and were no longer going to be taken into account in the FN's electoral strategy. Carl Lang, interviews with the author, Brussels, 1–2 July 1998.

24 Burrin, 'Le fascisme', p. 706.

25 This of course does not take into account the recent split in the FN; a split which has created a rival – but weak – version of the party headed by its former délégué général, Bruno Mégret, but a split which has also not fundamentally altered the view of Le Pen nor the party's general stance.

26 P. Jouve and A. Magoudi, *Les non-dits de Jean-Marie Le Pen: enquêtes et psychanalyse* (Paris: La Découverte, 1988).

27 J. L. Maisonneuve, *L'extrême droite sur le divan, psychanalyse d'une famille politique* (Paris: Imago, 1992).

28 Many of these studies, of which we have but listed two, should be understood as particularly indebted to an earlier stream of work concerned with the authoritarian personality in politics. The research carried out at Berkeley toward the middle of the 1940s by Adorno and his disciples, while discarded as methodologically inaccurate and politically tendentious, serves as the basis for much of the more recent research. Adorno's Freudian model which served as the basis of the – deeply flawed – 'fascism scale' led the way in studies on the authoritarian personality (see T. Adorno, *The Authoritarian Personality* (New York, NY: Harper Studies in Prejudice, 1950); Adorno's models were then criticised and amended by researchers such as Hans Jurgen Eysenck who, in his book *The Psychology of Politics* (Baltimore, MD: Baltimore University Park Press, 1954), suggests a reconceptualisation of political behaviour along two analytical axes: on the one hand a traditional Left/Right axis and, on the other, an axis measuring the two opposed attitudes of 'softeness' and 'hardness'. The study was also deeply flawed, most notably the technique for the interpretation of attitudes toward various social facts led to confusion between cause and effect. The study by Wilson on conservatism remains by far the most convincing. It suggests that conservatism is a general factor underpinning the entire field of social attitudes and that it should

thus be understood as a latent characteristic of any political behaviour rather than as a 'magic ingredient' which is present or absent from a particular psychological make up (see G. D. Wilson, 'A dynamic theory of conservatism', in G. D. Wilson, ed., *The Psychology of Conservatism*, New York, NY: Academic Press, 1973, pp. 527–66).

29 E. Plenel and A. Rollat, *L'Effet Le Pen* (Paris:Le Monde/La découverte, 1984).

30 People like Le Pen did not directly recuperate Left-wing thinkers. Other sections of the extreme Right, however, such as for example the *Groupement de Recherche et d' Etude pour une Civilisation Européenne* (GRECE) did. Most conspicuously, they recuperated the ideas of the Italian Marxist Antonio Gramsci and his concept of civil society: in other words, the GRECE adopted a crucial theoretician of the Left in order to be included in the French political debate. More interestingly for our purposes, groups such as the GRECE gradually succeeded in setting the new terms of the debate. The FN did not set out to do exactly that; they did not infiltrate the cultural and academic sphere as thoroughly as did the GRECE. However, the FN benefited a great deal from the reshaping of the political debate and more specifically from the rekindling of an explicitly Right-wing exclusionist discourse by a group which was clearly intellectual. In sum, while the FN and the GRECE always professed to be at odds, they can nevertheless be understood as largely complementary, the GRECE doing the initial work of legitimation and the FN capitalising on a newly forged image and series of opportunities. C. Fieschi, 'Le Pen and the discourse of ambiguity', pp. 108–10.

31 M. Souchard, S. Wahnich, I. Cuminal and V. Wathier, *Le Pen. Les mots* (Paris: Le Monde Editions, 1997).

32 Taguieff, 'La métaphysique', pp. 173–94.

33 Taguieff, 'La métaphysique', p. 193.

Chapter 6

A case study in presidentialisation: the *Front national* and presidential elections[1]

The FN, initially dismissed as a short-term protest-vote party, was, in 1995, the only progressing political formation in France, the only pole towards which there seemed to be any re-alignment. In other words, in the general context of a possible ongoing electoral de-alignment, Le Pen's party was the only one gathering what seemed like mainstream momentum. The evening of 23 April 1995 gave rise to yet another wave of disbelief as Le Pen's score rose to the 15 per cent mark. Le Pen had steadily increased his support through the 1980s in electoral contests (with the slight exception of the 1988 legislative elections). With a resounding and – as he was quick to point out – historic vote of 15.25 per cent, Le Pen, along with the Socialist candidate Jospin, was the 'winner' of the first round.

This section will illustrate that Le Pen's success should be seen as the result of an evolution of the candidate from proto-fascist political agitator to populist, quasi-respectable – although arguably no less politically menacing – populist figure. The following section consists of an analysis of his electoral performance to date, in the 1988, 1995 and 2002 presidential campaigns and relative electoral successes. The analysis sheds some light on the subtlety and complexity of Le Pen's shifting political persona and message and illustrates the abandon of fascism's radical outlook in exchange for a populist one as part of an adaptation to the Fifth Republic's institutional framework.

The words and style of the rally

Unlike de Gaulle's first two rallies in the Third and Fourth Republic, and unlike Poujade in 1956, Le Pen was able to use rally politics in order to gain a place within French politics: his rally did not need to exist 'alongside' normal politics, but it existed within a political system in which the rally drive had been institutionalised and, therefore, domesticated. Rally politics (which had hitherto either been consigned to times of crisis or met with strictly flash-in-the-pan success) had never been allowed such mainstream political access. The feat of Fifth Republican politics is not to have granted populism a window of opportunity but, rather, to have allowed rally politics – whether associated with populism or not – an institutionally defined space. The success of the FN should thus be understood as resulting from the institutionalisation of the rally drive through the presidentialisation of French politics and the concomitant evolution of a proto-fascist ideology into a populist one under the institutional pressures generated by presidentialism.

Political community as natural community

Le Pen's conception of politics is rooted in the main defining features of the rally: 'natural' communities rebelling against pernicious and artificially created categories on the one hand, and the desire to overcome these categories and bypass the man-made creations of representational politics on the other. His definition of politics illustrates the premium placed on natural communities and the disdain for the role of political parties:

> Politics is a science, the most important of all human sciences, that of the common interest of the people and of the nation. Political parties are not at liberty to do with it as they wish. But, politics is also a calling, that of service to the community, in the form of disinterested devotion to the cause of natural entities: Family, City and above all, Nation.[2]

What is also of interest in this definition of politics is the implicit notion, much as in de Gaulle's vision, that political sentiments and opinions (as well as emotions) are naturally ingrained in a people, that they need only be deciphered by someone like himself, who has the ability to do so because he is like them: 'I know your fears, your problems, your worries, your anxieties and your hopes because I have felt them and continue to feel them.'[3] Furthermore, the idea that only 'he' can hear them accentuates the gap between the corrupt existing elite and the people, and serves as the basis for the rejection of representative democracy, the rhetorical annihilation of the party drive and the concomitant privileging of the rally drive through his populist rhetoric.

Again much like de Gaulle and – even more so, Poujade – Le Pen's political career and his entry into politics were fuelled if not created by the resentment generated by a state which seemed to be unable to offer unifying or cohesive political solutions (let us not forget that Le Pen was a Poujadist deputy between 1956 and 1958). For de Gaulle, the resentment was directed against Pétain and Vichy; for Poujade, the Fourth Republic and the tax audit; for Le Pen, de Gaulle and Algeria. The resentment here is once again rooted in the fear of the break-up of the nation at the expense of the common people who sacrifice their lives for it and in favour of, not only a corrupt or inefficient or inept political class, but also of 'special interests' – fragments of the nation as opposed to the nation as a whole.

Unity as a political good

Crucially, the appeal is also rooted in the same notion that France exists as a unified entity which is being fractured by its own national elite. The fragmentation is presented in terms reminiscent of the rallies previously discussed:

> Hence, there sometimes emerge in the history of societies decadent elites, oligarchies who are far removed from the people whom they had the mandate to serve and whom they have betrayed to benefit their privileged interests.[4]

or

> Today, the defence of sectoral interests fragments national solidarity and stands to compromise the sacrifices necessary for the unity of our country. The common will for a shared destiny is being weakened.[5]

The belief is that the fragmentation of the nation is at the root of all the problems with which France is faced and that, concurrently, unity and cohesion – in the form of a rally – is the only political remedy.

The relentless appeals to unity ('*Sans unité nationale il n'y a plus de patrie*', (Without national unity there no longer is a homeland); '*le maintient de la nation passe par le rassemblement des Français*', (The safeguarding of the nation depends on the rallying of the French)) which pepper FN publications and speeches; the organisation of the

'*Caravanes FN*'[6] (for presidential elections, or against Maastricht) has
been well documented. Furthermore, the theatricality of FN meetings,
the organisers' use of the most sophisticated media and lighting tech-
niques, the content and rhetorical sweep of Le Pen's speeches, the
attention paid to creating a sense of privileged community as well as,
ultimately, the valorising of the gathering itself, all contribute to the
understanding of the FN as a professional organisation that can 'put on
a show'. These characteristics however, cannot solely be attributed to
the 'mediatisation' or Americanisation of politics. For those attending
the meetings, the *Fête Bleu-Blanc-Rouge* (one of the FN's mains
annual mass gatherings), the party congresses and yearly *Université
d'été* (the party's summer school) these are not media events, but rallies
of opinion whose value lies in great part in the gathering itself. At an
organisational level, that is for those who stage the meetings, the aim
of the rally is the rally; it is the achieving of a sense of togetherness, of
shared destiny, the arousal of common emotions and the conjuring of
a shared vision in order to create the illusion that this is not 'real' politics, that it is not a political meeting around a politician but rather a
rally of like-minded people around an exceptional leader. The rally is
designed to enhance – if not create – the sense that the leader is not a
politician like any other, since this is not 'really' politics (as real politics
are perceived as fragmenting). This in turn allows for the sense that the
party or rally is not in opposition, it is simply on a different plane, in a
different universe. The creation of a third locus of power which is
neither government nor opposition plays an important role in a situation where the presidential contest structures political life. Rally politics therefore – and in this case Le Pen's – should be perceived as
particularly well-suited to a presidential regime in which the president
– and perhaps more importantly the *présidentiable* – must appear to
inhabit this third locus of power.

Rally politics and the grooming of a présidentiable

During the 1988 presidential campaign, a few days prior to the first
round, a poll by the market research agency SOFRES revealed that
only 28 per cent of voters intending to vote for Le Pen believed that
he would make a good president.[8] The first round of the election was
already fulfilling a role of opinion outlet, and many of the votes
garnered by Le Pen were but protest votes.[9] The period from the early
1980s up to 1988 was characterised by a strategy of consolidating an

emerging power-base, and of asserting Jean-Marie Le Pen's presence
on the French political stage through a 'credibility' offensive. The
period from 1988 to the 1995 presidential elections saw the FN and
its leader move further into the political mainstream in order to
become *présidentiable* and dispel doubts about Le Pen's suitability as a
leader of the French Republic.

1972–84: Rallying to the rally

While the Le Pen phenomenon is doubtless greater than the sum of its
parts, Le Pen's career – and thus the evolution of the FN – can be
divided into four distinct stages: the first, from the FN's creation in
1972 to 1983/4 was marked by a barely disguised proto-fascism.
Dressed in combat gear and sporting a beret and eye-patch, Le Pen
cultivated an aggressive public image. In spite of this, when the leaders
of the far-Right movement *Ordre Nouveau* (founded in 1969 – hereafter ON) decided to create a movement more palatable to the electorate in the form of the FN, it was Le Pen whom they singled out as
capable of transforming the image of the far Right from a radical, anti-
system, proto-fascist current into that of a party which stood some
chance of electoral gain, however marginal, in the March 1973 legislative elections. In 1972, when Le Pen created his *Front national*, it was
with the distinct objective of re-integrating the far Right into the
parliamentary arena, a place it had briefly enjoyed in the 1950s with
the *Poujadiste* movement but from which it had been virtually
excluded since.[10] Le Pen's task, therefore, was to assemble under the
red, white and blue flame of his party's logo the diverse currents which
made up the far Right in France.

As outlined by P. Milza,[11] this was an arduous task in the light of
the failure of earlier far-Right movements since the war. Until 1984,
the gains were insignificant: no score in the 1973 legislative elections;
0.7 per cent in the 1974 presidential elections. In 1981, the FN did
not run in the presidential elections as Le Pen failed to gather the 500
necessary signatures, and in the legislative elections which took place a
month later the FN scored 0.3 per cent. Yet in the 1983 municipal
elections the FN candidate Jean-Pierre Stirbois gained 16.7 per cent of
the votes for the FN list in Dreux (Eure et Loir). The reasons behind
this surge in support remain to be explained but most often invoked is
a backlash effect against the Left (in power since 1981). Discontent
which might have stemmed from radical socialists disappointed in

Mitterrand's performance as well as from Right-wing supporters hardening their stance in view of the Left's power, account in part for the electorate's sudden interest in Le Pen's party. The 'Dreux effect', as it came to be known, signalled the beginning of the FN's electoral emergence and paved the way for the 1984 11.1 per cent breakthrough in the European elections. For the FN, these scores were a confirmation of the efficiency of their tactics: the strategic combination of extremist discourse and democratic allegiance had enabled the far Right to re-enter the realm of parliamentary politics.

Two points need to be stated as this stage of the argument. The first is that on its creation in 1972 the FN, despite the presence at its helm of Le Pen – who had been recruited to lead it – was very much the creation of the leaders of ON. The latter comprised such figures as Jeantet (a former supporter of Doriot and the *Croix de Feu*), Brigneau (a convinced Maurrassien) and Charbonneau (who had belonged both to *Action française* and then later on *Milice*). After pitiful results in the 1971 municipal elections in Paris the leaders of ON decided that the only solution to get out of the electoral impasse in which they found themselves was to attempt to federate the various groups which made up the far Right at the time. The overture toward Le Pen was to be taken also as a symbolic overture toward the former supporters of *l'Algérie française*. Further, Le Pen was perceived as cumulating the political experience of Poujadism, anti-Gaullism, and, finally, *Tixierisme*.[12] The Tixier-Vignancourt connection was important not only because it signalled Le Pen's multifaceted political experience but, also because the '*comités TV*' (as they came to be known) had succeeded in bringing together factions as diverse as the conservative anti-Gaullists (such as Pierre Arrighi) with the neo-fascists from *Occident* and the European neo-paganists such as Jean Mabire or Dominique Venner.[13] Le Pen thus embodied a potential for political federation and synthesis which appealed to the leaders of ON.

The first FN programme published in the November issue of *National*, reflects the compromise between '*les nationaux*' – those supporting Le Pen and associated with *l'Algérie française* and the '*comités TV*' on the one hand, and '*les nationalistes*' – those associated with ON and the former *Occident* figures, on the other. In terms of our framework for analysis, this can be interpreted as a recognition from the leaders of the ON of the necessity to create a structure for political participation. This in itself can be seen as a first response to the Fifth Republic whose two-round majority system creates – at the very least – a party-political imperative which forces groups, nebulous movements and smaller parties to federate into more mainstream political parties.

The 1973 legislative elections were thus prepared tactically and ideologically on the basis of a compromise and according to the developing logics of the two factions (*nationaux* and *nationalistes*) in the FN. So bleak were the results of the election (1.32 per cent) that ON recommended an intensification of activism and a retreat from electoral politics. Le Pen on the other hand began a campaign to strengthen the party and called for a deepening of the electoral strategy. This can be taken as the beginning of the second stage of adaptation, a stage at which Le Pen continued the strengthening of the party apparatus but during which the rally drive and rally politics were kept in check as the organisational imperatives continued to dominate the internal agenda.

On the 21 June 1973 as a consequence of ON's specifically anti-Semitic discourse and following clashes with the police, ON was dissolved and outlawed. The coast was clear for Le Pen. From then on it was up to him to recreate the FN without the members who had since its creation constituted its core and principal strategists.[14]

This leads us to a second point which is that, in 1974, while Le Pen had already recognised the limits of a proto-fascist radicalism and the importance of running in the presidential elections, it is clear that his attitude denotes the fact that he had not yet recognised the complex nature of the process which made leaders *présidentiables*.

As such from 1974 to 1979 Le Pen and the FN cannot be seen as having entirely rallied to the presidential game. This is evidenced by the FN's increasing reliance – particularly between 1974 and 1978 – during those years on revolutionary activists as well as by the fact that the party was then still in the hands of its most extremist members. The tendency is exemplified by François Duprat's joining the FN in 1974. Duprat was a professor of history, a former member of *Jeune nation*, *Occident* and ON and was a frequent contributor to a number of neo-nazi journals both in France and abroad.[15]

In the January 1974 issue (the first issue) of *Cahiers Européens*, Duprat revealed what he saw as the ideological foundations of the FN. These foundations comprised three elements: a strident anti-parliamentarianism and radical opposition to democratic systems; a recognition that all members of the FN should be allowed to belong to other political movements and parties; and – rather paradoxically – the acceptance of the need for punctual political alliances with the mainstream Right. The programme's incoherence was matched only by the abysmally low electoral results which it yielded in the next elections.

Two reasons however can be put forth as partial explanations for this tactical choosing of radicalism. The first was the need for the FN to demarcate itself from its main political rival of the time, the *Parti des forces nouvelles* (PFN) created in 1974. The second, and perhaps more important, reason is probably as argued by Jean Yves Camus the perceived necessity of incorporating into the FN a great many little groups and movements which constituted the nebula of the far Right at the time.[16] Most of these movements were ON dissidents who would not countenance the idea of compromising with their fascist or neo-fascist principles.[17]

Le Pen was therefore not immediately able to move away from the party's fascist roots. And electorally and politically the FN at the time seemed incapable of having any impact whatsoever on the French political scene. The 1977 municipal elections had the advantage of making the FN's dilemma absolutely clear as the party was forced to ally itself with the local mainstream Right.[18]

The 1978 legislative elections were to see the FN take its first steps toward a populist strategy. This year therefore marks the beginning of Le Pen's unwavering hold on the party as well as its outright 'rallification'. This year can thus be taken as stage three in the party's transformation from party to rally. Le Pen personally wrote and published an economic manifesto entitled '*Droite et démocratie économique*' ('The Right and economic democracy'). In this quintessentially populist appeal, the FN denounced the overblown French state, the arbitrariness of the fiscal regime and defended a liberalism which was designed to benefit small to medium-size firms and local shopkeepers. The manifesto's consequences were to pit – once again – the two wings of the FN against one another: the revolutionary elements disdained Le Pen's manifesto which they characterised as petit bourgeois while Le Pen consciously strove to veer away from what he saw as a cripplingly extremist discourse which was ill-adapted to the politics of a presidential regime.[19]

It is important to remember that at this time many of the FN's candidates and much of its personnel were either involved or had been involved in neo-fascist or neo-nazi groups. In 1978 one-third of the FN's 137 candidates in the legislative elections were allies of François Duprat or belonged to allied groups and movements. The result of the first round of the 1978 elections gave the FN 1.6 per cent of the votes but before the second round an incident which was to modify the FN's path to development significantly took place. François Duprat was killed by a bomb wired to his car. This incident was to mark the beginning of a significant ideological transformation of the FN as slowly Jean-Marie Le Pen fashioned himself into the uncontested leader of the party transforming it into a populist electoral machine and purging it of its most radical or neo-fascist elements.

Most commentators agree that Le Pen may only have been paying only lip-service to Republican and democratic ideals, values which, however scorned by supporters of the far Right, are nevertheless necessary to achieving a credible and respectable image.[20] Le Pen's increasing public allegiance to broad democratic ideals played a significant role in the rehabilitation of the far Right and in his political rise to power.[21] As Taguieff and Milza[22] make clear, the FN espoused a strategy consisting of a suave blend of legalistic tactics, centrist propositions and radical ideas in its conquest of the electorate.[23]

By 1984 a first step had been made; the FN was still perceived as a protest movement rather than as the expression of a coherent political opinion but it had succeeded in de-ghettoising the far Right.

1984–88: rally politics and political credibility

The period from 1984 to 1988 saw the FN establishing itself as a fixture in French political life. Whereas the ten preceding years had been spent using a strategy capable of yielding an electoral breakthrough, the period between 1984 and 1988 is characterised by the attempt to harness this emerging electoral strength to an even more 'democratic' image in order to achieve political credibility and, as a consequence, durability. 1984 marks the beginning of Le Pen's great democratic professions of faith as well as the beginning of his more insistent and public re-definition of himself through books and declarations. Also noteworthy in this respect is Le Pen's increasing need to re-define himself: for example he increasingly uses the term 'democrat' to label and define himself from 1984 onward;[24] in the same vein 1984 marks the beginning of his likening himself to Reagan, to Churchill, or to Mac Arthur.[25]

In terms of recruitment the FN began to diversify its membership by recruiting personalities with impeccable credentials: for example, alongside the FN's core of Right-wing extremists the party welcomed P. Descaves, former vice-president of the *Syndicats des Patrons Indépendants* (SNPMI), P. Forrestier, former secretary-general of the *Confédération Intersyndicale de Défense et d'Union Nationale d'Action des Travailleurs Indépendants* (CID-UNATI) (both trade unions supporting independent and small business people), A. Arette-Landress, former vice-president of the *Fédération française d'agriculture*; all of whom were recruited in part thanks to the FN's creation – in 1985 – of an association christened '*Entreprise moderne et libertés*', aimed at recruiting members from the business world.[26]

Organisationally, also, it is useful to remember the study by Birenbaum and François cited in Chapter 1: in it the two authors draw attention to the fundamental shift in personnel organisation which occurs from 1984 onwards as a result of the growing pressures stemming from electoral success and in an attempt to give the party a more 'professional' image. As highlighted by Birenbaum and François:

> New working rules (imposed not without provoking internal strife) were imposed, based on a differentiation of electoral and partisan functions, whose aim was to ensure the FN's representation by a new type of political actor: more specialised, more competent and more presentable.[27]

More particularly and in line with the FN's aim to broaden its membership base, 1984 marks the beginning of the reinforcing of national, regional, departmental and local party structures.

Finally, 1984 marks the beginning of the FN's ever closer links with the *Club de l'horloge*, a *Nouvelle Droite* think-tank that brought together intellectuals, writers and politicians of different Right-wing hues and whose members began to take an interest in the FN. The *Club de l'horloge* was created in 1974 by Yvan Blot, Jean-Yves Le Gallou and Henry Lesquen; until 1979–80 it remained connected to the GRECE, but – in part as a result of the controversy surrounding the GRECE in the summer of 1979 – the *Club de l'horloge* began to distance itself from GRECE in the early 1980s and re-label itself as a group of 'nouveaux républicains' in a marked attempt to appear politically trustworthy and respectable. The presence in the FN of key personalities from the Club de l'horloge (such as Le Gallou and Bruno Mégret) undeniably enriched the FN's programme and did much to grant the party a newfound respectability, connected as it was to well-established intellectual and political circles.

Le Pen's score of 14.39 per cent in the 1988 presidential election confirmed his political success but also the continuing reluctance, even of many of his supporters, to perceive him as more than a first-round presidential candidate. While he was credible enough to attract a vote which could not easily be dismissed by other politicians, another tactic was needed if he was to achieve a political image which could be harnessed to win the respectability necessary for 'presidentiability'.

1988–95: rally politics, respectability and setting the agenda

The attempt to achieve the necessary respectability to become *présidentiable* evolved along two lines, both of which were crucial. One concerned Le Pen's electoral attitude, the other a more general transformation of his discourse. Le Pen's discourse varied according to his audience. There was a marked difference between his rhetoric and discourse while on the campaign trail and the more radical and unashamedly racist and offensive discourse he was more well known for off the trail, in between major electoral contests. This was, for example, readily apparent in 1988, when, after having endlessly justified himself so as to regain a measure of credibility with respect to a statement in which he referred to the holocaust as a 'point of detail',[28] he slipped back into this mode shortly after the election with a pun on Nazi crematoriums.

The contrast between the 'campaigning' Le Pen and the 'real' Le Pen still existed at the time of the 1995 elections: while he was uncharacteristically subdued – as will be illustrated below – during the campaign, he was unable to contain his anger and frustration against all of his 'enemies' upon hearing of the definitive results of the first round, and thus could not resist the appeal of a rhetorical rampage. His anti-Semitic comments on the Jewish pop singer Patrick Bruel when the latter cancelled his shows in the cities where an FN mayor had been elected in the municipal elections of June 1995 were also revealing after his carefully controlled discourse during the presidential campaign. Even on that occasion, however, although anti-Semitic, Le Pen's attacks were again much less strident than those levelled against Jews earlier on in his political career. To this dual attitude dictated by electoral contests, one must, therefore, add a broader transformation of Le Pen's discourse between 1988 and 1995 rooted in his quest for respectability. The import of his discourse remained offensive, nationalistic and implicitly racist. But his rhetoric shifted from the crudely explicit to the more sophisticated.

While he still oscillated between his more radical non-campaigning persona and a softer electorally groomed personality, Le Pen also altered his general discourse qualitatively in order to appear more statesmanlike.[29] The debate surrounding the Maastricht treaty and the shape of the new Europe, as well as Le Pen's leadership of the *Groupes des Droites Européennes* afforded him a double opportunity to work on his more politically mainstream image. It first and foremost saw him speak to such distinguished assemblies as the European Parliament. More importantly, however, his notorious opposition to a federal Europe allowed him to target pro-European politicians and their 'cosmopolitan' views of Europe as the cause of unemployment (since it was their philosophies which allowed for growing numbers of immigrants into nations such as France). This in turn enabled him to attack all politicians more freely by accusing them of all being part of the same plot to annihilate the French nation. Well known examples from the 1988–95 period were Le Pen's puns on the '*Maastricheurs*' (the 'Maastricheats') and the '*Fédérastes*' ('federal' being equated in Le Pen's repertoire with 'pederast' as another abnormal compulsion). This period marked the beginning of the real shift in his discourse, a point at which the tell-tale signs of populism begin to make their appearance; for example attacking the politicians rather than the immigrants themselves in a move characteristic of populism's distrust of the professional politician. The debate on Europe, and more specifically, from 1992, on Maastricht, can be seen as having afforded Le Pen an opportunity to appear as a political actor preoccupied with affairs of state in a prestigious and validating environment. It also allowed him to alter his rhetoric without appearing to be selling out in the eyes of his supporters.

The 1995 presidential campaign came after yet another series of electoral successes. The 1988 elections were followed by an 11.8 per cent score in the 1989 European elections, 12.5 per cent in the 1993 legislative elections, and 10.5 per cent in the 1994 European elections. The 15.25 per cent 1995 presidential score appalled many, but surprised no one.

The 1995 campaign

Le Pen's 1995 presidential campaign was marked by little continuity and much subtle change. Continuity was apparent, in the electoral success, which was predictable and in line with what Le Pen had come to expect since 1988 and in terms of the organisation and timing of the campaign both of which did not differ significantly from those of the previous one. As in 1988, Le Pen began campaigning early: he officially announced his candidacy on 17 September 1994, but the campaign had already begun in fact as early as January of that year as he set out on his campaign for the cantonal elections, and then in the spring for the European elections. Both of these campaigns were for all intents and purposes pre-mobilisation exercises for the 1995 presidentials. By the time Le Pen officially declared his intention to run for the presidency in his closing speech of the *Bleu-Blanc-Rouge* meeting in September 1994 in Reuilly, he had already attained campaign momentum. And from September, Le Pen set out to canvass the country once more. Like Chirac's, his was a dynamic grass-roots campaign using whatever local support was available to create the feeling of an unstoppable popular wave spreading across France.[30] The consciously created appearance of a popular movement was one of the most striking aspects of Le Pen's 1995 campaign. This popular rubbing of elbows fitted neatly with the image of the 'little man' who has done well for himself yet not forgotten past setbacks, the ordinary person in touch with the plights and problems of average French citizens.

The manner in which he presented himself to the voters in his 1995 presidential manifesto is a good illustration the relationship between himself and the ordinary – potential – voter.

> As candidate to the post of President of the Republic, I am nothing more than a French citizen like any of you. War orphan, state-funded pupil, student activist, combat officer, businessman, family man, national and European MP, I know your fears, your problems, your worries, your distress and your hopes because I have felt, and continue to feel them.[31]

What emerges is the paradoxical image of a visionary pragmatist: in touch with both the prestige and honour of the French nation and the daily well-being of citizens. This ability to combine vision and ordinariness one of the requisite features of the populist leader.

The 1988 campaign was marred by Le Pen's dismissal in late September of 1987 of the holocaust as a 'point of detail'; no such monstrous remarks were made during the 1995 presidential campaign, and few offensive declarations were reported by the press.

However, although this campaign did not suffer from verbal media gaffes, it was placed under the sign of violence and the FN saw itself twice accused of having blood on its hands. On the night of 21 February 1995, FN supporters putting up posters murdered a young Comorian, Ibrahim Ali, and on 1 May (during the FN traditional May Day parade) a young Morrocan, Brahim Bouarram, drowned in the Seine after having been thrown off a bridge, allegedly by FN supporters. The loathsome and explicitly racist nature of both these crimes angered much of the French population and Le Pen was asked to justify himself and his party on several occasions. But on these two matters again, Le Pen succeeded in appearing circumspect (in the case of the second murder he refused to accept responsibility, blaming instead a 'Chiraquian manipulation'[32] destined to mobilise anti-racist opinion against the FN). The tone adopted by Le Pen on both occasions was almost appropriately regretful, in particular during his appearance on the French political show *La France en direct*, during which he reacted violently against an interviewer who insinuated that Le Pen could not have cared less about Ibrahim Ali's death in February.[33]

On neither occasion did Le Pen seem altogether 'repentant': of course, he did not accept responsibility for either 'accident' (as he called them), but his reaction was far removed from that which one might have expected in 1987 or 1988. It seems that the high cost of the 1987 pun, and of his virulent discourse more generally, might have led the FN leader to reappraise the efficiency of this sort of attitude, especially while on the campaign trail.[34] Furthermore, Le Pen seemed to have mastered the art of distancing himself from the FN at crucial times so as not to appear as one of its more radical elements, while at others, such as in times of electoral contests, he showed himself consistently capable of mobilising party support and activists. Thanks to this strategy, Le Pen often came across as the one whose strength and inspiration inspired the party, but who, nevertheless, could not be held accountable for members' individual actions and statements. This in turn enabled him to appeal to groups both on the far and on the mainstream Right.

Perhaps the most important point regarding Le Pen's respectability offensive during this campaign concerns his discourse surrounding immigration. Whereas Le Pen remained as opposed to immigration in 1995 as he had been in 1988, analysts such as Pascal Perrineau[35] noted a shift in Le Pen's discourse. First, Le Pen evoked the themes of immigration and insecurity far less in 1995 than in 1988, concentrating rather on unemployment. Secondly, the immigration issue was increasingly dealt with by attacking 'inept politicians' rather than the immigrants themselves. During several television interviews, Le Pen explicitly questioned government figures regarding the immigrant population in France; and he accused the French government of lying to the public, of doctoring official statistics and questioned its ability to maintain the distinction between legal and illegal immigrants.[36] Le Pen's attacks on politicians were not new, but whereas he had previously attacked the immigrant population itself, the professional politicians of both Left and Right were the exclusive targets of Le Pen's criticisms during the 1995 electoral campaign.

Le Pen's campaign flyers are a good illustration of the manner in which the treatment of the immigration issue evolved between 1988 and 1995. They also illustrate the broader evolution of Le Pen's discourse between the two elections, and the increased populist appeal of his discourse to a new group of voters, mainly the unemployed and those living in increasingly precarious conditions – in essence, those who would not vote for an outwardly racist discourse but would readily sympathise with his diagnosis that things were getting worse and that France's elite politicians were generally to be held responsible either as crooks or as incompetents. The comparison also illustrates Le Pen's bid for presidential credibility by portraying himself, as most other candidates traditionally do, as someone who is of the people but has an added experience of political life.

Le Pen's 1988 campaign claim that he was unlike any other running politician put him in a difficult situation for 1995: on the one hand, it was crucial that he maintain the requisite distance between himself and all the others in order to condemn political corruption without any risk of being assimilated to those he criticised. On the other hand, it was essential for the election that he shed his 'outsider' image which he had explicitly cultivated in 1988 (one of his three electoral posters pitched him against the background of a horse race with the caption *L'outsider défend vos couleurs* ('the outsider champions your interests').

The image of the outsider was precisely what Le Pen needed to transform into an image of someone who was as présidentiable as the other candidates. As such, where the 1988 flyer demarcated him from the rest of the political class, the 1995 flyer, while it could not afford to place him squarely on the 'inside' lest he be tainted, placed him *amongst us*. His insistence in 1988 that he was the only candidate able to offer such a programme, that he was a solitary visionary, was replaced in 1995 with a discourse of his belonging to France. 'I am like no one else' had been replaced by 'I am like you'. Where the 1988 flyer centred on what Le Pen would do were he to be elected, the message in 1995 centred on who Le Pen was and where he came from. In the 1995 *Appel aux Français* (on the reverse side of the flyers), presenting a programme became secondary to presenting Le Pen as a credible candidate for the presidency. Replacing 1988's risky *Osez voter pour vos idées, Osez voter Français* (Dare to vote for your ideas, Dare to vote French) with the bland 1995 caption *Avec vous une France pour tous les Français* (With you a France for all French people) confirmed the desire to turn a protest-vote into a mainstream vote. Even though a superficial knowledge of Le Pen's ideas cast exclusionary light on the words, their explicit message was tame. The *tous les Français* implied a broad notion of citizenship on the basis of a *jus solis* tradition (giving pre-eminence to place of birth) as well as the intended *jus sanguinis* (which privileges lineage and heritage).

In the corpus of the letter he refers to those who have lost their jobs, who fear for them, and those whose children have been unable to find a job. He then refers to those who fear for their pensions (an attempt at targeting the elderly population which had until then consistently been reluctant to vote for him: only 12 per cent of the over sixty-five vote in 1988).[37] Immigration is mentioned only once in the 1995 flyer, and then only amongst a variety of other elements. The 1988 flyer on the other hand gave a far greater impression of a nation under siege, with Le Pen referring to 'immigrants, assassins, terrorists and drug-dealers'. The urgency and violence of 1988 gave way to a more fashionable worried concern.

Lastly, the bullet-point section of the flyers of 1988 and 1995 was altered subtly. Two elements are readily apparent: the first is that Le Pen kept 1988's 'why would they [the political mainstream] do tomorrow what they couldn't do yesterday?' slogan. However, unlike the 1988 flyer which went on to swamp the reader with statistical information concerning numerous issues, the 1995 flyer simply reminds the reader of the other candidates' affiliation with the current (scandal-tainted) political class implicated in the nation's decline. The section closes with the caption 'A vote for Le Pen is a useful vote right from the first round', an ambivalent appeal to perceive Le Pen as both a 'useful' first-round candidate and an imaginable second-round one. This is not Le Pen the real outsider but a candidate asserting his rights to be considered a true insider.

The second change in the bullet points was that while both flyers organised the ten points by theme, the themes adopted in 1988 were all at once hard-hitting and static ('Immigration'; 'Security'; 'Housing' etc.), followed by very short, direct, aggressive descriptive paragraphs. The 1995 flyer also offers ten bullet points, but the thematic headings and the present infinitive infuse the sentence with a directness and sense of purpose: *Offrir un travail à chaque Français; Garantir la santé publique; Reconquérir la souveraineté française* (giving work to all French persons; guaranteeing public health; reconquering French sovereignty). Furthermore, unlike the agressiveness of 1988, the 1995 headings were more cryptic, giving the illusion of someone delineating both a programme and a vision rooted in classical values. For example,

1988's fifth point entitled *L'Europe: pour l'Europe des patries* (Europe: for a Europe of the fatherlands) is transformed into 1995's tenth and last point 'Reconquering French sovereignty' followed by several illustrative points of which renegotiating Maastricht is but one. Without going into further detail here, we can see that there is a shift between 1988 and 1995, from an emphasis on Le Pen's *knowledge* to an emphasis on his *vision*. The 1995 document targeted a much broader audience by means of a more mainstream Right-wing discourse. It targeted the large section of the electorate which was concerned with unemployment, pensions and security. Its language was therefore necessarily closer to the political mainstream than in 1988, as its aim was to present Le Pen as someone whose vision, broad understanding of issues and capacity for action made him an ideal candidate to the presidency.

The most striking aspect of the Le Pen's 1995 vote was not the score. His 15.2 per cent was indeed historic but it was not surprising, and, in fact, only represented a 0.8 per cent gain over the 1988 score. What evolved more dramatically between 1988 and 1995 (in fact, from 1986) was the social composition of his electorate. Le Pen's initial vote was in a sense a protest vote of the provincial 'petite bourgeoisie';[38] but by 1994, Le Pen had become the clear winner in the popular sectors and amongst workers.[39] 1995 also confirmed the geographical as well as the social penetration of Le Pen's constituency. It confirmed its hold on the eastern parts of France and the regions bordering the Mediterranean coast, and gained strength in the industrial north and centre of the country. Hervé le Bras (director of the *Laboratoire de démographie historique*) noted this shift and characterised it as one from a protest electorate to a disaffected electorate.[40] Le Bras also underscored the increasing differentiation between the electorate of the south of France and the electorate of the north. He refers to the southern 'ideological' vote and the northern 'sociological' vote[41] and points to Le Pen's capacity to tap into various forms of resentment, disaffection and fear. In essence, Le Pen developed a discourse and programme which exploited the resentment of the industrially burntout zones of northern France, the fears stemming from the insecurities bred by the living conditions and social isolations of the Parisian suburbs and, finally, the disaffection of a southern electorate which resented the strain of an ill administered, poorly managed and economically deprived immigrant population. The southern electorate had for a long time constituted Le Pen's main electoral pool, but the north and Paris represented a relatively new and growing phenomenon which could provide him with an expanding (and young) pool of voters.

In Jean-Marie Le Pen's presidential campaign, the factor of real importance was the deepening of the 'respectability' strategy and the tactics associated with it (toning down of the immigration issue, a relative absence of explicitly offensive remarks, and a generally more mainstream rhetoric); this accompanied a new drive for the diversification of the FN's electoral base. The results of this strategy are apparent, not so much in Le Pen's score, but in the sociological composition of his vote. The FN has been able to position itself as much more than a single-issue/single-electorate party and has the potential to act as a rallying point for the disaffected as a social category.

1996–2002: populism, presidentialism and the rallification of the republic

No event better illustrates the impact of the presidentialisation of French politics on Fifth Republican institutions than the impact of Le Pen's electoral score in the 2002 presidential contest.

In fact, the 2002 elections can be taken as a vivid illustration of a number of Fifth Republican mechanisms both functional and dysfunctional. On the dysfunctional side, rally politics and party politics were pitted against one another mercilessly as Le Pen's triumphant populism carved itself a space in the second round of the presidential elections eliminating the candidate of the 'Gauche plurielle' and bringing to a close the five years of consensual, pragmatic party politics of cohabitation. On the functional side, the 2002 elections set the context for the reassertion of Republican values by granting Chirac a landslide victory in the second round, and the RPR a secure majority in the legislative elections. During a time-frame of less than two months France was the theatre of an extraordinary drama in which the Fifth Republic's various facets and tendencies were revealed and acted out at break-neck speed.

For the FN, 2002 marked both its apogee and the very real limits imposed upon it by a system which it has permeated but cannot conquer. The final part of the FN's evolutionary cycle in terms of its permeation of the Fifth Republic's structure of political opportunity stretches from 1996 to 2002. Within this period there are three relevant moments: the 1998 regional elections, the party's much publicised split in 1998/1999 and, finally, the electoral cycle of 2002.

*The 1998 legislative elections: party drive
and rally drive within the FN*

What this book proposes is an understanding of the continued success of the FN as the result of rally politics being re-introduced and institutionalised in France through the Fifth Republic. Where traditionally one type of politics (rally or party) existed at the expense of the other in the various French republics, the Fifth – through Gaullism – brings these two contradictory drives together. The Fifth Republic thus ushers France into modern liberal politics, forcing it to accommodate these two types of politics through a specific set of institutions. As argued by Graham, the two drives are ever-present in all liberal democratic polities, but, they are also present within each party, each movement. For it is the contradictory pressures generated by modern democratic frameworks and governance that create the interlocking logic of the two drives, hence all parties – because they are subjected to these same demands – will also exhibit currents, tendencies toward both drives, toward both types of politics.

What we see clearly within the FN, from 1997 onward is the emergence of the contradictory pulls within the party. Paradoxically, the more the party adapted to the exigencies of the Fifth Republic, the better it became at playing the game, the more it exposed itself to the very same dangers as all other parties by being subjected to the very same dilemmas and external forces. As we have argued, Fifth Republican institutions are designed to force parties to address both styles of politics. In many ways this tests their limits by testing their organisational and ideological cohesion as well as their capacity to harbour a democratically conducted debate regarding the party's orientation. Given the make up of the FN and its diverse components, these pressures were bound to take a heavier toll on it than on other parties whose make up was less diverse and whose organisation was more open to contestation and debate.

1998 was a key year because the regional elections revealed two very different orientations within the party as well as a multitude of fault-lines which had been held together by Le Pen's leadership but which resurfaced as the party started to become successful at levels other than national politics (i.e. at levels where Le Pen's leadership could not be seen as the sole motivation behind the voters' willingness to cast a vote for the FN). The regional elections of 1997 are a good illustration of both of these phenomena occurring simultaneously: the FN's success at the regional level (and previously at the local level in

Toulon, Orange and Marignane) legitimated – within the party – leadership styles but also visions of the party and ideas within the party which were easily marginalized when Le Pen was the embodiment of the FN, but less so once these visions and these leadership styles could be held in part responsible for the FN's success. This meant a growing confidence on the part of factions within the FN to disagree with the Le Pen line and an increasing confidence in voicing alternative policy lines. In some ways therefore, it is impossible to separate the FN's score in the 1998 regional elections from the party's internal crisis which exploded in late 1998, for it was the successes of 1998 which emboldened the Mégretistes factions within the FN and ultimately led to the split.

As outlined above, it can be argued that the more successful the party, the stronger the pressure to balance the party and rally tendencies within it. The 1998 regional elections were the enactment of the FN's attempt to do just that. The split within the party one year later was the signal that it had failed.[42]

Five years after the event, the shock over the success of the FN across France in the regional elections of 1998 can hardly be overstated and is surpassed only by that following the first round of the 2002 elections.

For the public and analysts alike, the 1998 regionals were a belated confirmation of what the 1995 local elections had intimated: that the vote for the FN was no longer strictly a vote for Le Pen, but rather, was being transformed into the sort of party allegiance that might outlast the leader of the FN. Two aspects of the elections are thus particularly noteworthy for our purposes: the first is simply the level of support for the FN across France which was consistent with a steady increase in regional elections from 1986 to 1998. The second, more important aspect is that it created a situation known as '*triangulaires*' in a number of regions, in other words situations in which support for the FN was strong enough to rival support for the mainstream Left and the mainstream Right and in which therefore the FN was a potential alliance partner for the mainstream Right in the second round. In places where the electoral outcome was too close to call the mainstream Right might have been tempted to make a deal with the FN, promising seats for the FN on the regional council in exchange for the FN directing its first round supporters to vote for the mainstream Right in the second round. The choice was therefore between what was promptly depicted by the media as a 'pact with the devil' or a 'Republican front'. While much was made of the hesitation characterising certain politicians regarding this choice, two aspects of the situation were far more important. The first, and perhaps that which was truly responsible for the near-hysteria that gripped France in those few weeks, was the public's sentiment that the FN was able to set the political agenda, that what had begun as a 'tolerated', if not endorsed, form of political protest was moving beyond that and was plunging the legitimate, mainstream parties into chaos. More perversely perhaps, there was even a sense in which the FN was revealing a facet of mainstream politicians which many amongst the French public and analysts alike would have preferred to ignore: that they were indeed as malleable as ready to 'sell out' as the FN insisted they were.

But secondly, and more importantly for our purposes here, the situation of the *triangulaires* while it revealed a number of facts about the mainstream Right, was much more significant in terms of what it revealed about the FN, for it became quite apparent during the two weeks between the two rounds of the elections that opinions were divided within the FN as to whether the party should be pursuing this particular strategy. More specifically it became clear that while Mégret was the architect of what came to be known as the '*stratégiè de la main tendue*' (outreach strategy), Le Pen was far from convinced of its appropriateness and increasingly resentful of Mégret's readiness to dilute the FN platform in exchange for council seats. On this issue Le Pen's comments collected during an interview a few moths earlier in Brussels were that 'Bruno [Mégret] needs to learn that the FN can orchestrate a campaign without his help and be quite successful' and that the aim was not to govern at any cost but rather to preserve the integrity of the party.[43] In the days and weeks following the elections the full force of the disagreements between Le Pen and Mégret became increasingly public as a lukewarm Le Pen distanced himself from Mégret's public relations offensive.

With regard to our broader argument regarding a better understanding of the transformation of the FN and its persistence on the French political scene, a number of points can be made regarding this particular period. Firstly, as alluded to earlier in this section, the dynamic that played itself out in 1998 can be characterised as one of rally politics versus party politics. Where Le Pen continued to situate himself, and the identity of his party, on the periphery of the French political stage (in other words as an alternative to the ruling political elite), Mégret on the other hand saw himself as incarnating a 'new' FN, ready to govern in coalition, ready to enter into pacts and perhaps even ready to become more or less a part of the more mainstream Right (of

which he had been a part – in the Gaullist RPR – until his defection to
the FN in the mid-1980s). The words of Le Pen during these few
weeks were revealing of their radically different commitments and
visions of the party: where for Mégret the party was a vehicle, an
instrument designed to ensure participation in politics, for Le Pen the
aim of the party was the party itself – as rally. Mégret's reply that 'a
party is a political instrument, and when a instrument ceases to work
you change it' when he was asked about his views on the party
confirms the hypothesis that the two men had extremely different
views of the FN's function. Providing a context for rally politics in the
form of a contestatory populism defined Le Pen's commitment to the
party, whereas Mégret can be seen as having privileged the party politics – i.e. those dynamics which define a commitment to representation
and participation in the more pragmatic and procedural aspects of
democratic politics (precisely those aspects of democracy which a party
such as the FN is initially designed to contest).

Secondly, it is also clear that the juggling act between the two
drives or styles of politics became more pronounced as success
increased. Fifth Republican institutions create a structure of political
opportunity in which both drives need to be addressed and which privileges parties whose internal structure can handle the delicate juggling
act that this involves. So, while the institutionalisation of the rally
within the republic creates an opportunity for a party such as the FN,
creating incentives for the privileging of certain core ideological
concepts over others (for example populism over violence), it simultaneously generates pressures such as the pressure to find a balance
between rally politics and party politics or suffer the organisational
consequences. For parties whose forte lies not in compromise and
internal democratic debate this challenge is one that is not often met.

1998–99: and then there were two ...

The split within the FN can be read as the predictable failure of two
such different – though equally megalomaniac – political personalities
as Le Pen and Mégret to work together within the same rigid party
structure. But it is perhaps more accurate and interesting to see the
split as the resulting organisational consequence of the party's incapacity to maintain a balance between its populist rally politics and its more
pragmatic party politics (an understanding which does not nullify the
first but rather puts it into a broader context). Tensions at the heart of

the party had been apparent since as early as 1995, a year which for the FN marks the beginning of the rift between Le Pen and Mégret as Le Pen's 15 per cent score in the presidential elections is perceived by some in the party, including Mégret, as a disappointing score – proof that Le Pen's leadership was leading to stagnation rather than progression. Mégret's growing influence in the party is further evidenced by his wife's local victory in Vitrolles in February 1997 and the very public party struggles surrounding the FN's 1997 Strasbourg Congress,[44] while, as argued previously, Mégret's 1998 regional elections strategy further underlined his differences with Le Pen.

Thus far, the story is that of differences, disagreements and strained relations. However, April 1998 saw a sharp degenerating of the relationship between Le Pen and Mégret as a result of Le Pen's condemnation to two years ineligibility to run for elections as a result of a conviction for assault.[45] Le Pen's response to this is, shunning Mégret, to propose that his wife Jany take his place in all electoral contests thus provoking Mégret into publicly condemning this choice and putting himself forward instead.[46] Taking this as a counter-provocation, Le Pen immediately called for a 'deMégretisation' of the party and a new organisational blue-print for the party made up exclusively – aside from two names – of Le Pen supporters within the party. When everyone in the party thought that things were not likely to get much worse, Le Pen's ineligibility sentence was lightened thus allowing him to run both in the European elections of 1998 and the 2002 presidential elections. What should have simplified relations within the party had the opposite effect as Le Pen seized this opportunity to re-impose his authority over his organisation by threatening his internal enemies, wielding sanctions and humiliating detractors. This period of crisis is widely remembered by party workers and FN officials as one in which Le Pen's megalomania was unsurpassed. By the time of the national council meeting on 5 December 1998, the party was ripe for a split: during the meeting Le Pen's authority was repeatedly called into question and his leadership role undermined as the council degenerated into a brawl during which insults and blows were exchanged.[47] Following this meeting, Mégret, having secured the support of a number of key FN figures attempted to mount a leadership challenge against Le Pen by calling for an emergency party congress. Fully aware of Mégret's plot – and knowing perhaps that he would be powerless to stem a significant tide of discontent within the party – Le Pen categorically refused to call the congress and simply proceeded to exclude the 'guilty' members one by one from the organisation, finally formally expelling Mégret (whom he, by then, only referred to as 'Brutus'). Once expelled from the FN Mégret moved swiftly: on 23 January in Marignane he organised the first meeting of the dissident FN. This break-away FN, re-baptised *FN – mouvement national*, brought together a significant proportion of the FN's personnel and most of the FN's most influential and brilliant characters.

Le Pen's – and more broadly, the FN's – score in the 2002 elections can only be understood properly against the background of this long-brewing crisis and the resulting acrimonious split. Further, in terms of our argument concerning the role of Fifth Republican institutions, the split provides a useful illustration of the toll taken by institutions on political parties. The continued success of the party in the 2002 elections despite its serious internal crisis conversely illustrates the opportunities that persist despite the constraints imposed.

The 2002 elections

The 2002 presidential and legislative elections will no doubt be remembered for a number of things, but mainly for the post-first-round shock of finding Jean-Marie Le Pen as a second-round candidate. Contrary to all expectations and predictions, the presidential election witnessed the disqualification of the Left's main candidate by the rise of both the far Right and the far Left. The subsequent round gave a president once weakened by corruption scandals and the absence of a parliamentary majority the opportunity to be elected with a record 82 per cent of the vote and his party went on to claim an absolute majority of seats in the National Assembly a few weeks later. The paradox is that such upheaval took place in the context, and possibly as a result of, an uneventful period of cohabitation and an election campaign that had apparently bored the French population to unprecedented levels.

Much has been written on the reasons for Le Pen's unpredicted and unexpected presence in the second round – most commentators stress Lionel Jospin's (the incumbent prime minister) lack of media personality, point to the apparent impossibility of being perceived as *présidentiable* once one is prime minister in France given the lacklustre nature of the job, or blame the Left's multitude of break-away candidates. While all of these no doubt contributed to Le Pen's score, or, to the impact of his score, there are nevertheless two more puzzling and immediate questions: how did the FN, or Le Pen in particular, survive the crisis in the FN, the loss of a significant proportion of his party apparatus and supporters to the extent that his score in the presidential election had, not only matched, but increased as compared with the score in the 1995 elections (after all the 1999 European election scores suggested that both Le Pen and Mégret were now at the helm of insignificant parties)?[48] And why had political analysts, polling organisations and journalists been utterly unable to predict Le Pen's score and its consequences?

The answer to the first question, it seems, fits neatly with the symbolism of rally politics and with the populism that is granted a space within the Fifth Republic and characteristic of the FN. In fact, the answer is that while Mégret left the FN with some financial resources and significant personnel resources, Le Pen maintains his hold on the FN's symbolic capital. Where Mégret was seen to take with him the people associated with political savvy, expertise and intelligence (not least because of his association with the Right-wing think tank Le Club de l'horloge), as well as benefiting from a well-respected and vast network of contacts; Le Pen, on the other hand, was seen as retaining the truly devoted and trustworthy.[49]

In some respect Le Pen's constituency of FN faithful constituted a handicap for the FN – these supporters were seen to be lacking in intellectual credibility and strategic capacity, mainly thought of as men and women who are not 'political', but embody the volkish aspects of the FN, an aspect which Mégret never ceased to denounce and condemn as counter-productive. Yet, paradoxically, it is quite clear that the lack of political expertise and savvy, the less-than-stellar intellectual credentials constitute an important part of the function of the FN. As delineated earlier on, one of the FN's main platforms, in particular from the 1980s onwards, was its critique of day-to-day politics, their condemnation of a technocratic, emotionless politics which contributed to ordinary people's alienation from it, one of its main attractions was the promise of a politics that would be different from that proposed by professional politicians who were too intellectual, too removed from ordinary people to feel like them and speak like them. The split (while damaging because it made the FN look guilty of the sort of behaviour often condemned by the FN in other parties) nevertheless strengthened this particular aspect of the FN that remained Lepeniste. Le Pen was perceived as man of principles, unwilling to bend or sell out to the 'pros' in his party and prepared to suffer the consequences of a 'real fight'. Mégret might have consolidated his image as a political strategist, but Le Pen consolidated his image as a man of the people who stood by his people (and vice versa). This is one of the most likely reasons why Le Pen was able to regain so much political terrain between 1999 and 2002: despite a media black-out (having written him off, the French media were no longer interested in him), despite financial difficulties, Le Pen was seen by his supporters as coming out fighting despite this 'reversal of fortune'. Interestingly enough, until the 2002 campaign Le Pen accentuated the volkish aspects of the party: he deliberately espoused a style that was even more flamboyant in its humour, its propensity to break into song as well as relentless jokes and puns on the Mégret camp. In other words, Le Pen played the card of the 'ordinary man', capable of ordinary pleasures and ordinary talk. By 2002 he was once again ready to capitalise on the fidelity of the 'ordinary' voter. As Perrineau notes:

> [T]he implosion of a partisan organisation is one thing, the implosion of an electorate and the dwindling of the powerful springs that sustained its commitment is another. The hasty projecting of the first phenomenon upon the second led to an error of interpretation.[50]

Unlike the campaigns previously analysed here, the 2002 campaign was uncharacteristically subdued for Le Pen.

Le Pen launched his presidential campaign in his usual style: using his traditional 1 May speech to announce his intention to stand for election. He followed this traditional gesture by the no less traditional 'summer caravan', using this cross-national set of meetings to meet with FN supporters in informal holiday settings and staging impromptu gatherings, while the *Fête Bleu-Blanc-Rouge* of late September 2001 served to inaugurate the start of the campaign. Having kept up appearances and renewed with FN traditions thus far, this is where the similarities with previous campaigns stop. Following these three important events, Le Pen went on to stage a very different campaign to those previously undertaken.

The FN programme remained untouched and the contents of both manifestos and speeches were reminiscent of those of the 1995 campaign: hostility to Europe and, this time, the Euro, nationalism, immigration, law and order and an aggressively dynamic policy to redress the birth rate. Nothing new – in fact the pamphlet for the first round was eerily similar (down to the wording and layout) to the 1995 one.

The innovation came in the style of the campaign, a style which Le Pen seemed to have altered beyond recognition: subdued, calm, shying away from provocation: the image is one of the older politician who has been worn and 'rounded' by years of experience and by age. Where the press expected the usual bombastic routines and strident discourse, they found a more quietly humorous man willing to be photographed smoking an Arabic water-pipe in a notoriously racially mixed quarter of Paris or reciting a Verlaine poem set to rap music. 'I have not changed,' he said, 'I am still the same centre-Right man that I have always been.' The development of this character – the seemingly kinder, gentler Le Pen – is in part responsible for the media's misreading of the Le Pen threat: having grown used to Le Pen's style, the new style was taken as further evidence of the FN's decline and Le Pen's weakness as a candidate. Yet this was definitely to over-estimate the impact of the split on FN supporters. What the voters who had voted for him in the first round had clearly seen was something akin to the black-and-white picture which graced his second-round pamphlets in which he appears as a smiling older man, wearing a casual sailing sweater and expensively rugged watch. The result is a cross between a family photograph and a Rolex advert – quietly extolling the man with enough class and self-confidence to agree to an impromptu, almost intimate shot – wrinkles, receding hair-line and all. While the picture clearly was not enough to stem the tide in favour of Chirac, it did come across as the unveiling of another Le Pen: the photograph corresponded to the Le Pen whom traditional FN voters had continued to support, and whose effigy needed to be 'outed' in preparation for the second round. Paradoxically, this was the picture associated with the second half of the campaign which also saw Le Pen lose his newfound calm and revert to what many felt was a suicidally aggressive strategy.

All in all however, while the results of the presidentials were staggering for Le Pen's presence, the campaign itself was far from so.

For our purposes it is worth asking therefore what constituted the springs behind this unpredicted dynamic of support for the FN. In part, we can understand the continued support for Le Pen for the reasons outlined above: he was perceived as the leader of the far Right and had a powerful symbolic capital upon which he was able to draw. Secondly, it is clear that in terms of numbers the score was perhaps not so spectacular: there was an increase in support to the tune of an extra 150 000 extra votes for Le Pen in comparison to 1995, but it is arguable that Le Pen's presence in the second round had more to do with Jospin being a mere 200 000 votes short rather than a spectacular showing on the part of Le Pen. Nevertheless, the latter sheds some light on the effects of cohabitation in France and versions of coalition government in general. What is quite clear is that the long period of cohabitation, which inevitably gave the impression, if not of a happy partnership, certainly of a working partnership, played directly into the hands of Le Pen's populist rhetoric. What better way to illustrate the governing of the common people by a corrupt and collusive elite than to point to two sworn enemies managing to govern together? This is the sort of 'carve up' that serves as the basis of populist politics: an elite seemingly willing to make whatever compromise is necessary in order to remain in power and govern at the expense of the 'people'. Add to this the personalities of an 'intellectual' and a 'crook' and the balance is bound to shift – partly – in favour of the man perceived as able to transcend the politicking and reconnect with those who have been helplessly watching the double act from the sidelines. The cocktail is all the more explosive since policy failure in this context is interpreted as a double failure: 'two heads' and still no solution to what are perceived as the problems of day-to-day life. The context of cohabitation in France, coalition government in Austria, the politics of compromise and the Polder model in the Netherlands have all delivered stability and prosperity – they have also blurred cleavage-lines and can be held somewhat responsible for an increased willingness to vote for both extremes of the spectrum, but in particular for the populist options that seem to offer a 'different kind' of politics (in France the total votes for the far Right in the first round of the presidential elections was 19.2 per cent and for the far Left 10.4 per cent).

The scare provoked by Le Pen's vote, the collective dismay at the absence of a 'real' choice in the second round and the sense, however intuitive, that the past five years of cohabitation had led to this appalling result explains to a great extent both Chirac's artificially inflated support in the second round and the electorate's unwillingness to take any chances on another cohabitation during the legislative process.[51]

Finally however, it would seem that Le Pen's and the FN's 'success' in 2002 could be interpreted as the final adaptation of the FN to the Fifth Republican structure of political opportunity. What we have argued is that we see from the 1980s onward a transformation of the FN – an internal transformation which led it to abandon certain concepts and commitments constitutive of fascism as well as a transformation of its political campaigning style. We have tracked both of these transformations; with respect to the first, the party's internal commitments – in terms of party platform etc. – are highlighted. With respect to the second, we would argue that the transformation evolves in three stages: the first stage is one in which Le Pen still characterises himself as the outsider trying to get into the system; the second is a phase in 1995, where the notion of the 'outsider' has been abandoned and replaced with the idea that he is a politician with experience and but without a track record that might make him a professional/corrupt politician. The argument here is that 2002 represents the final stage in that in many ways, Le Pen takes a back seat to the dynamics imparted by the institutions and the institutionalisation of rally politics. One of the ways of characterising this is to say that while in the 1980s the situation is one of Le Pen attempting to gain entry into the system, in 1995 he is firmly within the system and more than ever able to contribute to the setting of the agenda. By 2002, one could argue that the dynamics of the Fifth Republic have as much adapted to the FN as the FN has adapted to the Fifth Republic. One could therefore go as far as to argue that given this symbiotic relationship, the phenomenon is destined to remain marginal in terms of actual political power but that the effects of this marginal phenomenon are far-reaching in institutional terms. In terms of rally politics and party politics, it is clear that the splintering of the first-round vote in France indicates a desertion by voters of what is being perceived as an overly procedural and pragmatic politics and the capacity of the FN to rally supporters despite heavy setbacks a couple of years prior to this is an indication of voters' readiness to privilege the rally elements of the republic. Even Chirac's victory can be interpreted as the result of the unexpected 're-rallification' of politics after the first round.

Notes

1 A version of a section of this chapter has appeared in chapter form under the title 'The other candidates: Voynet, Le Pen, de Villiers and Cheminade', in J. Gaffney and L. Milne, eds, *French Presidentialism* (Aldershot: Ashgate, 1997), pp. 135–64.
2 J. M. Le Pen, 'J'appelle la France à combattre le déclin, la décadence et la servitude', *National Hebdo* (12 November 1987).
3 J. M. Le Pen, 1995 presidential election campaign flyer.
4 Le Pen, 'Déstabiliser l'établissement', *Identité* (January 1990).
5 Le Pen, *Français d'abord*, 302 (July 1999), p. 3.
6 Le Pen first organised these 'caravanes' in the 1950s and 1960s. The first was for *L'Algérie française* in 1957, the second for the Tixier-Vignancourt campaign in 1965. He then began to organise them again in 1987 for example for his presidential campaign and the party has since then had recourse to them several times.
7 Le Pen's discourse and style of politics have been well researched and documented. The reader is referred to Catherine Fieschi, 'The discourse

of ambiguity', in H. Drake and J. Gaffney, eds, *The Language of Leadership in Contemporary France* (Aldershot: Dartmouth, 1996), pp. 107–32; M. Souchard, S. Wahnich, I. Cuminal and V. Wathier, *Le Pen. Les mots* (Paris: Le Monde Editions, 1997); P. A. Taguieff, 'La métaphysique de Jean Marie Le Pen', in P. Perrineau and N. Mayer, eds, *Le Front national à découvert*, second edition (Paris: Presses de Sciences Po, 1996), pp. 173–94; Christophe Hameau, *La campagne de Jean-Marie Le Pen pour l'élection présidentielle de 1998* (Université de Paris II, Travaux et recherches Panthéon-Assas, 1992).

8 SOFRES poll conducted 1 and 2 April 1988, cited by J. Jaffré in 'Le Pen ou le vote exutoire', *Le Monde* (12 April 1988).

9 Pierre Bréchon for example, describes the vote for the FN as a 'social protest vote' ('un vote de protestation sociale') in his article 'Qui choisit le Front National?', *Etudes*, 1 (January 1992), 47.

10 The extreme Right's previous public achievement had been the 4.3 per cent polled by Jean-Louis Tixier-Vignancourt in the 1965 presidential election.

11 P. Milza, 'Le Front National: droite extrême ou national-populisme?, in J-F. Sirinelli, ed., *Histoire des droites en France, Vol. 1* (Paris: NRF Gallimard, 1992), pp. 691–7.

12 Le Pen had been involved in coordinating Tixier-Vignancourt's campaign for the 1965 presidential elections. More particularly he had been directly responsible for the organisation of the *comités Tixier-Vignancourt*, TV's campaign support network.

13 When the *comités TV* disappeared they gave rise to two subsequent movements which are responsible for the political training of several personalities who then went on to belong to the FN. One movement was the *Alliance républicaine pour les libertés et le progrès* (ARLP) and the other was the *Mouvement jeune révolution* (MJR).

14 Members of the defunct ON massively converted to Giscardisme and supported his campaign for the 1974 elections.

15 Duprat's ideology was a mix of national socialism and propositions drawn from the Italian Fascist theoretician Julius Evola. His relentless anti-Semitism and the populist anti-capitalism of his discourse in the tradition of Edouard Drumont were reminiscent of the late-nineteenth-century anti-Jewish leagues.

16 J. Y. Camus, 'Origine et formation du Front national', in Perrineau and Mayer, eds, *Le Front national*, pp. 17–36.

17 These groups were groups such as *Devenir Européen* (based in Nantes), *Peuple et nation* (based in Lyon), the *Centre de Documentation Politique et Universitaire/CDPU* (Based in Aix-en-Provence) and of course the *Groupes nationalistes révolutionnaires* founded by Duprat. The *Front national jeunesse* was also founded at the same time with the help of the avowedly neo-nazi *Action Européenne* and the contributions of *Jeunesse d'Action Européenne*.

18 This is a little-known fact and yet the alliances were concluded in three medium-sized cities: Courbevoie on the outskirts of Paris, Merignac on the outskirts of Bordeaux and Villefrance-sur-mer in the south.

19 This is a point which Le Pen often makes. Interviews with the author.

20 The view that democratic values and the discourse associated with them
    were understood by Le Pen as nothing more than instruments in gaining
    electoral strength was even supported by Le Pen's ex-wife Pierrette who
    candidly admitted to the French weekly *L'événement du jeudi* that 'He
    thinks that authoritarian regimes are more efficient. Democratic regimes,
    he thinks that's just something you have to put up with for a while' (28
    March 1985).

21 The latter also points to the fact that Le Pen's feigned conversion to
    democracy and his endorsement of the republican framework should also
    be seen as part of a wider movement begun as early as 1962 by Europe-
    Action and followed by the rest of what was to be known as the French
    New Right, and which consisted in 'combat through wits and ideas rather
    than through force'. Thus spoke Dominique Venner, leader of Europe-
    Action, in *Défense de l'Occident* (26 November 1962), 46–52.

22 Some accused Le Pen of being a wolf in sheep's clothing and of harbour-
    ing authoritarian tendencies behind a veil of democratic discourse. Others,
    such as French historian and political scientist René Rémond – go as far
    as to wonder whether one could apply the 'extreme Right' label to an
    organisation 'whose relatively moderate and legalistic character would
    prevent one from associating it with the counter-revolutionary tradition
    and the agitation of the Leagues', cited in Milza, 'Le Front National',
    pp. 699–700.

23 This strategy, which forced commentators and adversaries of Le Pen to
    seek new lines of inquiry into the FN phenomenon and new ways of
    countering its brand of racism and radicalism, in no way diminishes the
    threat a figure such as Le Pen posed for the democratic process – quite the
    opposite. As Milza writes 'Strident anti-parliamentarianism and direct
    action can constitute some of the hallmarks of related organisations, but
    they do not exclude the presence of legalistic currents that are temporar-
    ily ready to play the parliamentary game for tactical reasons ... With
    regard to the FN as it stands today, and while we struggle to pinpoint the
    subtle difference between the extreme Right and the extremes of the
    Right, let us keep in mind that the leagues of the 1930s pale in compari-
    son with the activism of the FN's origins, the clearly expressed tactical
    choices of its founders who established that the FN was to camouflage its
    true colours and its consistently and resolutely anti-system discourse.
    Finally let us keep in mind its verbal violence which, in terms of the
    critique of the party system, of its xenophobia, of the denunciation of
    cosmopolitanism and its designation of minorities in more or less coded
    manner is again no tamer than that which we find in other explicitly
    extremist movements and parties of the inter-war years.' Milza, 'Le Front
    National', pp. 699–700.

24 On Le Pen's strategy of credibility and respectability between 1974 and
    1988 see specifically section II, part A/1 'Le vent en poupe: une stratégie
    prometteuse de crédibilisation et de respectabilisation' in Hameau, *La
    campagne*, pp. 55–66.

25 See in particular the article entitled 'Le Pen, un Reagan français?' in
    National Hebdo (13 June 1984).

26 On this see G. Birenbaum, 'Front national: les mutations d'un groupus-cule', *Intervention*, 15 (January–March 1986), 25–32.

27 G. Birenbaum and B. François, 'Unité et diversité des dirigeants fron-tistes', in Perrineau and Mayer, eds, *Le Front national*, p. 86.

28 For a discussion of this and other gaffes and their implications and conse-quences for the 1988 campaign see Hameau, *La campagne*, in particular annex 13.

29 See C. Fieschi, 'Jean Marie le Pen', pp. 107–32.

30 This was reminiscent of what in 1988 was dubbed the '*tournée des plages*' (the beach tour) which saw Le Pen on a summer campaign tour of major French beaches making the most of the opportunity to chat with locals and tourists.

31 J. M. Le Pen, *Appel aux Français*, 1995 presidential campaign flyer *Le Pen président* (Saint-Cloud: Publications du Front National, 1995).

32 On this occasion, Le Pen made specific reference to the desecration of a Jewish cemetery in Carpentras in 1990 of which Le Pen supporters had been hastily accused and which turned out to have been carried out by a gang of bored teenagers not even remotely associated with the FN. The accusation had been made in haste and far too pointedly for Le Pen not to seize the opportunity to masquerade as scape-goat and martyr. On Le Pen's declaration about the two murders, see Renaud Dely 'Le Pen se place dans l'opposition', *L'événement du jeudi* (8 May 1995), 11.

33 See Le Pen's inflamed reply on *La France en direct* (France 2 Television, 13 March 1995).

34 It is interesting to compare Le Pen's self-control with Chirac's who was incessantly portrayed in satirical television programmes as having the choice between keeping quiet or risking another gaffe; Chirac's puppet was thus constantly seen clasping his hands over his mouth and repeating mantra-like statements in an attempt to keep his cool and avoid costly slips of the tongue.

35 Robert Schneider, 'Qu'est-ce qui fait monter Le Pen ...' interview with Pascal Perrineau, *Le Nouvel Observateur* (6 April 1995), 30–1.

36 *La France en direct* (France 2 Television, 13 March 1995); *Face à la une* (TF1 Television, 23 March 1995). See also Le Pen's *Appel au Français* 1995 presidential campaign flyer.

37 Hameau, *La campagne*, p. 101.

38 R. Schneider, 'Qu'est ce qui fait ...?', 31.

39 R. Schneider, 'Qu'est ce qui fait ...?', 31.

40 Hervé Le Bras, interview in *Le Monde* (14–15 May 1995).

41 Hervé Le Bras, *Le Monde*.

42 C. Fieschi, 'Rally politics and political organization: an institutionalist perspective on the French far right', *Modern and Contemporary France*, 8: 1 (February 2000), 71–89.

43 Le Pen, interview with the author, Brussels, 4 November 1997.

44 Two aspects of the 1997 congress were remarkable – the first was the cross-national mobilisation against it. Bus-loads of protesters descended upon Strasbourg to protest against the FN and, indeed, the city's Socialist mayor Catherine Trautmann encouraged the city's inhabitants to mobilise against the Le Pen's party. The second remarkable aspect was the obvious

internal strife within the FN regarding Le Pen's possible successor. To observers at the time, the contest was between Bruno Mégret, seen as the party strategist, and Bruno Gollnisch, perceived as the faithful lieutenant. Le Pen was at pains to stress that no succession plan was under way. He famously remarked that the FN 'only has one leader and that is me'. The congress was nevertheless followed by an internal restructuring of the party, designed in great part to avoid the creation of an easily designated heir to the leadership.

45 Le Pen's condemnation was for physically assaulting a Socialist deputy in Mantes-la-Jolie in May 1997.

46 B. Mégret 'La candidature de Jany Le Pen n'est pas une bonne idee', *Le Parisien* (24 August 1998).

47 The best, and perhaps most entertaining, account of this meeting is to be found in R. Dely, *Histoire secrète du Front national* (Paris: Grasset, 1999), pp. 256–69.

48 In the European elections of 1999, Le Pen's FN scored 5.69 per cent of the vote (five seats) and Mégret's FN-MN scored 3.28 per cent and no seats.

49 This is underscored by V. Rillardon, 'Front contre Front', *Modern and Contemporary France*, 8: 1 (2000), 99–102.

50 P. Perrineau, 'La surprise Lepeniste et sa suite legislative', in P. Perrineau and C. Ysmal, eds, *Le Vote de Tout les Refus* (Paris: Presses de Science Po., 2003), pp. 199–222.

51 Once Chirac was elected president therefore, it seemed the only campaign available was one against cohabitation: the French electorate drew lessons from the presidential election and reluctantly dragged itself to the polling booths to give the President a clear majority in the Assembly.

Conclusion

The counter-revolutionary inheritance of the FN would have never allowed it to evolve into the national party which it is today. What has allowed the party to profoundly modify the topography of the French Right (regardless of its internal disarray), is its ability to draw on the rally politics of populism.

Under the guidance and leadership of Jean-Marie Le Pen, the FN has moved from a party governed by fascists, whose concerted anti-parliamentarianism was often and stridently affirmed, to a party whose allegiance to democracy may well be circumstantial but is nevertheless a working allegiance which – tactically or not – is embodied in the manifestos it puts forth.

It can be argued that Fifth Republican France pushes all political parties to embrace the rally drive – those parties that are fundamentally defined by this drive rather than by the duality of the rally and the party, will therefore find it easier, at least in the medium term, to find a niche. One of the results of presidentialism in France is to make parties more aware of the rally politics tradition which has always been at play there; this rallying to rally politics means that to some extent all political parties, by converting to a presidential form of politics, will use the resources of populist politics. It is the institutionalisation of rally politics and presidentialism which makes French Fifth Republican politics so easily permeable to populism – of the Left but even more so, of the Right.

This book's main conclusion is that the *Front national*'s success should be understood as the results of the party's capacity to draw on the institutional changes brought in by the Fifth Republic (and in particular the presidentialisation of French politics). In order to benefit from this new structure of political opportunities, the FN privileged one of its ideological components – populism – and marginalised the others, in order to exploit the institutionalisation of rally politics in France. A first set of set remarks should serve as an overview of the book's main arguments.

The arguments revisited

This book has established, firstly, that while theories of political opportunity structures are useful to understand the opportunities and constraints with which political actors are faced in a given institutional and political context, such theories might benefit from more refined definitions of institutions such as those put forward by neo-institutionalist approaches. In particular, historical institutionalism – with its emphasis on history and practice – was shown to establish a definition of institutions which allowed for a appropriate understanding of the role and impact of political institutions. As an institution, the French presidency's political effects (presidentialism) presented a useful set of political opportunities for movements or parties such as the FN by giving rise to a presidentialism that allowed for the reconciliation of two opposing drives in liberal democracies, the rally drive and the party drive.

Until the Fifth Republic, rally politics in France were condemned to exist either alongside normal politics, or emerge in times of crisis. The Fifth Republic's reconciliation of these two drives through a presidential system meant that rally politics for, better or for worse, was integrated into French politics.

Second, the project has illustrated the links between institutional arrangements and ideologies through an examination of fascism in France. While France did not produce a fascist regime, fascism's role and impact (if not as a regime but as a party-political and cultural option) in France should not be under-estimated.

Finally, we have shown that the latent populism of the FN (part of its original fascist core) benefited from the institutionalisation of rally politics. The FN moved away from its fascist roots, and toward an espousal of populism more conducive to a measure of success within the political institutions of the Fifth Republic.

Two further sets of conclusions can be drawn here. The first concern the FN as a political phenomenon; the second the methodology adopted for this project.

Political conclusions

The break-up of the FN (over the months of December 1998 and January 1999) – which seemed to signal the end of the party's more marked and mainstream success – has been pinned on the inherent instability of far-Right movements, because these movements harbour deep ideological divisions. This could well be true but the effects of ideological division were still played out within the opportunities and constraints associated with Fifth Republican political institutions.

The institutions of the Fifth Republic exacerbate rivalries for *présidentiables*. This competition takes its toll more heavily on parties in which leadership contests are not resolved, thus more often in parties in which deep ideological divisions persist and give rise to organisational instability. This is the main reason for which ideological divergences should not be under-estimated, not simply because they exist as divergences but because far-Right parties, while to some extent more intrinsically unstable than others for the reasons mentioned above, are placed in a context in which mainstream parties are subject to the same sets of exogenous pressures, pressures which (as revealed by the fortunes of most mainstream French parties) render all parties organisationally fragile.

Le Pen was able to turn an extremist movement into a populist rally and was granted – unlike Poujade – more scope to do so. Unlike Poujade's UDCA, the FN was therefore able to make a lasting impact on the French political scene and to participate in – if not set the agenda for – French politics for two decades. But while the Fifth Republic has succeeded in institutionalising the dual party and rally drives, the FN had not succeeded in achieving this balance within its party organisation. This tension within the party contributed to its fragmentation. Mégret's technocratic style, his insistence on an alliance strategy with the mainstream Right (particularly during the regional elections of 1998), the importance placed on conquering municipalities and his procedural approach to the party's organisation, all suggest a privileging of the party drive. It goes almost without saying that Le Pen's quasi-caricatural opposition to Mégret reveals his unsurprising commitment to the rally aspects of the FN. Given the circumstances of cohabitation and the remaining cloud of accusations of corruption over Chirac, it is hardly surprising that the FN (as well as options on the far Left) held some appeal for a somewhat disgruntled and bored electorate. The consequences of these results largely confirm what has been abundantly clear for years, namely that Le Pen does well in

presidential elections; that the FN does less well – though not cata-
strophically badly – in legislative contests; and that while anywhere
between 10 and 15 per cent of the French public is willing to cast a
vote for Le Pen, ultimately it is not ready to grant him any real governmental power.

What is most interesting from the point of view of the French case
is that it illustrates the impact of those largely 'unintended' – to use
March and Olsen's expression – consequences of institutional design as
well as institutions' power to impart a long-term, path-dependent logic
to the actions of political actors.

Methodological and theoretical conclusions

Neo-institutionalist theories in conjunction with theories of political
opportunity structures allow the researcher to view institutions as both
constraints and opportunities. Such a view of Fifth Republican institutions does much to shed light on the success of the FN as well as its
recent setbacks. For our purposes three points are noteworthy.

First, while the well-documented history of the French far Right
leaves no doubt as to the fact that French political culture provides a
hospitable context for the FN's ideological stance, the re-integration of
the FN into a broader institutionalist and comparative analysis is
important. The Fifth Republic's institutional framework has had a
dramatic impact on the domestication of the rally drive in France. The
presidentialisation of the regime has allowed for the constitutional and
institutional expression of the rally drive and thus for the integration
into French politics (and more importantly French government) of a
form of personalism which had been (unsuccessfully) marginalised
since the Revolution of 1789, and even more so since 1870. These
changes facilitated the entry into French politics of a rally party such as
the FN at a time when far-Right ideas were marginalised.

The second important point is that the institutionalisation of rally
politics appeals to an ingrained tendency in French politics to bypass
parties in favour of a version of Republicanism rooted in the
Rousseauist conception of the General Will. The Fifth Republic did
not simply create a political space structured by the duality of the rally
and party drives; it created the possibility of a third type of power
which can be considered a version – the French version – or the
outcome of the dialectical tension between the two drives.

Finally, a historical institutionalist conception of institutions is more conducive to a dynamic understanding of politics and the political process. The real potential of historical institutionalism remains largely untapped. Altering this state of affairs will depend upon addressing the role of ideas in institutional formation and political change, and the impact of institutions on ideational and ideological development and adaptation. This book has hopefully contributed to this endeavour.

Bibliography

Adamson, W. 1975. *Avant-garde Florence*. Cambridge, MA: Harvard University Press.

Adorno, T. 1950. *The Authoritarian Personality*. New York, NY: Harper Studies in Prejudice.

Almond, G. 1988. 'The return to the state', *American Political Science Review*, 82: 2, 853–74.

Altemeyer, B. 1996. *The Authoritarian Specter*. Cambridge, MA: Harvard University Press.

Amenta, E. and Y. Zylan. 1995. 'It happened here: political opportunity, the new institutionalism and the Townsend movement', in S. M. Lyman, ed., *Social Movements, Critiques, Concepts, Case-Studies*. London: Macmillan, pp. 199–233.

Apter, D. E., ed. 1964. *Ideology and Discontent*. New York, NY: Collier Macmillan.

Aristotle. 1962. *The Politics*. Translated by T. H. Sinclair. London: Penguin Classics.

Baechler, J. 1976. *Qu'est-ce que l'idéologie?* Paris: Gallimard.

Bardèche, M. 1948. *Nuremberg ou la terre promise*. Paris: Sept Couleurs.

Barrès, M. 1966. *Le culte du moi*. Paris: Livre de Poche.

Barrès, M. 1959. *Du sang, de la voplupté et de la mort*. Paris: Plon.

Barrès, M. *Mes cahiers. Vol. 2*. Paris: Plon.

Barrès, M. *Scènes et doctrines du nationalisme*. Paris: Editions Felix Juven.

Bartolini, S. and S. Mair. 1990. *Identity, Competition and Electoral Availability: The Stabilisation of European Electorates, 1885–1985*. Cambridge: Cambridge University Press.

Beetham, D. 1993. 'In defence of legitimacy', *Political Studies*, XLI: 3, 488–91.

Beetham, D. 1991. *The Legitimation of Power*. London: Macmillan.

Berger, P. and T. Luckmann. 1966. *The Social Construction of Reality*. New York, NY: Anchor Books.

Berstein, S. and O. Rudelle, eds. 1992. *Le modèle Républicain*. Paris: PUF.

Berstein, S. and P. Milza. 1991. *Histoire de la France au XXème. siècle – 1945–1958*. Paris: Editions Complexes.

Betz, H. G. and S. Immerfall, eds. 1998. *The New Politics of the Right: Neo-populist Parties and Movements in Established Democracies.* London: Macmillan.

Betz, H. G. 1994. *Radical Right-Wing Populism in Western Europe.* New York, NY: St. Martin's Press.

Betz, H. G. 1993. 'The new politics of resentment: radical right-wing populist parties in Western Europe', *Comparative Politics*, 25: 4, 413–27.

Bihr, A. 1992. *Pour en finir avec le Front national.* Paris: Syros.

Birenbaum, G. and B. François. 1996. 'Unité et diversité des dirigeants frontistes', in P. Perrineau and N. Mayer, eds, *Le Front national à découvert*, second edition. Paris: Presses de Science Po, pp. 83–106.

Birenbaum, G. 1992. *Le Front national en politique.* Paris: Balland.

Birenbaum, G. 1986. 'Front national: les mutations d'un groupuscule', *Intervention*, 15 (January–March), 25–32.

Blinkhorn, M. 1990. *Fascists and Conservatives.* London: Unwin.

Blot, Y. 1985. *Les racines de la liberté.* Paris: Albin Michel.

Borne, D. 1977. *Petits bourgeois en révolte? Le mouvement Poujade.* Paris: Flammarion.

Bréchon, P. and S. Kumar Mitra. 1992. 'The National Front in France: the emergence of an extreme right protest movement', *Comparative Politics*, 25 (October), 63–82.

Bréchon, P. 1992. 'Qui choisit le Front National?', *Etudes*, 1 (January), 41–50.

Burrin, P. 1992. 'Le fascisme', in J. F. Sirinelli ed., *Histoire des droites en France, Vol. 1.* Paris: Gallimard, pp. 603–52.

Burrin, P. 1986. *La dérive fasciste.* Paris: Seuil.

Cameron, D. 1984. 'Social democracy, coporatism, labor quiesence and the representation of economic interests in advanced capitalist society', in J. Goldthorpe, ed., *Order and Conflict in Contemporary Capitalism.* Oxford: Clarendon Press, pp. 143–78.

Cameron, D. and R. Hofferbert. 1973. 'Continuity and change in Gaullism: the General's legacy', *American Journal of Political Science*, 17: 1, 78–83.

Cameron, D. 1972. 'Stability and change in patterns of French partisanship', *Public Opinion Quarterly*, 36 (Spring), 19–30.

Cammack, P. 1992. 'The new institutionalism: predatory rule, institutional persistence and macro-social change', *Economy and Society*, 21 (November), 397–429.

Campbell, J. 1998. 'Institutional analysis and the role of ideas in political economy', *Theory and Society*, 27, 377–409.

Campbell, P. 1957. 'Le Mouvement Poujade', *Parliamentary Affairs*, 10: 3, 362–65.

Camus, J. Y. 1996. 'Origine et formation du Front national', in P. Perrineau and N. Mayer, eds, *Le Front national à découvert*, second edition. Paris: Presses de Sciences Po, pp. 17–36.

Canovan, M. 1999. 'Trust the people! Populism and the two faces of democracy', *Political Studies*, 47: 1, 2–16.

Canovan, M. 1981. *Populism.* London: Junction Books.

Cerny, P. 1982. 'Non-terrorism and the politics of repressive tolerance', in P. Cerny, ed., *Social Movements and Protest in France.* London: Frances Pinter.

Chebel D'Appolonia, A. 1988. *L'extrême droite en France de Maurras à Le Pen*. Paris: Editions Complexes.

Chiarani, R. 1995. 'The Italian far right', in L. Cheles, R. Ferguson and M. Vaughan, eds, *The Far Right in Western Europe*. London: Longman.

Codreanu, C. 1995. 'The programme of the iron guard', in *Die eiserne Garde*. Berlin: Brunnen Verlag, 1940.

Coste-Floret. 1946. *Journal Officiel*, 20 August, p. 3185.

Crewe, I. and D. Denver. 1985. *Electoral Change in Western Democracies: Patterns and Sources of Electoral Volatility*. London: Croom Helm.

Crouch, C. and A. Pizzorno. 1978. *The Resurgence of Class Conflict in Western Europe Since 1968*. London: Macmillan.

Crozier, M. 1970. *La société bloquée*. Paris: Seuil, p. 95.

Daalder, H. 1993. 'The comparative study of European party systems: an overview', in H. Daalder and P. Mair, eds, *Western European Party Systems, Continuity and Change*. London: Sage, pp. 1–27.

Dahl, R. 1961. *Who Governs? Democracy and Power in an American City*. New Haven, CT: Yale University Press.

Dalton, R. J. and M. Kuechler. 1990. *Challenging the Political Order: New Social and Political Movements in Western Democracies*. Cambridge: Polity Press.

De Felice, R. 1977. *Interpretations of Fascism*. Cambridge, MA: Harvard University Press.

De Gaulle, 1970. *Discours et messages, Vol. 1. Pendant la guerre, juin 1940-janvier1946*. Paris: Plon.

De Gaulle, 1970. *Discours et messages, Vol. II. Dans l'attente, février 1946-avril 1958*. Paris: Plon.

Debré, M. 1981. 'The constitution of 1958: its raison d'etre and how it evolved', in W. G. Andrews and S. Hoffmann, eds, *The Impact of the Fifth Republic on France*. New York, NY: SUNY Press.

Declair, E. G. 1999. *Politics on the Fringe: The People, Policies and Organisation of the French National Front*. Durham and London: Duke University Press.

Dely, R. 1999. *Histoire secrète du Front national*. Paris: Grasset, pp. 256–69.

Dely, R. 1995. 'Le Pen se place dans l'opposition', *L'événement du jeudi* (8 May), 11.

Diani, M. 1992. 'The concept of social movement', *The Sociological Review*, 40: 1, pp. 1–25.

Downs, A. 1957. *An Economic Theory of Democracy*. New York, NY: Harper and Row.

Duhamel, O. 1980. *La gauche et la Vème République*. Paris: PUF.

Duverger, M. 1980. 'A new political system model: semi-presidential government', *European Journal of Political Research*, 8, 165–87.

Duverger, M. 1951. *Les partis politiques*. Paris: Arnand Colin. Translated into English and published by Methuen, London, 1954.

Duyvendak, J. W. 1994. *Le poids du politique: nouveaux mouvements sociaux en France*. Paris: L'Harmattan.

Duyvendak, J. W. 1993. 'Une communauté homosexuelle en France et aux Pays-Bas; de blocs, tribus et liens', *Sociétés*, 39, 75–81.

Eagleton, T. 1991. *Ideology*. London: Verso.

Eatwell, R. 1998. 'The drive toward synthesis', in R. Griffin, ed., *International Fascism*. London: Arnold, pp. 189–203.

Eatwell, R. 1996. 'On defining the fascist minimum: the centrality of ideology', *Journal of Political Ideologies*, 1: 3, 303–19.

Eatwell, R. 1995. 'Toward a new model of generic fascism', *Journal of Theoretical Politics*, 4: 2, 174–85.

Eatwell, R. 1993. 'Ideologies: approaches and trends', in R. Eatwell and A. Wright, eds, *Contemporary Political Ideologies*. London: Frances Pinter, pp. 1–22.

Eisinger, P. 1973. 'The conditions of protest behavior in American cities', *American Political Science Review*, 67, 11–28.

Elgie, R. 1996. *Electing the French President: The 1995 Presidential Election*. London: Macmillan.

Errson, S. and J. E. Lane. 1982. 'Democratic party systems in Europe; change and stability', *Scandinavian Political Studies*, 5: 1, 67–96.

Eysenck, H. J. 1954. *The Psychology of Politics*. Baltimore, MD: Baltimore University Park Press.

Fieschi, C. 2000. 'Rally politics and political organization: an institutionalist perspective on the French far right', *Modern and Contemporary France*, 8: 1 (February), 71–89.

Fieschi, C. 1997. 'The other candidates: Voynet, Le Pen, de Villiers and Cheminade', in J. Gaffney and L. Milne, eds, *French Presidentialism and the Election of 1995*. Aldershot: Ashgate, pp. 135–64.

Fieschi, C. 1996. 'Jean Marie Le Pen and the discourse of ambiguity', in H. Drake and J. Gaffney, eds, *The Language of Leadership in Contemporary France*. Aldershot: Dartmouth, pp. 107–32.

Flanagan, S. C. 1984. 'Patterns of realignment', *Electoral Change in Advanced Industrial Democracies*. Princeton: NJ: Princeton University Press, pp. 95–103.

France, P. M. 1976. *La vérité guidait leur pas*. Paris: Gallimard.

Freeden, M. 1998. *Ideologies and Political Theory: A Conceptual Approach*. Oxford: Oxford University Press.

Freeden, M. 1994. 'Political concepts and ideological morphology', *Journal of Political Philosophy*, 2, 140–64.

Gaffney, J. and L. Milne, eds. 1997. *French Presidentialism and the Election of 1995*. Aldershot: Dartmouth.

Gaffney, J. 1989. *The French Left and the Fifth Republic: The Discourses of Communism and Socialism in Contemporary France*. London: Macmillan.

Gaffney, J. 1989. 'Introduction: French presidentialism and the Fifth Republic', in J. Gaffney, ed., *The French Presidential Elections of 1988*. Aldershot: Dartmouth.

Gentile, E. 1975. *Le origini dell'ideologìa Fascista*. Roma: Laterza.

Gentile, G. 1925. *Che cosa è il fascismo*. Florence: Valecchi.

Gergen, K. J. and K. E. Davis. 1985. *The Social Construction of the Person*. New York, NY: Springer-Verlag.

Giddens, A. 1971. *Capitalism and Modern Social Theory: An Analysis of the Writings of Marx, Durkheim and Max Weber*. Cambridge: Cambridge University Press.

Girardet, R. 1983. *Le nationalisme Français. Anthologie, 1871–1914.* Paris: Seuil.

Giurati, G. 1931. 'I giovani e il partito', *Gioventù Fascista*, 1: 6, 3.

Goguel, F. 1957. *Géographie des élections du 2 janvier 1956.* Cahiers de la Fondation nationale des sciences politiques, n. 82, Paris: Armand Colin.

Goldstone, J. 1998. 'Initial conditions, general laws, path dependence, and explanation in historical sociology', *American Journal of Sociology*, 104: 3, 829–45.

Gourevitch, P. 1986. *Politics in Hard Times.* Ithaca, NY: Cornell University Press.

Graham, B. D. 1993. *Representation and Party Politics.* Oxford: Blackwell.

Gregor, A. J. 1974. *Interpretations of Fascism.* Morristown, NJ: General Learning Press.

Griffin, R., ed. 1998. *International Fascism.* London: Arnold.

Griffin, R. 1996. 'The 'post-Fascism' of the Alleanza Nazionale: a case study in ideological morphology', *Journal of Political Ideologies*, 1: 2, 123–45.

Griffin, R., ed. 1995. *Fascism.* Oxford: Oxford University Press.

Griffin, R. 1993. *The Nature of Fascism.* London: Routledge.

Gurr, T. 1970. *Why Men Rebel.* Princeton, N.J.: Princeton University Press.

Haas, P. 1992. 'Introduction: epistemic communities and international policy coordination', *International Organization*, 46, 1–35.

Hagopian, F. 1990. 'Democracy by undemocratic means? Elites, politial pacts and regime transitions in Brazil', *Comparative Political Studies*, 23: 2, 144–70.

Hall, P. 1993. 'Policy paradigms, social learning and the state: the case of economic policy-making in Britain', *Comparative Politics*, 25: 3, 175–96.

Hall, P. 1992. 'The movement from Keynesianism to monetarism: institutional analysis and British economic policy in the 1970s', in S. Steinmo *et al.*, eds, *Structuring Politics: Historical Institutionalism in Comparative Analysis.* Cambridge: Cambridge University Press, pp. 90–113.

Hall, P. 1989. 'Conclusion: the politics of Keynesian ideas', in P. Hall, ed., *The Political Power of Economic Ideas.* Princeton, NJ: Princeton University Press, pp. 361–91.

Hall, P. 1986. *Governing the Economy: The Politics of State Intervention in Britain and France.* New York, NY and Oxford: Oxford University Press, p. 19.

Hall, P. and R. Taylor. 1998. 'The potential of historical institutionalism: a response to Hay and Wincott', *Political Studies*, 46: 5 (December), 958–62.

Hall, P. and R. Taylor. 1996. 'Political science and the three new institutionalisms', *Political Studies*, 44: 5, 936–57.

Hameau, C. 1992. *La campagne de Jean-Marie Le Pen pour l'élection présidentielle de 1988.* Université de Paris II, Travaux et recherches Panthéon-Assas.

Hamilton, M.B. 1987. 'The elements of the concept of ideology', *Political Studies*, 25, 18–38.

Hartley, E. L. 1946. *Problems in Prejudice.* New York: King's Crown Press.

Hay, C. 1998. '"Punctuated evolution" and the uneven temporality of institutional change: the "crisis" of Keynesianism and the rise of neo-liberalism in Britain'. Paper presented to the *Eleventh Conference of Europeanists*, Baltimore, 26–28 February.

Hay, C. and D. Wincott. 1998. 'Structure, agency and historical institutionalism', *Political Studies*, 46: 5 (December), 951–7.

Hayward, J. 1993. 'From republican sovereign to partisan statesman,' in J. Hayward, ed., *De Gaulle to Mitterrand: Presidential Power in France*. London: Hurst and Company, pp. 1–35.

Hayward, J. 1983. *Governing France: The One and Indivisible Republic*, second edition. London: Weidenfeld and Nicholson, pp. 23–4.

Hazareesingh, S. 1994. *Political Traditions in Modern France*. Oxford: Oxford University Press.

Hoffmann, S. 1967. 'Heroic leadership: the case of Modern France', in L. J. Edinger, ed., *Political Leadership in Industrial Societies: Studies in Comparative Analysis*. New York, NY: Wiley, pp. 253–74.

Hoffmann, S. 1967. 'Le héros politique: Pétain, De Gaulle, Mendès-France', part I, *Preuves* (June), 25–45; Part II, *Preuves* (July), 286–93.

Hoffmann, S. 1956. *Le Mouvement Poujade, Cahiers de la fondation nationale des sciences politiques*. Paris: Presses de la fondation nationale des sciences politiques.

Ignazi, P. 1996. 'Un nouvel acteur politique', in P. Perrineau and N. Mayer, eds, *Le Front national à découvert*, second edition. Paris: Presses de Science Po, pp. 63–80.

Ignazi, P. 1995. *Postfascisti?* Bologna: Il Mulino.

Ignazi, P. 1992. 'The silent counter-revolution: hypotheses on the emergence of extreme right-wing parties in Europe', *European Journal of Political Research*, 22, 3–34.

Ignazi, P. 1992. 'New and old extreme right parties: the French Front national and the Italian Movimento Sociale', *European Journal of Political Research*, 22, 101–21.

Ignazi, P. 1989. *Il polo escluso. Profilo del Movimento Sociale Italiano*. Bologna: Il Mulino.

Immerfall, S. 1998. 'The neo-populist agenda', in H. G. Betz and S. Immerfall, eds, *Parties and Movements in Established Democracies*. London: Macmillan.

Immergut, E. 1998. 'The theoretical core of the new institutionalism', *Politics and Society*, 26 (March), 17.

Inglehart, R. 1990. *Culture Shift in Advanced Industrial Society*. Princeton, NJ: Princeton University Press.

Inglehart, R. 1987. 'Value change in industrial society', *American Political Science Review*, 81, 1289–303.

Inglehart, R. 1977. *The Silent Revolution: Changing Values and Political Styles amongst Western Publics*. Princeton, NJ: Princeton University Press.

Ionescu, G. and E. Gellner, eds. 1969. *Populism: Its Meanings and National Characteristics*. London: Weidenfeld and Nicholson.

Irvine, W. 1991. 'Fascism in France and the strange case of the Croix de Feu', *Journal of Modern History*, 63, 271–95.

Jaffré, J. 1988. 'Le Pen ou le vote exutoire', *Le Monde*, 12 April.

Jones, E. 2002. 'Politics beyond accommodation? The May 2002 Dutch parliamentary elections', *Dutch Crossings*, 26, Summer, 61–78.

Jouve, P. and A. Magoudi. 1988. *Les non-dits de Jean-Marie Le Pen: enquêtes et psychanalyse*. Paris: La Découverte.

Katzenstein, P. 1978. *Between Power and Plenty*. Madison, WI: University of Wisconsin Press.

Khalil, E. 1995. 'Organizations versus institutions', *Journal of Institutional and Theoretical Economics*, 151: 3, 445–66.

Kirchheimer, O. 1966. 'The transformation of Western European party systems', in J. LaPalombara and M. Weiner, eds, *Political Parties and Political Development*. Princeton, NJ: Princeton University Press, pp. 177–200.

Kitschelt, H. (with R. McGann). 1995. *The Radical Right in Western Europe*. Ann Arbor, MI: University of Michigan Press.

Kitschelt, H. 1994. *The Transformation of European Social Democracy* (Cambridge: Cambridge University Press).

Kitschelt, H. 1993. 'Social movements, political parties, and democratic theory', *Annals of the American Academy of Political Science*, 528, 13–29.

Kitschelt, H. 1988. 'Left libertarian parties: explaining innovation in competitive party systems', *World Politics*, 40, 194–234.

Kitschelt, H. 1986. 'Political opportunity structures and political protest: anti-nuclear movements in four democracies,' *British Journal of Political Science*, 16, 57–85.

Knight, J. 1992. *Institutions and Social Conflict*. Cambridge: Cambridge University Press.

Krasner, S. 1988. 'Sovereignty: an institutional perspective', *Comparative Political Studies*, 21: 1, April, 66–94.

Krasner, S. 1984. 'Approaches to the state: alternative conceptions and historical dynamics', *Comparative Politics*, 16: 2 (January), 223–46.

Kriesi, H. P. 1995. 'The political opportunity structure of new social movements: its impact on their mobilization', in J. C. Jenkins and B. Klandermans, eds, *The Politics of Social Protest: Comparative Perspectives on States and Social Movements*. London: UCL Press, pp. 167–98. Initially published in 1991 by Wissenschaftszentrum Berlin für Sozialforschung, FSIII 91-103.

Kriesi, H. P., R. Koopmans, J. W. Duyvendak and M. Giugni, M. 1992. 'New social movements and political opportunities in Western Europe', *European Journal of Political Research*, 22, 219–44.

Laclau, E. 1977. *Politics and Ideology in Marxist Theory: Capitalism – Fascism – Populism*. London: NLB.

Ladrech, R. 1989. 'Social movements and party systems: the French Socialist Party and the new social movements', *West European Politics*, 12: 3, 262–79.

Lancelot, A. and M.T. Lancelot. 1987. 'L'évolution de l'électorat français', in G. Ross and S. Hoffman, eds, *L'expérience Mitterrand: continuité et changement dans la France contemporaine*. Paris: PUF, pp. 105–31.

Le Bras, H. 1997. 'Les trois composantes des moeurs en France', in N. Mayer, ed., *Les modèles explicatifs du vote*. Paris: l'Harmattan.

Le Bras, H. 1995. Interview in *Le Monde*, 14–15 May.

Le Pen, J. M. 1999. *Français d'abord*, 302 (July), 3.

Le Pen, J. M. 1995. *Face à la une*. TF1 Television, 23 March.

Le Pen, J. M. 1995. *La France en direct.* France 2 Television, 13 March.

Le Pen, J. M. 1995. *Appel aux Français,* presidential campaign flyer *Le Pen président.* Saint-Cloud: Publications du Front National.

Le Pen, J. M. 1990. 'Déstabiliser l'éstablisshment', *Identité* (January).

Le Pen, J. M. 1987. 'J'appelle la France à combattre le déclin, la décadence et la servitude', *National Hebdo* (12 November).

Le Pen, J. M. 1985. 'Pour une vraie révolution française', *National Hebdo,* 62.

Le Pen, J-M. 1984. *Les Francais d'abord.* Paris: Carrère, p. 70.

Lewis-Beck, M. 1984. 'France: the stalled electorate', in R. Dalton, S. Flanagan and P. A. Beck, eds, *Electoral Change in Advanced Industrial Democracies: Realignment or Dealignment.* Princeton, NJ: Princeton University Press, pp. 428–33.

Lijphart, A. 1994. 'Presidentialism and majoritarian democracy: theoretical observations', in J. Linz and A. Valenzuela, eds, *The Failure of Presidential Democracy.* London: The Johns Hopkins University Press, pp. 91–105.

Lijphart, A. 1984. *Democracies: Patterns of Majoritarian and Consensus Government in Twenty One Countries.* New Haven, CT: Yale University Press.

Linz, J. 1994. 'Presidential or parliamentary democracy: does it make a difference?', in J. J. Linz and A. Valenzuela, eds, *The Failure of Presidential Democracy.* London: The Johns Hopkins University Press, pp. 8–16.

Lipset, S. M. and S. Rokkan. 1967. ' Introduction', *Party Systems and Voter Alignments.* New York, NY: Free Press.

Lipset, S. M. 1964. 'The changing class structure and contemporary European politics', *Daedalus,* 93, 271–303.

Luther, K. R. (2000) 'Austria: a democracy under threat from the Freedom Party?', *Parliamentary Affairs,* 53: 3, 426–42.

Lyttelton, A. 1996. 'The crisis of bourgeois society and the origins of fascism', in R. Bessel, ed., *Fascist Italy and Nazi Germany.* Cambridge: Cambridge University Press, pp. 12–22.

Lyttelton, A. 1973. *Italian Fascisms: From Pareto to Gentile.* London: Jonathan Cape.

MacEwan, A. 1988. 'Transitions from authoritarian rule', *Latin American Perspectives,* 58: 15: 3, 115–30.

MacRae, D. 1967. *Parliament, Parties and Society in France 1946–1958.* New York, NY: St Martin's Press.

Maguire, M. 1983. 'Is there still persistence? Electoral change in Western Europe, 1948–1979', in H. Daalder and P. Mair, eds, *Western European Party Systems Continuity and Change.* London: Sage, pp. 67–94.

Mainwaring, S. 1993. 'Presidentialism, multipartism and democracy: the difficult combination', *Comparative Political Studies,* 26: 2 (July), 198–228.

Mair, P. 1992. 'La trasformazione del partito di massa in Europa', in M. Calise, ed., *Come cambiano i partiti.* Bologna: Il Mulino, pp. 99–120.

Maisonneuve, J. L. 1992. *L'extrême droite sur le divan, psychanalyse d'une famille politique.* Paris: Imago.

March, J. G. and J. P. Olsen. 1984. 'The new institutionalism: organizational factors in political life', *American Political Science Review,* 78, 734–49.

Marinetti, F. 1973. 'Benito Mussolini', appendix to Antonio Beltramelli, *L'Uomo Nuovo*. Milan: Mondadori, pp. iii–vi.

Martin, P. 1996. 'Le vote Le Pen', *Notes de la Fondation Saint-Simon*, Paris, October–November, pp. 1–12.

Marx, K. 1972. 'The eighteenth Brumaire of Louis Bonaparte', in Robert C. Tucker, ed., *The Marx-Engels Reader*. New York, NY: Norton.

Massot, J. and G. Vedel. 1997. 'Alternance et cohabitation sous la Vème République', special issue of *Notes et Etudes Documentaires*, 5058 (August).

Massot, J. 1987. *L'arbitre et le capitaine. Essai sur la responsabilité présidentielle*. Paris: Flammarion.

Maurras, C. 1954. *Oeuvres capitales*. Paris: Flammarion.

Mayer, N. 1999. *Ces Français qui votent FN*. Paris: Flammarion.

Mayer, N. 1998. 'La perception de l'autre', in P. Perrineau and C. Ysmal, *Le vote surprise: les élections législatives des 25 mai et 1er juin 1997*. Paris: Presses de Science Po, 1998, pp. 267–84.

Mayer, N. 1997. 'Du vote lepéniste au vote frontiste', *Revue française de science politique*, 47: 3–4 (June–August), 438–53.

McGregor, A. J. 1979. *Young Mussolini and the Intellectual Origins of Italian Fascism*. Berkeley, CA: Berkeley University Press.

Mégret, B. 1998. 'La canditature de Jany Le Pen n'est pas une bonne idee', *Le Parisien* (24 August).

Mellucci, A. 1980. 'The new social movements: a theoretical approach', *Social Science Information*, 19, 199–226.

Meyer, J. W. and B. Rowan. 1991. 'Institutionalised organizations: formal structure as myth and ceremony', in W. W. Powell and P. J. DiMaggio, eds, *The New Institutionalism in Organizational Analysis*. Chicago, IL: The University of Chicago Press.

Milza, P. 1992. 'Le Front National: droite extrême ou national-populisme?', in J-F. Sirinelli, ed., *Histoire des droites en France*. Paris, Gallimard, pp. 691–7.

Milza, P. 1992. 'L'Ultra droite des années trente', in M. Winock, ed., *Histoire de l'extrême droite en France*. Paris: Seuil, pp. 165–71.

Milza, P. 1987. *Fascisme français. Passé et présent*. Paris: Flammarion.

Milza, P. 1985. *Les fascismes*. Paris: Imprimerie nationale.

Minkenberg, M. 1997. 'The new right in France and Germany. Nouvelle Droite, Neue Rechte and the new right radical parties', in P. Merkl, ed., *The Revival of Right-wing Extremism in the Nineties*. London: Frank Cass, pp. 65–90.

Minkenberg, M. 1992. 'The new right in Germany: the transformation of conservatism and the extreme right', *European Journal of Political Research*, 22 (July), 55–81.

Monzat, R. 1992. *Enquêtes sur la Droite Extrême*. Paris: Le Monde Editions.

Morris, P. 1997. 'Presidentialism in France: a historical overview', in J. Gaffney and L. Milne, eds, *French Presidentialism and the Election of 1995*. Aldershot: Dartmouth, pp. 5–21.

Mosse, G. 1979. *International Fascism: New Thoughts and Approaches*. London: Sage.

Mudde, C. 2000. *The Ideology of the Extreme Right*. Manchester: Manchester University Press.

Mudde, C. 1995. 'Right-wing extremism analyzed: a comparative analysis of three alleged right-wing extremist parties (NPD, NDP,CP'86)', *European Journal of Political Research*, 27, 204–24.

Mussolini, B. 1932. *Il fascismo: Dottrina e instituzzioni*. Rome: Ardita.

Nolte, E. 1970. *Le fascisme dans son époque, Vol. I, L'Action française*. Paris: Julliard.

North, D. 1990. *Institutions, Institutional Change and Economic Performance*. Cambridge: Cambridge University Press.

Nowak, M. 1987. *Une éthique economique*. Paris: Editions du Cerf.

O'Donnell, G. 1991. 'Democracia delegativa?', *Novos Estudios, CEBRAP*, 31 (October).

O'Donnell, G., P. Schmitter and L. Whitehead, eds. 1986. *Transitions from Authoritarian Rule: Latin America (Vol. 2)*; *Transitions from Authoritarian Rule: Comparative Perspectives (Vol. 3)*; *Transitions from Authoritarian Rule: Tentative Conclusions about Uncertain Democracies (Vol. 4)*. Baltimore, MD: The Johns Hopkins University Press.

O'Kane, H. T. 1994. 'Legitimacy and political science', *Political Studies*, XLII, 103–4.

O'Kane, H. T. 1993. 'Against legitimacy', *Political Studies*, XLI: 3, 471–87.

O'Sullivan, N. 1980. *Fascism*. London: Dent.

Offe, C. 1996. 'Institutions in East European transitions', in R. E. Goodin, ed., *The Theory of Institutional Design*. Cambridge: Cambridge University Press, pp. 199–226.

Offe, C. 1985. 'New social movements: changing boundaries of the political', *Social Research*, 52, 817–68.

Orrù, M., N. Woolsey Biggart and G. G. Hamilton. 1991. 'Organizational isomorphism in East Asia', in W. W. Powell and P. J. DiMaggio, eds, *The New Institutionalism in Organizational Analysis*. Chicago, IL: The University of Chicago Press, pp. 361–89.

Passmore, K. 1997. *From Liberalism to Fascism: The Right in a French Province, 1928–1939*. Cambridge: Cambridge University Press.

Passmore, K. 1995. 'The Croix de Feu: Bonapartism, national populism or fascism?', *French History*, 9: 1, 67–92.

Passmore, K. 1993. 'The French Third Republic: stalemate society or cradle of fascism?', *French History*, 7: 4, 417–49.

Paxton, R. 1995. 'Les fascismes: Essai d'histoire comparée', *XXème siècle*, 45 (March), 3–13.

Payne, S. 1995. *A History of Fascism, 1914–1945*. Madison, WI: University of Wisconsin Press.

Payne, S. 1983. *Fascism: Comparison and Definition*. Madison, WI: University of Wisconsin Press.

Perrineau, P. 2003. 'La surprise Lepéniste et ses suites legislatives', in P. Perrineau and C. Ysmal, eds, *Le vote de tout les refus*. Paris: Presses de Science Po, pp. 199–222.

Perrineau, P. 1997. *Le symptôme Le Pen: radiographie des électeurs du Front national*. Paris: Fayard.

Perrineau, P. 1997. 'Les étapes d'une implantation électorale', in P. Perrinau and N. Mayer, eds, *Le Front national à découvert*, second edition. Paris: Presses de Sciences Po, pp. 37–62.

Perrineau, P. and N. Mayer, eds. 1996. *Le Front national à découvert*, second edition. Paris: Presses de Sciences Po.

Perrineau, P. 1995. 'La dynamique du vote Le Pen: le poids du gaucho-lepénisme', in P. Perrineau and C. Ysmal, eds, *Le vote de crise: l'élection présidentielle de 1995*. Paris: Presses de Science Po, pp. 243–61.

Perrineau, P. 1995. *Le Monde*, 26 April.

Pickles, D. 1953. *French Politics: The First Years of the Fourth Republic*. London: Methuen and Co. Ltd.

Pierson, P. 1993. 'When effects become cause: policy feedback and political change', *World Politics*, 45, 595–628.

Plenel, E. and A. Rollat. 1984. *L'Effet Le Pen*. Paris: Le Monde/La découverte.

Poujade, P. 1955. *J'ai choisit le combat*. Saint-Céré: Société Générale des Editions et des Publications.

Przewoski, A. 1991. *Democracy and the Market: Political and Economic Reforms in Eastern Europe and Latin America*. Cambridge: Cambridge University Press.

Przeworski, A. 1986. 'Some problems in the study of transitions to democracy', in G. O'Donnell *et al.*, eds, *Transitions form Authoritarian Rule, Vol. 3*. Baltimore, MD: The Johns Hopkins University Press, pp. 47–63.

Przeworski, A. and H. Teune. 1970. *The Logic of Comparative Inquiry*. New York, NY: Wiley Interscience.

Rémond, R. 1982. *Les droites en France*. Paris: Aubier.

Ricoeur, P. 1981. *Hermeneutics and the Human Sciences*. Cambridge: Cambridge University Press.

Riedlsperger, M. 1998. 'The Freedom Party of Austria: from protest to radical right populism', in H.G. Betz and S. Immerfall, eds, *The New Politics of the Right: Neo-Populist Parties and Movements in Established Democracies*. London: Macmillan, pp. 27–43.

Rillardon, V. 2000. 'Front contre Front', *Modern and Contemporary France*, 8: 1 99–102.

Rioux, J. P. 1980. *La France de la quatrième République, I. L'ardeur et la nécéssité 1944–1952*. Paris: Seuil.

Rose, R. and D. Urwin. 1970. 'Persistence and change in Western Party systems since 1945', *Political Studies*, XVIII: 3, 287–319.

Sartori, G. 1976. *Parties and Party Systems: A Framework for Analysis*. Cambridge: Cambridge University Press.

Sartori, G. 1969. 'Politics, ideology, and belief systems', *American Political Science Review*, 63, 398–411.

Sartori, G. 1968. 'The sociology of parties: a critical review', in O. Stammer, ed., *Party Systems, Party Organisation and the Politics of the New Masses*. Berlin: Institut für Politische Wissenschaft an der freie Universität.

Sauer, W. 1967. 'National socialism: totalitarianism or fascism?', *American Historical Review*, 73: 2 (December), 408–22.

Savage, J. 1985. 'Postmaterialism of the left and right: political conflict in postindustrial Society', *Comparative Political Studies*, 17: 4 (January), 431–51.

Schneider, R. 1995. 'Qu'est-ce qui fait monter Le Pen ...?', interview with Pascal Perrineau, *Le Nouvel Observateur* (6 April), 30–1.

Scott, W. R. 1995. *Institutions and Organizations*. Thousand Oaks, CA: Sage Publications.

Scott, W. R. 1994. 'Institutions and organizations: towards a theoretical synthesis', in W. R. Scott and J. W. Meyer, eds, *Institutional Environments and Organizations: Structural Complexity and Individualism*. Thousand Oaks, CA: Sage Publications.

Scott, W. R. 1991. 'Unpacking institutional arguments', in W. W. Powell and P. J. DiMaggio, eds, *The New Institutionalism in Organizational Analysis*. Chicago, IL: The University of Chicago Press, pp. 164–82.

Searle, J. 1969. *Speech Acts: An Essay in the Philosophy of Language*. Cambridge: Cambridge University Press.

Seurin, J-L. 1986. *La présidence de la République en France et aux Etats-Unis*. Paris: Economica.

Shamir, M. 1984. 'Are Western party systems frozen? A comparative dynamic analysis', *Comparative Political Studies*, 17: 1, 35–79.

Shepsle, K. 1986. 'Institutional equilibrium and equilibrium institutions', in H. Weisberg, ed., *Political Science: The Science of Politics*. New York, NY: Agathon Press, pp. 51–81.

Shugart, M. and J. Carey. 1992. *Presidents and Assemblies: Constitutional Design and Electoral Dynamics*. New York, NY: Cambridge University press.

Siegfried, A. 1964. *Tableau politique de la France de l'Ouest sous la Troisième République*. Paris: Armand Colin.

Skocpol, T. 1992. *Protecting Soldiers and Mothers: The Political Origins of Social Policy in the United States*. Cambridge, MA: Belknap Harvard.

Skocpol, T. 1985. 'Bringing the state back in: strategies of analysis in current research', in P. Evans *et al.*, eds, *Bringing the State Back In*. Cambridge: Cambridge University Press.

Skocpol, T. and K. Finegold. 1982. 'State capacity and economic intervention in the early new deal,' *Political Science Quarterly* (Summer), 255–78.

Snyder, D. and C. Tilly. 1972. 'Hardship and collective violence in France, 1883–1960', *American Sociological Review*, 37, 520–32.

Souchard, M. S. Wahnich, I. Cuminal and V. Wathier. 1997. *Le Pen. Les mots*. Paris: Le Monde Editions.

Soucy, R. 1987. 'France', in D. Mühlberger, ed, *The Social Basis of European Fascist Movements*. London: Croom Helm, 190–212.

Soucy, R. 1986. *French Fascism, The First Wave, 1924–33*. New Haven, CT: Yale University Press.

Soucy, R. 1972. *Fascism in France. The Case of Maurice Barrès*. Berkeley, CA: University of California Press.

Steinmo, S., K. Thelen and F. Longstreth, eds. 1992. *Structuring Politics: Historical Institutionalism in Comparative Analysi*s. Cambridge: Cambridge University Press.

Stepan, A. and C. Skach. 1993. 'Constitutional frameworks and democratic consolidation', *World Politics*, 46 (October), 1–22.

Sternhell, Z. 1985. *Maurice Barrès et le nationalisme français*. Paris: Editions Complexes.

Sternhell, Z. 1983. *Les origines françaises du fascisme*. Paris: Seuil, Coll. Points.

Sternhell, Z. 1983. *Ni droite, ni gauche: l'idéologie fasciste en France*. Paris: Seuil.

Streel, J. 1942. *La révolution du vingtième siècle*. Brussels: Nouvelle société d'édition.

Suleiman, E. 1994. 'Presidentialism and political stability in France', in J. Linz and A. Valenzuela, eds, *The Failure of Presidential Democracy*. London: The Johns Hopkins University Press, pp. 137–62.

Suleiman, E. 1987. *Les Notaires. Les pouvoirs d'une corporation*. Paris: Seuil.

Suleiman, E. 1986. 'Toward the disciplining of parties and legislators: the French Parliament in the Fifth Republic', in E. Suleiman, ed., *Parties and Parliamentarians in Democratic Politics*. New York, NY: Holmer and Meier, pp. 79–105.

Suleiman, E. 1980. 'Presidential government in France', in R. Rose and E. Suleiman, eds, *Presidents and Prime Ministers*. Washington: American Enterprise Institute.

Suleiman, E. 1974. *Power and Bureaucracy: The Administrative Elite*. Princeton, NJ: Princeton University Press.

Svåsand, L. 1998. 'Scandivanian right-wing radicalism', in H.G. Betz and S. Immerfall, eds, *The New Politics of the Right: Neo-Populist Parties and Movements in Established Democracies*. London: Macmillan, pp. 77–93.

Swyngedoun, M. 1998. 'The extreme right in Belgium: of a non-existent Front National and an omnipresent Vlaams Blok', in H.G. Betz and S. Immerfall, eds, *The New Politics of the Right: Neo-Populist Parties and Movements in Established Democracies*. London: Macmillan, pp. 59–75.

Taguieff, P. A. 1996. 'La métaphysique de Jean-Marie Le Pen', in P. Perrineau and N. Mayer, eds, *Le Front national à découvert*, second edition, Paris: Presses de Sciences Po, pp. 173–94.

Taguieff, P. A. 1990. 'Mobilisation national-populiste en France; vote zéno-phobe et nouvel anti-sémitisme politique', *Lignes* (March), 91–136.

Taguieff, P. A. 1986. 'La doctrine du national-populisme en France', *Études*, 364: 1, pp. 27–46.

Tarrow, S. 1994. *Power in Movement: Social Movements, Collective Action, and Politics*. Cambridge: Cambridge University Press.

Tarrow, S. 1989. *Struggle, Politics and Reform: Collective Action, Social Movements and Cycles of Protest*, second edition. Ithaca, NY: Cornell University, Western Societies Program Occasional Paper 21.

Tarrow, S. 1983. *Struggling to Reform: Social Movements and Policy Change during Cycles of Protest*. Ithaca, NY: Cornell University, Western Societies Program Occasional Paper 15.

Theleweit, K. 1989. *Male Fantasies*. 2 vols. Cambridge: Polity Press.

Tilly, C. 1994. 'The time of states', *Social Research*, 61: 2, 269–95.

Tilly, C. 1984. 'Social movements and national politics', in C. Bright and S. Harding, eds, *Statemaking and Social Movements*. Ann Arbor, MI: University of Michigan Press, pp. 297–317.

Tilly, C. 1978. *From Mobilisation to Revolution*. Reading, MA: Addison-Wesley.

Touchard, J. 1978. *Le Gaullisme, 1940–1969*. Paris: Seuil, Points Histoire, pp. 238–41.

Touchard, J. 1956. 'Bibliographie et chronologie du Poujadism', *Revue Française de Science Politique*, 6: 1.

Touraine, A. 1981. *The Voice and the Eye*. Cambridge: Cambridge University Press.

Trevor-Roper, H. 1981. 'The doctrine of fascism?' in S. J. Woolf, ed., *European Fascisms*. London: Weidenfeld and Nicholson.

Turner, S. 1992. 'Introduction,' in S. Turner and D. Kasler, eds, *Sociology Responds to Fascism*. London: Routledge, pp. 1–16.

Venner, D. 1962. *Défense de l'Occident* (26 November), 46–52.

Weber, M. 1968. *On Charisma and Institution Building: Selected Papers*, ed. and with an introduction by S. N. Eisenstadt. Chicago, IL: University of Chicago Press.

Weber, E. 1962. 'Nationalism, socialism and national-socialism in France', *French Historical Studies*, 2: 3, 273–307.

Weber, M. 1949. *The Methodology of the Social Sciences*. Illinois: Glenoce, p. 22.

Weir, M. 1992. 'Ideas and the politics of bounded innovation', in S. Steinmo *et al.*, eds., *Structuring Politics: Historical Institutionalism in Comparative Analysis*. Cambridge: Cambridge University Press, pp. 189–216.

Wildavsky, A. 1959. 'A methodological critique of Duverger's political parties', *The Journal of Politics*, 21: 2 (May), 303–18.

Wiles, P. 1969. 'A syndrome, not a doctrine', in G. Ionescu and E. Gellner, eds, *Populism: Its Meanings and National Characteristics*. London: Weidenfeld and Nicholson.

Williams, P. 1958. *Crisis and Compromise: Politics in the Fourth Republic*. London: Longman.

Williamson, O. E. 1991. 'Comparative economic organizations: the analysis of discreet structural alternatives', *Administrative Science Quarterly*, 36, 269–96.

Wilson, G. D. 1973. 'A dynamic theory of conservatism', in G. D. Wilson, ed., *The Psychology of Conservatism*. New York, NY: Academic Press.

Winock, M. 1990. *Nationalisme, anti-sémitisme et fascisme en France*. Paris: Seuil.

Wolinetz, S. 1979. 'The transformation of the Western European party system revisited', *West European Politics*, 2, 4–28.

Wright, V. 1989. *The Government and Politics of France*, third edition. London: Unwin Hyman.

Zimmerman, E. and T. Saalfeld. 1993. 'The three waves of West German right-wing extremism', in P. H. Merkl and L. Weinberg, eds, *Encounters with the Contemporary Radical Right*. Boulder, CO: Westview Press, pp. 50–74.

Front national publications

300 Mesures pour la renaissance de la France – Front national, Programme de gouvernment, 1993. Paris/Saint Cloud: Editions nationales.

Français d'abord! Le magazine de Jean-Marie Le Pen (bi-monthly)
National Hebdo (weekly)

Interviews with *Front national* personnel

Bernard Antony, *Dirécteur Institut Français d'action culturelle Front national*, MEP, Brussels, 1 July 1998.
Bruno Gollnish, *Secrétaire Géneral Front national*, MEP, Brussels, 2 July 1998
——, Paris, 8 July 1998.
Carl Lang, *Vice-Président Front national*, MEP, Brussels, 1 July/2 July 1998.
Jean-Yves Le Gallou, *Secrétaire National aux élus Front national, Conseiller Général d'Île-de-France*, Paris, 8 July 1998.
Jean-Marie Le Pen, *President Front national*, Paris, 3 June 1998.
——, Brussels, 1 July 1998.
——, Brussels, 4 November 1998.
——, Paris, 6 July 2000.
——, Paris, 10 July 2001.
——, Paris, 20 July 2002.

Index

Note: 'n.' after a page reference indicates the number of the note on that page.